The Carter Years

The Carter Years

The President and Policy Making

Edited by
M. Glenn Abernathy
Dilys M. Hill and
Phil Williams

St. Martin's Press, New York

Printed in Great Britain

First published in the United States of America in 1984

Library of Congress Cataloging in Publication Data

Main entry under title:

The Carter Years.

    Includes Index.
    1. United States--Politics and Government--1977-1981--
addresses, essays, lectures. 2. Political Planning--United
States--Addresses, essays, lectures. 3. Carter, Jimmy,
1924-   --Addresses, essays, lectures. I. Abernathy. M. Glenn"
(Mabra Glenn), 1921-   . II. Hill, Dilys M.
III. Williams Phil.
JK271.c277 1884   973.926   83-40061

ISBN 0-312-12286-1

Contents

Contributors

M. Glenn Abernathy   Olin D. Johnston Professor of Government, University of South Carolina, Columbia, South Carolina

Q. Whitfield Ayres   Department of Government and International Studies, University of South Carolina, Columbia

Dilys M. Hill   Reader in Politics, University of Southampton

Donald A. Marchand   Director, Institute of Information Management, Technology and Policy and Associate Professor, Department of Management Science, University of South Carolina, Columbia

Clifton McCleskey   Professor, Department of Government and Foreign Affairs, University of Virginia

Pierce McCleskey   Graduate School, University of Virginia

Raymond A. Moore   Professor of Government and International Studies, University of South Carolina, Columbia

Phil Williams   Department of Politics, University of Southampton

Stephen Woolcock   Royal Institute of International Affairs (Chatham House)

Tinsley E. Yarbrough   Professor and Chairman, Department of Political Science, East Carolina University, Greenville, North Carolina

1 Introduction

Dilys M. Hill and Phil Williams

Few recent presidents can have come to office after such a meteoric political career as Jimmy Carter who, in a matter of months, went from obscurity to the White House. Indeed, Carter's arrival in office generated enormous expectations: here was a new president untainted by America's domestic and foreign problems. Four years later Carter returned to obscurity after only one term in power amidst charges that he had been incompetent, inefficient and unable to design or implement effective policies. The Carter Presidency, which had started with such promise, ended in disarray. What were widely accepted as indecision and weakness on domestic issues were compounded in foreign policy by a series of humiliating events, especially the hostage crisis, which cast doubt on American power and policies. Indeed, by the presidential election of 1980, Jimmy Carter suffered from what is perhaps best described as a confidence gap. Although he had avoided the excesses of some of his predecessors, he had demonstrated an inability to offer the kind of decisive leadership that many Americans had once again come to demand from their president. Yet there had been few hints of this in the election campaign of 1976 when candidate Carter had promised not only new formulas but effective implementation.

During this campaign Carter also claimed to have been influenced by James Barber's book, *The Presidential Character: Predicting Performance in the White House.*[1] Almost inevitably, he was asked by journalists how he saw himself fitting into Barber's categorization of presidents. Carter's reply was interesting and, in retrospect, some would argue founded on delusion. Not only did he state that he hoped to prove himself an active-positive president but went on to suggest that he would enjoy the job. This enthusiasm was particularly contagious, coming as it did after Nixon's disgrace and Gerald Ford's apparent inability to do anyting more than muddle through in a clumsy and undistinguished manner.

Carter's self-confidence, however, obscured crucial questions about his ability to cope with the kind of problems that would confront any president in the latter half of the 1970s. In addition, it overlooked the difficulties that an 'active-positive' president was likely to create for himself. Barber was to point out that the typical virtues of an active-positive character— goal orientation and an emphasis on rational problem-solving —could be offset by the failure of such a person to take account of the irrational in politics.[2] And politics in Washington, while not irrational, was enormously complex. For any outsider the intricacies of power and policy could be baffling. As Jimmy Carter saw it, however, the problem was not how to come to terms with the cynicism, the compromises and the sordidness which often characterized politics in Washington, but how he could transcend these features. Although this appears at first sight to be simply a matter of style or taste, its implications were far-reaching. Unless he understands the institutional structures, the political constraints and the policy processes, a president has little chance of being effective. A transcendental strategy is no substitute for an acute awareness of the limitations of the possible in either domestic or foreign policy, and a distaste for the use of power is no basis from which to overcome these limitations. In other words, Carter's character and style reinforced rather than weakened the structural and political constraints that are a problem for all presidents.

This is not to deny that these constraints themselves were extremely powerful if not wholly intractable. Indeed, Jimmy Carter probably had to contend with a more restrictive atmosphere than any president since World War II. It is one of the ironies of the Carter Presidency that the very disillusionment which had led many Americans to vote for an outsider for president also made it enormously difficult for that president to function effectively. To some extent, of course, this goes back to the earlier points about style: the qualities which had helped Carter obtain the presidency were different from the qualities required to make his incumbency an effective and successful one. Even if Carter's style had been more compatible with Washington, however, he would still have faced overwhelming difficulties. In 1980 Carter was berated for his lack of leadership; yet the events of the 1960s and 1970s had left many

Americans highly suspicious of presidential power and determined to avoid any repetition of the Johnson and Nixon years.
Congressional desires to circumscribe the authority of the
President combined with the changes in the internal structure
of Congress to render presidential leadership so difficult that
some analysts suggested that the 'Imperial Presidency' had been
replaced by an 'imperilled Presidency'. Carter faced a Congress
that was not only extremely assertive and suspicious but was
also highly fragmented and individualistic. In other words,
Jimmy Carter arrived in office at a time when the presidency as
an institution had been severely weakened and the problems
of coalition-building in Congress had become formidable.
Any president in his place would have encountered similar
problems.

Whether or not another President would have been able to
cope better with these structural problems is difficult to decide.
Much would obviously have depended on his personality and
leadership style. Yet style and structure are not the only considerations which need to be taken into account in any assessment of the Carter Presidency. Equally important was the
growing public mood of fiscal and social conservatism—a mood
reflected in an increasingly conservative Congress. The changes
were especially apparent in the Senate. In the early 1970s the
liberals in the Senate were in the forefront of all the attempts to
restrain the Imperial Presidency. In the aftermath of the 1978
elections the Senate as a body was not only much more conservative, but its liberal members had become something of an
endangered species, targeted as they were by the growing number of right-wing pressure groups determined to reverse what
they regarded as a number of highly dangerous trends in American policy and politics. By 1980 this conservative mood had
become the dominant theme in American politics and a conservative Republican was swept to victory on a domestic and
national security programme well to the right of his Republican
predecessors. From this perspective the Carter Presidency
appears not only as an interregnum between two periods of
Republican rule but as an aberration in a rising tide of conservatism in American life. If this is so then Carter's achievements should be judged against the external constraints rather
than against the goals he established.

The broader implication of this point concerns the difficulties of establishing criteria to evaluate presidential performance. Should a conservative president be assessed according to different standards than a liberal president? Should the analyst focus on aspirations or outcomes? How much weight should be given to the bureaucratic and political obstacles which hinder the attainment of goals? How does one compare persistent efforts to overcome these obstacles with strategies designed to accommodate them? Is the most appropriate focus the endeavour or the result?

The contributors to this study have not all given the same answers to these questions. Indeed, there are significant variations in the questions they have focused on. Nevertheless, all the authors attempt, to a greater or lesser degree, to trace the interaction of style and structure, to consider the tensions and incompatibilities between the personal preferences of the President and the public and congressional mood, and to offer judgements about the performance of the Carter Administration in particular issue areas. Several take as their starting point the situation inherited by Carter; others focus initially on the President's own attitudes and aspirations; but all offer insights into the difficulties which probably confront all presidents, but which seem particularly acute for Democrats, especially those with unlimited aspirations and limited experience. Throughout all the chapters there are several unifying themes. The first concerns the nature and extent of the difficulties which confronted the President. How intractable were those difficulties? Could they have been overcome with better management or were they so fundamental and deep-rooted that any improvements in managerial skills by the White House would have had little more than cosmetic effect? The second and closely-related question relates to President Carter's managerial and political skills: were these sufficiently well developed to take maximum advantage of the limited freedom of action which was available or were they so sparse that the President could only succeed in exacerbating the very difficulties he was trying to overcome? The third question follows from the second: if there were weaknesses in Carter's approach, what kind of weaknesses were they? Were the problems those of policy design or those of implementation? Or was it simply that Carter failed to project his goals in a way which convinced others that they were either appropriate or attainable? In other words, was Carter a potentially effective

President overwhelmed by unkind circumstances and poor public relations or an inept amateur who obtained the presidency only because of a reaction against the Washington insiders and then proceeded to demonstrate the dangers of electing outsiders?

The key to understanding certain problems in domestic policy lies in the clash which occurred between the president's style and the choices he made when faced with the labyrinth of Congress through which policy had to be implemented. As Dilys Hill's chapter reveals, the president's managerial penchant for rationality and problem-solving led to an ambitious programme which was difficult to handle effectively. The large number of legislative proposals caused difficulties for Congress. But Carter's search for an overall strategy rather than piecemeal solutions was, in his view, the only way to clear up the Washington 'mess' and address some of the outstanding problems of the times—energy, government reorganization, economic regeneration and social reform—which he had promised the American people he would tackle. But the comprehensive approach took time—while vital interest groups pressed impatiently for action—and the complexities and conflicts of the process among White House aides, Cabinet members and the bureaucracy exhausted participants and puzzled onlookers. This policy process, though based on a comprehensive philosophy, was liable to produce plans which were complex, detailed, and which frequently gave the impression of lacking vision or priorities.

In the field of economic policy, as Stephen Woolcock demonstrates, the aims of the Carter Administration were to reduce unemployment; to balance the budget and reduce federal outlays; to increase social spending within a balanced budget; and to produce tax changes over the four-year term. These objectives were based on a somewhat optimistic assumption about economic growth. The programme was a compromise between Carter's conservative preferences and the more liberal Democrats in Congress, and how to reconcile the two became the problem. But the Administration gave the impression that it was uncertain in its handling of the economy, and this was accompanied by a lack of confidence in the President's handling of inflation. Initially, however, there was some success as the economy was already recovering, and unemployment fell. But things began to go wrong in 1978 and Carter's priorities switched to fighting inflation. During 1979 this effort intensified and the search began for cuts in domestic programmes in order to cut the budget deficit. Monetary policy also suffered as the dollar fell. In fact the Carter Administration, unlike its predecessors, had a positive international economic order, but there were criticisms of what was seen as the Administration's amateurish approach and the ineffectual attempts to stabilize international money markets. The conclusion must be that Carter's record on economic policy was mixed: after initial progress in the domestic economy its significant failure was one of devising means of controlling inflation.

During his election campaign Carter had been critical of America's foreign policy and of the Kissinger diplomacy. Ray Moore's chapter shows that the outcome of his actions rested on a combination of politics, character and commitment. The Carter Administration's image of the international system was of interdependency. The cornerstone of foreign policy was to be human rights, but there were difficulties over what this meant and of charges of double standards. Foreign policy-making was marked by rivalry between Vance and Brzezinski and this problem was enhanced when the reorganization of the National Security Council gave Brzezinski Cabinet status. Brzezinski represented Carter's bold side; Vance his more traditional and methodical side. But it is characteristic of Carter's approach that with Brzezinski, as with Stuart Eizenstat in Domestic Policy, the President came to rely heavily on a few senior advisers whom he trusted and to whom he gave more and more influence over the final form of the ideas reaching him and the decisions themselves. Carter's efforts on SALT II and human rights are worthy of recognition, as is the calibre of the people he appointed and his willingness to innovate and to tackle issues. But his image of the international system was seriously flawed, and his lack of realism and his inconsistency were to prove shortcomings in his overall record.

In defence, Phil Williams argues that the President was only one actor among many in a complex system in which there were powerful, bureaucratic and industrial interests. Carter's record is ironic. He came into office with deeply-held views on the need for a more moralistic and less militaristic approach; for a reduced preoccupation with Moscow in favour of a more pluralistic view; for reduced defence spending. But he ended up by presiding, if reluctantly, over the need for increased defence budgets and no SALT II ratification. Carter's defence policy went through three stages. Until early 1979, Carter's own preferences were to the fore. Through 1979, Carter made compromises on spending in an attempt to obtain the Senate's consent to the ratification of SALT II. In 1980, following the invasion of Afghanistan, Carter adopted the tough approach which his critics had been demanding. In addition, the Carter Administration spent a long time, and intense effort, in wrangling over the production of a defence policy. Almost inevitably, this led to failures of communication—as it did in other spheres of policy-making—in which the President either did not make his views understood clearly enough or his advisers did not understand exactly what his aims were. The year 1979 was one of transition in which President Carter's defence preferences became subordinate to those of his advisers and to political expediency. The attempt to get the Senate to ratify SALT II became the dominant issue, and this then broadened into a much wider debate on the strategic balance and the Soviet threat. The difficulty was that Carter made no attempt to build a constituency either with Congress or with the public. He did not seem to understand that presidential power is the power to persuade and must be used to the full if implementation is to succeed.

What did characterize his style was that sense of duty which, as Glenn Abernathy demonstrates, marked his stance in domestic civil rights. His search for ways in which to promote racial equality primarily through executive and agency action rather than through legislative initiatives was evidence of that wider attitude which was to lead to charges of a 'passionless presidency'. In fact Carter's record in pursuing racial equality, privacy, equal rights in housing, civil justice-reform and women's rights was generally good, and Carter deserves more credit than he has been given for his wide-ranging concerns for domestic civil rights. Carter's success rate with Congress— even though many of his proposals were not particularly novel —was extremely small. The key, as with all of his legislative behaviour, was that the proposals were *many, complex* and gave no indication of *priorities* to guide Congress. Nor did the White House appear to make any concerted attempt to lobby or to get pressure group support and this meant a virtual absence of leadership from the White House *vis-à-vis* Congress.

The Carter Administration is unique in that the President neither courted his party's cadres nor yielded much to them, as the McCleskeys' chapter shows. But Carter's deliberate 'man of the people' candidature was more than a campaign ploy; it reflected his personality and his political values. It was also to have important implications for his conduct of the presidency. And Carter, who had not sought the support of the party leaders or of important groups in his path to the White House, remained at a distance from the mainstream of his party. But in spite of his well-publicized contretemps with Congress, with the party and with influential groups, the fact that he was the incumbent President tempered fears among his staff over the renomination. Nevertheless, as Carter's popularity in the polls declined and the battle with Kennedy intensified, the issue of Carter's renomination moved to the centre stage. In the end Kennedy's personal and political difficulties, and Carter's success in those states using the caucus or convention system of delegate selection, gave Carter the renomination. As a party leader, Carter must be judged a failure. His personality and style, and his conception of the political process, made it extremely difficult for him to lead other Democratic public officials and activists.

The key to presidential effectiveness lies in the people the president appoints and the way he uses his staff. Whitfield Ayres' chapter on the White House reveals that although individual aides were commended, the evaluation of the staff as a whole was overwhelmingly negative. On the surface, the Carter White House seemed to be constantly evolving, though in fact these changes were less radical than appeared. The changes which followed the July 1978 famous 'malaise' speech were more significant. Hamilton Jordan was formally instituted as Chief-of-Staff, and Jimmy Carter gave up two and a half years of trying to act as his own supremo. Ayres' judgement is that the White House staff would have enjoyed a better reputation if the initial structure had included a chief-of-staff filled by someone with substantial management experience. Although President Carter has himself flatly rejected the view that the reputation of the White House suffered from a poor fit between people and jobs, this was in fact an important factor in at least two cases—Hamilton Jordan and Frank Moore. Carter accused, rather, a vindictive and biased press. This did contribute to the problem but it was less important than the structure of the staff organization and the fit of personnel and jobs—especially given the staff's inexperience in the ways of Washington politics.

Although there was intense criticism of his effectiveness, Carter in fact had a moderately successful legislative record, as Tinsley Yarbrough shows. And it has to be stressed that many of the obstacles to President Carter's legislative successes were beyond the control of either his, or his Administration's, efforts. After problems in the first year, the White House/congressional liaison system then seemed to work more smoothly. But the liaison system was remote from Carter and he never showed that close interest in it which Johnson displayed. The problem was exacerbated by the fact that Democratic leaders in Congress could have forgiven Carter's 'outsider' style if he had won a resounding popular victory; as it was, many of them felt they owed little to him. Carter was not only an 'outsider' to Washington but also to the mainstream of his own party. This alienated some of his potential congressional support which sought a more expansionist and liberal set of policies. Carter also repeated in Washington a strategy he had used in Georgia of sending a large number of proposals to Congress on the basis that at least some would succeed. This was a miscalculation in Washington where congressional independence—and intransigence—reduced the likelihood of such a strategy being successful.

Donald Marchand's chapter shows why this was the case. Jimmy Carter was both an 'outsider', critical of the way government was run, and a managerialist with very definite views of how it might be put right. As incoming President he launched a number of management initiatives to further this aim. The most important moves were to create a Special Assistant to the President for Reorganization, to set up a Presidential Reorganization Project in the Office of Management and Budget, and to request approval of Congress to submit reorganization plans. The resulting management review was arguably the most comprehensive since the Hoover Commission of the 1950s. There were successes with civil service reform and the establishment of new Departments of Energy and Education. But, unlike the situation in Georgia, Carter had to seek the active support of the 'iron triangles' of the system—interest groups/congressional committees/federal bureaucrats—not spurn them. This meant that Carter underestimated the strong links between Congress and federal agencies until too late. His managerial style also hampered his effectiveness. The modern presidency is a very powerful post from which to exercise leadership but a very poor one from which to manage the details of administration.

The aim of this book is thus to show the contradictions and complexities of the modern presidency, and particularly the constraints which a Democrat faced in pursuing his policy objectives. Jimmy Carter's Southern populist beliefs—to aid the poor, uneducated, and minorities, but within the limit of 'good housekeeping'—marked his presidential style. To a Southerner, the goals of humanity, management efficiency and fiscal prudence were not inherently antithetical. On the national scene, however, they posed strains and contradictions which could not survive the transition to federal politics. Populism was overwhelmed in an unfavourable national political climate of a resurgent Congress and an increasingly conservative public mood. This presented an incoming Democratic President with a need to commit himself to a strong leadership position, to lobby extensively, to set priorities and to impose a vision. It is in these factors that, as this book tries to show, an analysis of the problems with which Carter had to deal most fruitfully lies.

Notes

1. James D. Barber, *The Presidential Character: Predicting Performance in the White House*, second edn., Prentice-Hall, Englewood Cliffs, New Jersey, 1977, p. 498.
2. Barber, op. cit., pp. 12–13.

Part I
Substantive Policies

2 Domestic policy

Dilys M. Hill

Among the most important goals in the Southern brand of populism was to help the poor and aged, to improve education, and to provide jobs. At the same time the populists tried not to waste money, having almost an obsession about the burden of excessive debt. These same political beliefs—some of them creating inherent conflicts—were to guide me in the Oval Office.[1]

Jimmy Carter's domestic policy achievements, though by no means as meagre as some critics alleged, were disappointing. In part this disappointment stems from an over-ambitious policy style. In his first year in office, Congress was bombarded with initiatives and this, combined with the search for comprehensive solutions, gave rise to highly publicized, long-drawn-out legislative wrangles which muted the victories when they did come. In assessing the outcome, therefore, this chapter takes three broad perspectives: the policy agenda; policy process and policy style; and policy achievements.

The policy agenda

(i) *Promises and expectations*

Candidate Jimmy Carter outlined a series of domestic commitments: job-creation, de-regulation of major industries, government reorganization, welfare and health policy reforms, tax reform, civil service reform, an energy plan and a balanced budget. The nucleus of the domestic agenda was contained in a hundred-page draft prepared during the transition by Stuart E. Eizenstat, as Chief Domestic Policy Adviser. The priorities were an economic stimulus package; the renewal of presidential authority to make changes in the executive branch, subject to congressional veto; an energy plan; and welfare reform. Initially,

*I am grateful to Stuart E. Eizenstat and other members of the Administration and Federal Civil Service who granted me interviews in March 1983, and to members of the Brookings Institution and Urban Institute. I would like to thank the British Academy for making the project possible.

the outlook was remarkably hopeful. In February the Emergency Natural Gas Act (to combat maldistribution between producing states and the North-East and northern Midwest in a particularly severe winter) was passed by Congress in less than a week. In April the bill granting Carter executive branch reorganization authority was successful. And in May the economic stimulus package (the Anti-Recession Fiscal Assistance Act) was passed. Originally enacted by Congress in 1976, to run until September 1977, it was extended to September 1978 and additional funds provided, together with a tax-cuts bill (though Carter had withdrawn his original request for a $50 tax rebate). The jobs programme, the Comprehensive Employment and Training Act, CETA, was given an extension in June.

By April, however, substantial doubts were emerging. The sheer weight of proposals swamped Congress and posed severe problems for overworked Cabinet Secretaries and White House staff in explaining and selling the proposals. Inflation became an issue, to the concern of organized labour and black leaders calling for more stimulation of the economy. Thus, in spite of expectations, it was economic issues which dominated the initial legislative agenda. Only then was it possible to pursue seriously the two substantive issues of the domestic policy agenda—energy and welfare.

(ii) Energy

Candidate Carter promised a strong energy policy which would emphasize conservation, reduce dependence on foreign oil and amalgamate the different federal agencies into one energy department. The initial problem, however, was more pressing. The severe winter led to shortages of natural gas. This was an early test of President Carter's leadership. It was also one which confirmed his own views of his office: as he had said in his campaign, only the President could speak for the government 'with a clear and simple voice' and that in the absence of presidential leadership there was no leadership.[2] The Emergency Natural Gas Act was submitted to Congress on 26 January and passed on 2 February, and the President used the drama of the emergency to publicize his call for a national energy plan. On 2 February President Carter gave his first television 'fireside chat'—his first policy speech. But it was curiously low-key: Carter appeared to be playing down his authority, seeking voluntary co-operation and avoiding mandatory controls.[3] At the same time, a bill was prepared (it was sent to Congress on 1 March), proposing the creation of a Department of Energy which would consolidate nineteen separate energy programmes and abolish three federal agencies with overlapping jurisdictions.

President Carter announced that he would send a comprehensive energy plan to Congress on 20 April—an ambitious timetable. Part of this planning involved a massive 'outreach' operation in which the public were invited to submit suggestions. By contrast, Congress complained that it had been excluded from the consultations. Secretary-designate James Schlesinger and his fifteen-strong team had evolved the plan in private, consulting neither Congress nor government agencies, because of pressure of time. This process, with its 'outreach' operation, reflected the populism of the Carter philosophy. The White House sought, however, to minimize friction with Congress by an extensive campaign to explain what the energy plan would entail. The difficulty, from Congress's viewpoint, was that 'explanation' fell far short of consultation and appeared to be a case of Carter propounding a plan (as, in his view, 'the people' expected him to do), and congressional leaders seeing that it became law.

President Carter's televised speech on energy on 19 April, on the eve of the plan's presentation to Congress, was grave, calling the issue 'The Moral Equivalent of War'.[4] The plan's highlights were: increased gasoline taxes from 1979; taxes on oil from 1978; tax rebates to consumers; penalties for high-consumption cars; price de-regulation of *newly-discovered* natural gas; heavy taxes to deter the use of natural gas by industry and the public utilities; tax credits for home insulation; support for the development of new fuels; de-control of gasoline prices; restructuring of utility rates; use of 'light-water' nuclear reactors, and the Clinch River project (the controversial nuclear breeder reactor in Tennessee) to be deferred indefinitely. There was a strong suggestion that the President could win approval of the plan only by going over the head of Congress to appeal directly to the people. Already, a congressional feeling was emerging that the gasoline tax was doomed and that natural gas de-regulation would be opposed.

There was early success for Carter, however, when, under Speaker O'Neill's guidance, the House of Representatives approved the creation of a select committee to co-ordinate the energy legislation that would otherwise have had to go to nine committees and sub-committees.[5] But conflict was still entrenched in Congress's procedures. First, although a single committee had been set up to deal with the energy proposals in the House, no such procedure was available in the Senate, where both the Energy and Natural Resources Committee (Chairman, Henry Jackson, D–Washington) and the Finance Committee (Chairman, Russell Long, D–Louisiana, and widely regarded as a supporter of his state's oil interests[6]) had jurisdiction. Second, there was a division between Democrats from industrial areas opposed to price de-regulation and Congressmen from producing states, and Republicans, who were in favour. Third, and in Carter's eyes a malevolent force, there was the influence of the lobbyists.[7]

These difficulties exacerbated what would in any event have been a lengthy legislative process, given the plan's complexities. Work on setting up the Energy Department went ahead more rapidly: Congress established the Department at the beginning of August 1977, but even there it showed its independence by denying the Secretary of Energy the power to set natural gas prices, establishing instead a new five-member Federal Energy Regulatory Commission, housed in the Department but independent of its Secretary. On the energy plan, work in the House went relatively smoothly, and the bill was approved at the beginning of August. The bill was broadly in line with the President's policy, though without the proposed increases in gasoline tax. At the same time, however, Senator Long revealed, ominously, that he was unenthusiastic about President Carter's energy proposals. By the middle of September it was clear that the Senate battle would be bitter. The opposing forces appeared at deadlock, and the eight-day filibuster by Senate liberals was only broken by controversial rulings by Vice-President Mondale on 3 October. It was followed by the approval of the de-regulation of all natural gas prices (which Carter at that stage opposed). Carter then decided to delay his already overdue tax proposals, even though it jeopardized their prospects in 1978, to avoid any action that would further impede the energy legislation emerging in the Senate.

On 31 October the Senate passed the last of five energy bills —very different in their tax imposts from Carter's original plans—and Carter again addressed the nation, on 8 November. The speech was the familiar exhortation but, in saying that energy legislation was not a contest of strength between himself and Congress, the President did attempt to assuage growing tensions.[8] As the House–Senate Conference met in November the President announced that he was cancelling his overseas tour in order to urge passage of the energy bill. But he made it clear that he was not prepared to compromise with Senator Long[9] even though his general stance signalled that he was willing to make concessions in order to end an intolerable period of governmental inaction and get the law passed. On 12 December, however, the White House conceded the impossibility of getting energy legislation through Congress in 1977 and President Carter announced that he would leave for his deferred foreign tour on 29 December. What was to have been the domestic centrepiece of the President's first year in office, the 'comprehensive energy programme', languished, and Carter conceded that the delay and conflict over the bill were a 'major failure'.[10] The energy bill remained deadlocked in Conference for the first three months of 1978; Carter, meanwhile, was undergoing a further test of his leadership, during the crisis of the extended coal strike. On the deadlocked bill, it was argued, Carter and his congressional liaison team had made no special efforts to resolve the impasse, and the expectations raised by the dramatic postponement of the foreign tour were soon dissipated.[11]

In April 1978, after returning from a two-day meeting with his Cabinet and senior White House staff at Camp David, President Carter made a forceful appeal to Congress to 'fulfill its duty to the American people' and enact an energy programme. This more assertive stance appeared to reflect the Camp David deliberations about the widespread criticism of the Administration's indecisiveness. In response, the Senate–House conferees agreed, in late May, on legislation on natural gas prices which would also allow for gradual de-regulation. But the Senate again baulked at oil taxes to cut imports. By August Speaker O'Neill was threatening a 'lame-duck' session after the November elections to pass the energy package. Carter again attacked Congress for its intransigence, and the White House sought to present a picture of a beleaguered President acting in the national interest but thwarted by a Congress ridden by special interest groups. The President cut short his holiday in the Grand Tetons to lobby for the bill. It was finally signed into law (the National Energy Act) by President Carter on 9 November 1978, in a form which fell notably short of what had been proposed by the Administration eighteen months earlier. But that was the paradox. The final version of the bill would normally have been seen as a major achievement, but because Carter's demands were for such a wide-ranging measure, public comment centred on what had been rejected by Congress, rather than what had been achieved. The major change was that instead of continued control of most natural gas prices, de-regulation was to be enacted by 1985—a political price which Carter was eventually willing to pay.[12]

Events during 1979 did not deal kindly with the energy plans. Though there were few new energy initiatives from the Administration, difficulties arose when the Iranian revolution and OPEC price rises resulted in long gasoline queues. President Carter, due to deliver a televised energy speech on 5 July, instead held a domestic 'summit' meeting at Camp David which reassessed the course of his Administration. But the reassessment of the energy issue appears to have stemmed from a memorandum sent to President Carter in Tokyo by Stuart Eizenstat proposing that the President should both reassess the approach to the energy crisis (long queues and price rises) and the managerial problems of the Energy Department (because of its allocations system) on his return. Otherwise, said Eizenstat, the Administration would suffer severe political damage.[13] The postponed energy speech was given on 15 July and emphasized what the President called the American people's spiritual 'crisis of confidence' and their need to meet the challenge of the energy crisis. But the effects of the speech were soon lost in the 'July Massacre' of Cabinet sackings.[14]

The new policies to emerge from the July decisions, and which were the Administration's priority through to 1980, were the tax on 'windfall profits', resulting from the de-control of domestic oil prices (which the Administration had introduced late in 1979 by executive order), subsidies for synthetic fuel production, and an Energy Mobilization Board to smooth the way for new energy projects. These met with modest success. By the end of May 1980 a Senate–House Conference committee had approved the Energy Mobilization Board, and agreed a generous programme of loans and subsidies for synthetic fuel projects and conservation measures. In April Carter had signed into law the 'Windfall Profits Tax'.[15] But Congress also overrode, in June, a Presidential veto of congressional legislation rejecting a $4.62 per barrel oil import fee—the first time in twenty-eight years that Congress had overridden a veto by a President of its own majority party. Late in June the House also referred the Energy Mobilization Board bill back to the House–Senate Conference (the Synthetic Fuels bill did get passed). The Energy Mobilization Board foundered, as liberals feared it would mean the evasion of environmental controls while conservatives opposed it as unnecessary. Again, the feeling was that President Carter and his aides had not learnt the ways of Congress. And the fight for a national energy policy, of which this was the final stage, had taken three years.

(iii) Welfare

If energy was President Carter's prime issue for the first year of his presidency, welfare reform was an issue about which he had long felt a passionate concern. He believed that the welfare 'system' was irrational, unfair and wasteful. As with his other policy approaches, he wanted an overhaul of the system which would be comprehensive, would stress jobs ('workfare, not welfare') and would prevent families from being split up—but which would not increase costs. It had also appeared from his campaign that he was willing to agree that the Federal government should relieve the states and big cities of most of their crippling welfare burden (in the event, only a small—10 per cent—subsidy was offered in the final plan). In many ways, in fact, Carter's goals were similar to those of Nixon's Family Assistance Plan which sought to reduce the numbers of people eligible for, and the levels of, benefit.

To achieve his aims, Carter appointed Joseph A. Califano, Jr. as Secretary of Health, Education and Welfare (HEW). Califano had been Special Assistant for Domestic Affairs to President Johnson and was responsible for the co-ordination of the Great Society programmes. President Carter called for a welfare plan to be presented to him for consideration by 1 May 1977. The complexities of the proposals, the difficulties of timetabling and costing, the congressional infighting and, not least, the influence of the personalities involved (the President, Joseph Califano, Stuart Eizenstat, Senator Long and Congressman Ullman) have been extensively analysed.[16] What emerges is that, if the judgement of the energy plan has been too harsh (legislation was passed, even if the 'comprehensive' expectations were misplaced), welfare has been judged, and rightly, a failure. Many argue that to try to achieve radical, comprehensive reform of a 'system' which has grown up in piecemeal fashion and is the archetypical example of Charles Lindblom's 'disjointed incrementalism' (if not *ad hockery* gone wild[17]) was itself a misjudged aim. President Carter, however, felt that he had campaigned on a comprehensive platform and that it was up to Congress to provide the legislation. But reform meant different things to different people. To Senator Long, Chairman of the Senate Finance Committee, it meant cutting the welfare rolls; Al Ullman, Chairman of the House Ways and Means Committee, also prefered public service employment to cash handouts. But Mayors and Governors wanted federal fiscal relief. Liberal Democrats, including James Corman, Chairman of the Ways and Means Committee's Subcommittee on Public Assistance, wanted to extend welfare coverage and benefit levels. Organized labour favoured a massive economic stimulus.

In spite of the very tight timetable, Califano began his task vigorously, seizing on the opportunity to appoint staff from the expert welfare field. He formed the Welfare Reform Consulting Group—from government agencies, congressional committees and state and local interest groups—to try to avoid some of the pitfalls of previous reform efforts.[18] Progress of the plan was impeded, however, by a straitjacket of competing power bases, personalities and expectations. Califano felt that the timetable was too tight and the 'no cost increase' target unrealistic. He has also met with Senator Long and Representative Ullman and was in no doubt about how difficult reform would prove to be.[19] President Carter, though seeking a comprehensive plan, thought that both Califano and Ray Marshall (Secretary, Department of Labor, DOL) should manage the plan and stressed the need for inter-agency consultation. But there was conflict between the two departments, and also an uneasy relationship between HEW and the White House. Califano was not happy with what he believed were over-zealous White House aides and this led to friction.[20]

Following a series of briefings by Califano and Marshall, President Carter, having insisted on the 1 May deadline, decided to make the statement but to announce principles only, not the expected detailed programmes. What lay behind this lack of detail in the 2 May announcement was that the policy process, which in its final stages had been heavily influenced by Stuart Eizenstat and his staff, had presented the President with a complex list of proposals to accept or reject, virtually on the eve of publication. On 6 August the plan, the detailed Program for Better Jobs and Income, was announced. This consolidated the cash programmes of Aid for Dependent Children (AFDC) and Supplemental Security Income (SSI) with the food stamps programme and extended coverage to the working poor, intact families and single adults. The no-cost increase limitation was replaced by a $2.8 billion increase (with only a minimal 10 per cent relief for the states, mentioned above) and proposed the establishment of 1.4 million public service jobs.

The immediate response was favourable (though Senator Long was strongly opposed to the number of people it would make eligible for benefits, and organized labour feared the effect of the jobs programme on labour markets). All, however, were sceptical of the Administration's cost estimates. The main problem, though, was that of steering such comprehensive legislation through Congress. Speaker O'Neill was able, as with the energy plan, to set up a special subcommittee to co-ordinate the legislation.[21] In the Senate, however, Senator Long began almost immediately to push his own bill for welfare reform.[22]

By the end of 1977 Carter was conceding that welfare reform would not be passed in 1978 and the plans were not included in his January 1978 State of the Union message. Late in March 1978, faced with the complexities of the other legislative proposals, and Carter's anxiety to press ahead with tax reform, the Administration decided to abandon the plan and search instead for limited, compromise proposals. Various attempts were made by senators to introduce bipartisan compromise bills and HEW, DOL and the New Coalition (a lobby of state and city groups) worked out a draft plan. But all this came to nothing since the public mood turned more conservative after the passage of Proposition 13, and Senator Byrd, the Senate Majority Leader, indicated to Speaker O'Neill that prospects for reform in the Senate were remote even if the

House passed a bill.[23] Inspite of this impasse three measures did get passed: the purchase requirement for food stamps was eliminated;[24] earned income tax credit was expanded; and CETA was renewed and targeted more effectively on the most disadvantaged.

In June 1977 a more modest welfare plan was sent to Congress in two separate bills: the Work and Training Opportunities Act and the Social Welfare Reform Amendments Act.[25] But the impetus had gone out of reform, as Carter struggled with the problems of Iran and with renomination battles with Senator Kennedy, and he turned instead towards domestic expenditure cuts. The jobs bill was effectively killed when, in March 1980, Eizenstat forwarded the Administration's request that funding be delayed until 1982 and the cash bill never got off the ground in the Senate.

Three factors contributed to welfare reform's failure. First, there was a lack of effective communication (between the White House and Califano, and in transmitting the President's wishes generally). Second, Carter's technocratic approach and his use of deadlines to force action was inappropriate for such a highly political and value-laden issue. Third, the costings and the evaluation of management factors was inadequate.[26] The leading actors became trapped in the dilemmas of zero-based budgeting, political manœuvring and 'comprehensive' imperatives.

Closely associated with the politics of welfare reform was the President's commitment to hospital-cost containment and a national health insurance plan. The issue was complicated by the intricacies of committee jurisdiction in the House and Senate (again, Senator Long's Finance Committee, and its Health sub-committee chaired by conservative Herman Talmadge, had jurisdiction over Medicare and Medicaid), and by the burden of legislation which Congress already faced. The issue was further compounded by rivalry between the President and Senator Edward M. Kennedy, which increased as the elections loomed. Although Califano set up an Advisory Committee on National Health Insurance in April 1977, progress was slow. Carter's attention was really focused on energy, welfare and the re-financing of the ailing Social Security system (whose taxes were raised in December 1977). As congressional unease at comprehensive health proposals grew, President Carter became increasingly concerned with hospital-cost containment and saw this as having priority in his anti-inflation battles. It would also, he felt, add to the viability of the welfare reform proposals (the Medicaid costs of which would be reduced by reduced hospital costs).

As with his other proposals, President Carter sought a compromise plan, but without increased costs. He met with Senator Kennedy and labour leaders on 6 April 1978 and reaffirmed his commitment to national health insurance and also said that, although the plan was not preconditioned on the passage of the hospital-cost containment bill, the latter was very important to him.[27] By midsummer the Administration itself was split (a row which became public knowledge) between the economic advisers arguing for a limited approach on the one hand, and Eizenstat and Califano on the other calling for a comprehensive plan requiring employers to provide coverage, with the government providing 'catastrophic' coverage for others.[28] But the issue faded over the congressional summer recess and then took a backseat to inflation and energy and the coming congressional elections. The issue again languished through 1979 as both Senator Long and Senator Kennedy sought to introduce their own (and very differing) bills. Carter, while not willing to yield his party's political ground to either of the Senators, was still more concerned with inflation and budget cuts and delayed introducing a proposal (a phased National Health Plan was finally announced on 12 June 1979). But it was clear that congressional politics would prevent its passage. With hospital-cost containment the problem was not the President's failure to move but the combination of legislative complexities and powerful lobby opposition.[29] The bill was defeated in the House in 1978 and though Carter became more involved in 1979, when the bill was reintroduced and was one of the Administration's key anti-inflation measures, it was finally defeated in November 1979.

(iv) Education: urban policy

Candidate Carter had campaigned for a strong federal role in education and felt this could only be achieved if the service were removed from HEW and a separate Department of Education established. This fulfilled a campaign promise to the National Education Association (NEA) but led to conflict with

HEW Secretary Califano, who opposed the move. President Carter did not announce a new department immediately on entering office but in April 1977 set up a study group inside the President's Reorganization Project (PRP). In November PRP recommended a broad-based department. This was opposed, not only by critics on the budget side of the Office of Management and Budget (OMB) but also by White House aides who foresaw great problems of political bargaining at a time when energy should be devoted to other battles. Lobbying for the department, especially from the NEA, continued to be strong, and the president still appeared to favour a broad programme base.

A bill was sent to Congress in March 1978 but sustained, complex negotiations on the part of the Administration were only forthcoming at a late stage. This was particularly damaging, following the length of time which it had taken President Carter and his aides to persuade the reluctant Representative Jack Brooks (Chairman, Government Operations Committee and generally unsympathetic to reorganization) to sponsor the bill in the House. Opposition in the House increased from those opposed to the splitting up of HEW to those who wanted to keep their favoured programmes—Headstart, child nutrition, Indian education—out of the new department's jurisdiction. Congress adjourned at the end of 1978 without voting on the bill. NEA lobbying intensified and the Administration became more willing to bargain. The bill which was passed in July 1979 was a much narrower version than originally proposed. The new department, which opened in May 1980, was essentially the old education division of HEW plus only one other programme.

The conclusion must be that this reorganization had a symbolic rather than a structural interest for the President and that a more restructured change would have needed a strong, involved leadership from the President, which was not in effect forthcoming. Instead, different groups of staff—in the White House, in PRP, in the agencies—had differing beliefs about what the President wanted, and cohesion was lacking.[30]

Carter's urban initiative was the first such 'urban policy' to be adopted by an American President.[31] The policy was produced by a special inter-agency task force, the Urban and Regional Policy Group, over a twelve-month period. In July, and again in November 1977, Vernon Jordan, Executive

Director of the Urban League, criticized the lack of progress. Again, the President emphasized the need for a comprehensive policy approch and a tight cost constraint. The year-long process was characterized, and in part caused, by well-publicized jurisdictional battles between departments, notably Housing and Urban Development (HUD), Commerce and HEW. Stuart Eizenstat became more heavily involved after December 1977 (when Carter rejected a brief requiring specific item decisions and called for an overall policy) and worked with Secretary Patricia R. Harris of HUD to prepare further briefs.[32] The process then intensified but the President's March 1978 deadline eventually left Carter only forty-eight hours to decide on some seventy-six detailed proposals. Carter's only previous involvement appears to have been meetings with leading aides in December and March, memorandums, and private communication with Eizenstat.[33]

The process lacked substantive guidance; there was no 'the President wants' or 'the President expects' and Carter only became involved right at the end when he could only *react* to Eizenstat and Harris. The President's dominant concern with controlling the budget and the scope of federal intervention did, however, prevail, though his other policies— against the Urban Development Bank—did not.[34] The urban policy, 'A New Partnership to Conserve America's Communities: A National Urban Policy', was announced on 27 March 1978. It was a series of proposals for jobs, tax incentives and grant, loan and public works efforts. In implementing policy, federal agencies were to be guided by targeting (giving resources to people and places in most need); leveraging (encouraging private investment); and management reform.

The policy had a mixed reception. The general feeling was, however, that it would depend on the money made available, while Vernon Jordan called the policy 'disheartening' and a 'missed opportunity'. A number of congressional committees handled different parts of the policy. These involved expansion of existing programmes, re-authorization of anti-recession measures and tax and job incentives. Congress was reluctant, in the prevailing mood of fiscal conservatism, to push ahead. Carter did have some success in 'targeting' aid to large cities under the Community Development Block Grant and General Revenue Sharing provisions. But the most effective of such programmes, the Urban Development Action Grants, had in fact been passed earlier, in the Housing and Community Development Act of 1977. The central planks of Carter's urban policy—anti-recession aid and the Urban Development Bank—failed when Congress did not renew the counter-cyclical fiscal measures which lapsed in 1978 and rejected the Urban Bank. In the spring of 1979 Carter decided not to re-submit the Urban Development Bank as a separate measure but to include it in the financing of the Economic Development Administration, EDA. This too was unsuccessful.

Two measures which did succeed depended on administrative, not legislative, action. These were the establishment of an Inter-agency Co-ordinating Council (under Jack Watson, the President's Assistant for Intergovernmental Relations) in May 1978 and the Urban and Community Impact Analysis, requiring federal policy-makers to review the local impact of their decisions, established by Presidential executive order in July 1979. But the urban policy had, arguably, faded long before that as, towards the end of 1978, President Carter turned his attention to domestic expenditure cuts.

Policy process and policy style

The framework for domestic policy-making consisted of three elements: Cabinet government, congressional procedures and behaviour, and the domestic policy staff. Carter, like many presidents before him, came into office committed to Cabinet government and decentralized decision-making.[35] In the early days of his presidency, Cabinet meetings were on a weekly basis but this pattern lapsed after the first year.[36]

The problems of congressional procedure and behaviour— the complexities of committee jurisdiction and the 'turf wars' to which they gave rise; the decline of strong party leadership and the dispersal of chairmen's power; the intensity of lobby politics—have become a familiar theme of the post-Watergate years. They were exacerbated in President Carter's case by two very powerful forces, both, it appears, of the Administration's own making. One was the deficiencies of the White House– congressional relations which are described elsewhere in this book. The other was that the President's own approach to domestic policy-making both compounded the complexities of the system and, because this then led to extended delays, caused damaging publicity repercussions for an incumbent claiming to be a 'can do' President.

Comprehensive proposals for energy, welfare and health and for the establishment of new Departments of Energy and Education had to face the jurisdiction of several congressional committees and sub-committees. Although it was possible in energy and welfare, after Speaker O'Neill's heroic efforts, to set up special committees in the House to deal with the legislation, no such procedures were available in the Senate. In this procedural and political fragmentation (and where Carter came to see lobby politics as a major obstacle) what was needed was sustained and pervasive presidential lobbying. This leadership style was alien to the 'Washington outsider', which President Carter had claimed with pride to be; significantly, where he did use it, as over the Panama Canal treaties, he was successful.

The Domestic Policy Staff, and their interactions with Cabinet members, in fact dominated the domestic policy process. Carter had abolished the Domestic Policy Council of Nixon and Ford and the staff was grouped into the Domestic Policy Staff directly responsible to the President through Domestic Policy Adviser Stuart E. Eizenstat. Eizenstat was widely regarded as very influential (he was one of the few advisers to see Carter daily). His role as Executive Director of the Domestic Policy Staff was crucial since he was responsible for the Presidential Review Memoranda (finally instituted in February 1978) and thus structured the opinions which the President received. He was heavily involved in the final stages of the energy, welfare and urban plans.

The policy process was complicated by the President's 'engineer's' style and his commitment to government reorganization. He believed that his success in governmental reorganization in Georgia—on a much smaller scale—could be achieved in Washington. The President's Reorganization Project (PRP) was established in OMB, and the staff had access to the President through OMB's Director (first Bert Lance, then James McIntyre). But for the Director this work was unlikely to have priority.[37] Moreover, the White House staff saw reorganization as separate from, not integral to, policy. In 1979 they were instrumental in rewriting the proposals for economic assistance, which they saw as politically sensitive. Instead of economic development programmes being combined with HUD to form a new Department of Development Assistance, they were to be put into Commerce, leaving HUD largely intact. In this the reorganization staff were the losers.

The effective life of the Reorganization Project was some two and a half years. It was successful in helping to establish the Energy and Education Departments and civil service reform. Later it drew up (after difficult and conflictful consultations with federal agencies and hostility from the Domestic Policy Staff and congressional interests) plans to consolidate federal programmes in four areas. These were: community and economic development; natural resources; food and nutrition and trade.[38] These were to become the responsibilities of four new Cabinet departments. By early 1979 it was clear that only natural resources was politically viable and likely to be put to Congress. But even that failed when Carter decided to drop the plan in May.

Initially, however, Carter's reorganization hopes prospered. In May 1977 he signed into law the bill giving him power to reorganize the federal bureaux and agencies (though not whole departments). At the same time he began to introduce zero-based budgeting (another Georgia legacy) which was a process requiring fuller justification of expenditures by departments. This affected relations between presidential choice and the federal bureaucracy and, importantly, between Congress and the bureaucracy—only the White House had the basic information on which the choices were made. But the main philosophy —that reorganization was a central and achievable aim for a revitalized government—did not make the passage from Georgia to Washington. It took too long; it lacked committed and sustained leadership; it foundered on poor relations with congressional staff. And those involved in substantive policy resisted the integration of organization proposals with their work. Above all, it lacked a public constituency, as public attention faded.

The decentralized style which permeated the philosophy of the first eighteen months of the Carter administration did not necessarily mean that decisions themselves were decentralized. The style leaned heavily on a system of task forces to develop policy options, in which Cabinet departments were collegial equals and White House aides were the co-ordinators and mediators. But the effect was to pull back practically all significant decisions into the White House. There, the President had to act as final arbiter, and became embroiled in detail. Nevertheless, the President was not wholly satisfied with the system which presented him—as with the urban policy for example—with too little time to study detailed policy options. Carter had announced in July 1977 that he was going to use a Presidential Review Memorandum process similar to that used by the National Security Council. At the same time Eizenstat was given clear responsibility for managing the way in which domestic policy issues were prepared for presidential decision. And in the last two years of the Administration the aim was, by contrast with the earlier period, to focus the President's involvement on a few selected issues and to reduce the policy agenda.

In 1979, as his difficulties with Congress and with the economy increased and his popularity fell, the President made changes. Following the retreat to Camp David in July he called for the resignation of his entire Cabinet. Five Cabinet members left the Administration: James Schlesinger (Energy), Griffin Bell (Attorney General), Brock Adams (Transportation), Michael Blumenthal (Treasury) and Joseph Califano (HEW). The last two, in particular, had been criticized for their too-independent stance. Hamilton Jordan was made chief of the White House staff. The effect of the changes was to tighten the political control of the White House over the executive Departments, to enhance Jordan's power, and generally to centralize authority in the White House.

Achievements

As President Carter says in his memoirs, 'Discretionary domestic spending, in real dollars, increased less than one per cent during my term of office'.[39] In 1980 Carter had said that he was not trying to balance the budget on the backs of the poor. Nevertheless, many of the proposed cuts were achieved by reducing or deferring programmes included in the January budget, among them economic development, anti-recession aid, welfare reform, the state portion of revenue-sharing, education, and CETA jobs. The domestic agenda for 1980 had few initiatives but reintroduced proposals which had been defeated in Congress the previous year, including hospital-cost containment, health insurance and stand-by gasoline rationing. None of these were successful.

Over the four-year term, however, there were some satisfying achievements. New Departments of Energy and Education had been set up and major reform of the Civil Service and de-regulation of the airlines had been achieved. In the early days of the Administration Congress had passed the Natural Gas Emergency legislation and the economic stimulus package of public service jobs and financial aid. Tax reduction was passed —though not the major reform of the tax system which Carter had wanted. Congress had finally passed a (much modified) five-part energy programme—but one which included natural gas de-regulation which Carter had originally intimated that he did not want. Later, in April 1980, a windfall profits tax was approved. In his anti-waste campaign, Carter was bruised in his early efforts to eliminate 'wasteful' water projects from congressional appropriations and late in 1977 he had to com-promise (in retrospect he reflected that he should have vetoed them).[40] In 1978 he took a harder line and in October was sup-ported by the House when he vetoed the public works appropria-tions bills containing water projects. The 'ethics in government' proposals, covering all three branches of government, were successful, as was the extension of grants to college students.

The four years were not easy ones, however, for a president who had pledged to balance the budget, halt inflation and curtail oil imports. Not only did these goals prove unattainable, they imposed fundamental constraints on the major programme reforms—in welfare, health and urban policy—which Carter hoped to achieve without significant extra costs. All met with only minor success. Oil imports were not curtailed and the crude oil equalization tax was not passed. The comprehensive approach, however, had more extensive drawbacks than just the impossibility of achieving broad changes alongside financial stringency. These drawbacks were, as this chapter has out-lined: an emphasis on technicity when political leadership was essential; a failure of communications between the Presi-dent and his aides and Cabinet members over the real goals to be pursued; and the inappropriateness of the comprehensive approach when the congressional policy process was over-whelmingly incremental and partial.

Was it the case, then, that the President's handling of domestic issues was 'panicked by one of Washington's fickle moods', as the July 1979 postponement of the energy speech was called?[41] In a paradoxical way, the answer must be 'Yes'. The White House proved better at crisis management (the Panama Canal treaties, the Russian invasion of Afghanistan, the natural gas shortage of early 1977) than when it had to follow through with domestic programmes requiring involved consultations, extensive coalition-building and sustained leadership. Perhaps the epitaph should be, as one observer put it: 'Bold initiatives quickly go stale, however, if promised results do not materialize'.[42] In domestic policy, the Carter years were a period when it was recognized that major, wide-ranging reforms presented hurdles that could not be overcome—and certainly not in one four-year term. If Congress did not see the 'rightness' of the solutions, only frustration and impasse could result. It is also true that an overall philosophy—the ends which domestic policy in fact sought—seemed to be missing. That tenacity of purpose, that vision, that sense of personal involvement[43]—that passion—were not transmitted by a president so overtly committed to change.

Notes

1. Jimmy Carter, *Keeping Faith: Memoirs of a President*, Bantam Books, New York, 1982, p. 74.
2. Charles Mohr, 'Carter, Putting Leadership to Test, Again Asks Saving of Heating Fuel', *New York Times*, 1 January 1977.
3. James Reston, 'An Uncertain Trumpet', *New York Times*, 4 February 1977.
4. The unfortunate acronym to which this gave rise—MEOW—was to haunt the administration for the next two years. The President was quoting, unattributed, from William James.
5. The 37 member *ad hoc* committee on energy was chaired by Representative Thomas Ashley (D–Ohio).
6. The Senate majority leader, Senator Robert C. Byrd, was regarded as not giving the necessary lead on this issue which Speaker O'Neill had given in the House; cf. Steven Rattner, 'Senate Dismantling Carter's Energy Bill', *New York Times*, 26 September 1977. He reaffirmed his minimalist leadership stance later in the year as the Energy Bill was deadlocked in Conference: Adam H. Clymer, 'The Energy Bill; Procedural Snags on Procedure', *New York Times*, 24 December 1977.

32   *Dilys M. Hill*

7. Jimmy Carter, op. cit. and Richard Corrigan, 'Lobbyists are Putting the Blitz on Carter Energy Program', *National Journal*, 26 November 1977, pp. 1836–40.
8. *New York Times*, 9 November 1977.
9. President Carter was reported as saying at his 30 November news conference, 'I've never had any conversation with Senator Long that would either encourage or require me to change my position from what it was last April', *New York Times*, 1 December 1977. Observers were divided as to whether he would veto the eventual bill or not.
10. *International Herald Tribune*, 16 December 1977.
11. Austin Ranney, 'The Carter Administration', in A. Ranney (ed.), *The American Elections of 1980*, American Enterprise Institute for Public Policy Research, Washington, DC, 1981, p. 9.
12. Not included in the bill were the Crude Oil Equalization tax; standby tax on gasoline; coal conversion policies; utility rate reform; rebates for buyers of economy cars; continued control of gas prices.
13. Dom Bonafede, 'A Turning Point . . .', *National Journal*, 14 July 1979, p. 1170. See also *Keeping Faith*, op. cit., pp. 116–17.
14. Austin, Ranney, op. cit., p. 31.
15. The Tax was not permanent, as Carter had requested. It was to expire either in October 1993 or when $227 billion in taxes had been collected.
16. The major work is Laurence E. Lynn Jr. and D. de F. Whitman, *The President as Policymaker: Jimmy Carter and Welfare Reform*, Temple University Press, Philadelphia, 1982. See also Joseph A. Califano Jr., *Governing America*, Simon & Schuster, 1981; Jimmy Carter, op. cit.; J. R. Storey, R. Harris, A. Fechter and R. C. Michel, *The Better Jobs and Income Plan: A Guide to President Carter's Welfare Reform Proposal and Major Issues*, The Urban Institute, Washington, DC, 1978.
17. S. M. Miller, 'Social policy on the defensive in Carter's America', *New Society*, 1 November 1979, pp. 244–7.
18. The appointment of staff was later to become controversial. President Carter and the White House had originally intimated that Cabinet Secretaries should go ahead and appoint their own staff. Later, the White House complained about the appointments not being cleared with the President's staff and the issue became part of the 'disloyalty' charges which preceded the Cabinet dismissals of July 1979. The consulting group, in the event, did not make any formal recommendations. The head of the group was Assistant Secretary Henry Aaron, formerly of Brookings, and author of 'Why is Welfare so Hard to Reform?'.
19. At a press briefing on 2 May 1977, Califano called welfare reform 'the Middle East of domestic politics'; Califano, op. cit., p. 321.

20. Lynn and Whitman, op. cit., p. 51.
21. The Welfare Reform Sub-committee was made up of the Chairman of Ways and Means, members of the Ways and Means Sub-committee on Public Assistance and Unemployment Compensation, and the Chairmen of (and representatives from) the Agriculture Committee and Education and Labor Committee. It was chaired by James Corman.
22. In the view of the *Congressional Quarterly Weekly Report*, Senator Long was poised to influence domestic policy in a way few legislators have done in this generation. Vol. 35, No. 37, 10 September 1977, p. 1905.
23. Lynn and Whitman, op. cit., pp. 262–71.
24. But the Food Stamps Act of 1977 introduced the requirement to register for, and seek, work. This was a central feature of all Carter's welfare reforms.
25. These two measures set a national minimum payment, covered intact families, replaced food stamps with consolidated cash payment for aged, blind and disabled, and funded a modest special jobs program.
26. Lynn and Whitman, op. cit.
27. Califano concluded from this meeting that from then on it would be a case of Kennedy and Labor versus President Carter and that President Carter had not responded strongly enough to Kennedy over the alleged delays. Califano, op. cit., pp. 105–6.
28. Califano, op. cit., p. 112.
29. Of the 234 in the House who voted to kill the hospital-cost containment legislation on 15 November 1979, 202 had received campaign contributions from the American Medical Association. The bill faced four health sub-committees (two in each House), five full committees (two in the Senate and three in the House) and the floor of both chambers.
30. Willis D. Hawley and Beryl A. Radin, 'Executive Politics and Domestic Policy-Making: Understanding the Organization of the U.S. Department of Education', March 1983.
    I am grateful to Dr Radin for this paper, which is to appear in Nelson & Hargrove, *The Presidency and the Political System*, Congressional Quarterly Press.
31. A move which reflected Congress's own mood. Title VI of the Housing and Community Development Act, passed in October 1977, amended the original 1970 Act to require the development of a national urban policy and a biannual report on that policy by the President to Congress.
32. A comprehensive account of the process is given in Harold L. Wolman and Astrid A. E. Merget, 'The Presidency and Policy Formulation: President Carter and the Urban Policy', *Presidential Studies Quarterly*, Vol. 10, 3, Summer 1980, pp. 402–15.

33. *Congressional Quarterly Weekly Report*, Vol. 36, 1 April 1978, p. 785.
34. Wolman and Merget, op. cit., p. 409.
35. Candidate Carter had read Stephen Hess's, *Organizing the Presidency*, Brookings, Washington DC 1976, in which ideas for a revitalized and more collegial Cabinet are explored, and had sought his advice.
36. Jimmy Carter, op. cit., p. 60.
37. For a critique, see Lester M. Salamon, 'The Goals of Reorganization: a Framework for Analysis', *Administration and Society*, 12, 4, February 1981, pp. 471–500; and Peter Szanton, *Government Reorganization: What Have we Learned?*, Chatham, NJ, Chatham House Press, 1981. Both Salamon and Szanton were involved in the project.
38. 'Organizing for development', *Final Report* of the Reorganization of the Study of Federal Community and Economic Development Programs, President's Reorganization Project, OMB, Washington DC, February 1979, and P. Szanton, op. cit.
39. Jimmy Carter, op. cit., p. 78.
40. Jimmy Carter, op. cit., p. 79.
41. Robert J. Samuelson, '. . . or an Empty Charade?', *National Journal*, 14 July 1979, p. 1171.
42. Dick Kirschten, 'Carter's Latest Anti-Inflation Plan—Waiting for the Verdict to Come In', *National Journal*, 12, 12, 22 March 1980, p. 478.
43. J. Lynn and D. de F. Whitman, op. cit., p. 3.

3 The economic policies of the Carter Administration

Stephen Woolcock

The legacy of the Ford Administration

The Carter Administration came to office at a time when the United States and world economies were beginning to recover from the 1974/75 economic recession. Unemployment in the United States had fallen from its peak of 9 per cent in 1975, but was still close to 8 per cent in 1976. There was a budget deficit of $66.4 billion in 1976, which was equivalent to 4.1 per cent of GNP (Gross National Product), a record for the United States. Although the budget deficit was planned to fall to $44 billion in 1977, as a result of cuts in spending and permanent reductions in taxation, some of the countercyclical programmes introduced in the 1974/75 recession were still to work their way through the budget, with the result that spending was growing at about 10 per cent per annum.[1] The scale of the federal debt was cause for widespread concern, and both President Ford and Mr Carter pledged to balance the federal budget.

A measure of the degree of governmental involvement in the economy is the share of federal outgoings in GNP. In 1976 this was 22.6 per cent, and Mr Carter pledged to reduce it to 21 per cent during his presidency. In addition to the inbuilt growth in the budget from the earlier countercyclical expansion programmes, there were also rising costs for social programmes. In particular, the social security and unemployment programmes were becoming more and more costly. The social security system was also in need of significant increases in funds if it was not to collapse under the pressure of demographic trends. The costs of medical services to the government were also rising, largely because of inflation in medical charges.

Faced with these issues, President Ford had decided to adopt a cautious approach to economic growth. In his proposals for the 1977 budget he sought to cut spending on social programmes in order to reduce the budget deficit, but he also intended to increase defence spending significantly. Fiscal and monetary policies were devised, with the objective of achieving modest but non-inflationary growth.

During his presidential campaign Mr Carter criticized this policy. He argued that the economy was weakening and that President Ford's policy would bring to a halt the economic recovery that had been under way in 1976. For Carter and the Democrats unemployment at 7.5 per cent was still unacceptably high. He therefore argued that while the budget should be balanced it should be balanced at a higher level of economic activity. Mr Carter was also critical of Ford's lack of action on a number of structural issues. The most important of these was energy policy, but Mr Carter also criticized the lack of action on tax and welfare reforms. In international economic relations he argued that the United States had to take active measures to support the international economy if protectionist pressures and Third World debt were not to fundamentally undermine the liberal multilateral economic order.

In early 1976 it appeared that economic policy would not be a major issue in the election. During the third quarter of 1976, however, the indicators pointed to a slowdown in the economy. This clearly helped Mr Carter because the shift in economic indicators suggested that Carter was correct and that there was indeed a need for a further stimulation of the economy. In actual fact, the slowdown was only temporary, and even before President Carter had a chance to implement a more expansionary policy, the economy was already experiencing more vigorous growth. The Carter Administration was therefore fortunate in the sense that the economy appeared bad enough for a majority to believe that its policies were needed, but not so bad as to present it with immediate problems.

The objectives of the Carter Administration

The general objectives of the Carter Administration were to reduce unemployment to 4.5 per cent by 1981, which was considered to be the full employment level of unemployment at that time. The budget was to be balanced and the share of federal outlays in total GNP reduced to 21 per cent. In addition, there were plans to inject $60 billion into the economy in increased spending on social programmes and tax changes over the full four years.[2] These targets or objectives were based on some rather optimistic assumptions concerning economic trends. Given the proposed stimulation of the economy it was assumed that the average growth over the four years would be 3.75 per cent per annum; that inflation would average 5.5 per cent; and that this would yield a total GNP of $2.9 trillion in 1981.[3]

These proposals represented a compromise between Mr Carter's more conservative preferences and the more liberal Democrats in Congress whose five-year programme to obtain full employment would have cost more than Mr Carter was prepared to spend.[4] The problem was, therefore, how to reconcile President Carter's own more conservative economic preferences and the more liberal-spending Democrats.

Early uncertainties

The option chosen for solving this dilemma was to have a stimulative package based on a once-and-for-all tax concession.[5] This method was chosen because a permanent tax reduction would have reduced revenues in the long term, and thus made subsequent balancing of the budget difficult. Furthermore, it was recognized that tax reductions would be needed in order to 'buy' the major tax reforms which President Carter planned to initiate. Even on the early, fairly optimistic assumptions of growth and inflation there was little scope for large-scale tax cuts, so that permanent cuts would have to be deferred to coincide with tax reform. In early 1977, and before President Carter had initiated the stimulative package, his Council of Economic Advisors revised their assessment of potential future GNP, and thus tax revenue. On this new assessment it seemed less likely that targets for spending and tax cuts could be squared with a balanced budget.

The stimulative package which finally emerged consisted of $15 billion in once-and-for-all tax cuts in 1977, and $15 billion in longer-term job creation for 1978. The latter took the form of urban aid programmes, public works and education programmes. The tax concession attracted much criticism for being inflationary, only contributing to increased consumption and not promoting investment. By early 1977, however, it became clear that the economy was growing fast without the need for a stimulative package. After some delay President Carter finally announced that the tax cuts would no longer be made, but that the longer-term measures for 1978 would go ahead as planned.

This early reversal of a policy decision gave the impression that the Administration was uncertain in its judgement of the state of the economy. It came at a time when the new Administration was under attack from those who felt that its policies were inflationary, and tended to confirm that the reconciliation between the more liberal-spending and fiscal conservatives in the Administration would weaken the resolve of the Government to make difficult decisions on economic priorities. The decision not to proceed with the reflationary package in 1977 also undermined the efforts of the United States to get the Germans and Japanese to reflate their economies in a co-ordinated manner, because it came only shortly before the United States met with the leading world economic powers. After deciding against reflation for itself, the United States could not press others to expand their economies.[6]

While much was made of this early indecision concerning the stimulative package, it was a lack of confidence in President Carter's policy on inflation which was of more importance. The Carter Administration expected inflation to fall from 7 per cent in 1976 to 6 per cent in 1977 and 1978, and to 5 per cent in 1979 and 1980. This assumption was based on the rather optimistic view that inflationary expectations had worked their way through the system, and that there would be enough slack in the economy not to increase inflationary pressures as the economy moved toward full employment. It is difficult not to conclude that these views contained a good deal of wishful thinking.

The anti-inflation programme announced in spring 1977 failed to convince the sceptics that President Carter's policies would not lead to an acceleration of inflation. The main reason for this was that the policies had little political support and faced the opposition of strong constituencies. The proposals were based on a voluntary approach to price and wage restraint. Before his election, Mr Carter had decided against the use of mandatory wage and price controls in order to placate the business community, which would otherwise have increased prices in anticipation of controls. Despite this move there remained some business opinion which still envisaged controls when the policies finally failed, as they inevitably would.

President Carter's preference was for a wage and price control policy based on a kind of social contract in which balanced non-inflationary growth could be achieved if people were prepared to be reasonable.[7] The 1977 anti-inflation policy was based on the belief that inflationary expectations would decline; that earlier price increases were, in part, due to the fear of price controls; that the buffer stocks, which the Administration intended to introduce for energy and raw materials, would help stabilize prices and minimize the risks of external shocks leading to inflation; and that firm commitment to a balanced budget would show that the Administration was serious about controlling inflation.[8] The anti-inflation policy consisted of voluntary price and wage control; the active use of anti-trust legislation to enhance domestic competition; and the absence of import controls to ensure a degree of import competition. Competition would be expected to hold down prices. The role of the Council on Wage and Price Stability was to be enhanced so that it could follow, on a micro scale, the price and wage developments in any given sector. As no one wishes to be held responsible for causing inflationary pressures, the Administration could use the threat of publicizing price and wage trends, it was argued, as a means of restraining inflationary wage settlements.

Organized labour opposed the policy because it felt that voluntary measures would inevitably discriminate against wages, and that the only way of guaranteeing fairness was indeed to have a mandatory system. On the other hand, the business community and financial communities did not believe that inflation could be controlled without a tighter control of the money supply. In the early days of the new Administration, Arthur Burns, the Chairman of the Federal Reserve, also consistently criticized the policy, arguing that it would lead to high rates of inflation. These early doubts about the economic policies of the Carter Administration meant that it had an uphill struggle convincing Congress of the need to support its policies.

The Carter Administration

The economic team President Carter assembled was technically qualified to deal with the complexities of the modern economy.

The fact that the economic policy-makers were technically on top of most of the issues meant that there were few major problems in formulating complex policy proposals. The economic team did, however, lack some political weight, which may go some way towards explaining why it had so much difficulty getting its proposals through Congress. The Administration also lacked a clear spokesperson on economic policy, which caused some confusion about the direction of policy and led to conflicting signals on more than one occasion.[9]

President Carter brought Bert Lance from Georgia to head the Office of Management and Budget (OMB). Lance was a close political ally of the President, and could be relied upon to support him in the event of differences with more liberal Cabinet members.[10] It was, therefore, a significant setback for Carter when Lance was forced to resign after a long, and very public, investigation of his credit dealings as a private banker. President Carter had sought to defend Lance against what he saw as an irresponsible press campaign throughout the spring of 1977, but in the end the 'Lancegate' affair cost him a close political ally and undermined confidence in his Administration. Lance was replaced by James McIntyre, who lacked the political weight of his predecessor.

Charles Schultze was brought back to government as Chief Economic Advisor. Schultze had had nearly twenty-five years' experience in economic policy formulation, starting with the Eisenhower Administration in which he was on the staff of the Council of Economic Advisors. In the Kennedy Administration he joined, and under Johnson became head of, the Bureau of the Budget (now OMB). Schultze came in for some criticism on the grounds that under Johnson he had presided over one of the most marked increases in federal spending in United States' history. It would be wrong, however, to classify Schultze as a freespender. Under Carter he probably occupied the middle ground between those, including the President, who wanted a balanced budget, and those who placed higher priority on economic growth.

Breaking with the convention of appointing a banker as Secretary of the Treasury, Carter chose Michael Blumenthal for this post. Blumenthal, who probably gave the Administration something of a liberal slant, was described as being profit-conscious but socially aware.[11] Blumenthal was also more internationalist in his outlook than most Treasury secretaries. Much of his experience and interest lay in international eco- nomic issues. He had been Deputy Assistant Secretary for Economic Affairs in the State Department, where he had led the US delegation to the Kennedy Round of multilateral trade negotiations. He had also been very involved in international economic issues as a leading member of the Trilateral Com- mission, to which a number of other officials, and the President himself had belonged. The presence of Blumenthal at the Treasury, together with other members of the Cabinet who, by tradition, adopt a more international view of economic problems, such as the Secretary of State and the US Trade Representative, meant that the leading members of the Carter Administration were probably more outward-looking on eco- nomic issues than most US administrations. The other core members of the Economic Policy Group (EPG) were Richard Cooper from the State Department, Juanita Kreps from Com- merce and Ray Marshall from the Department of Labor.

In pursuit of the Administration's policies on the co- ordination of macro-economic policies and trade negotiations, Vice President Mondale immediately travelled to Europe and Richard Cooper to Japan to seek agreement on global economic expansion and a swift conclusion to the GATT trade talks. In the trade field, the task of negotiating the Tokyo Round, and equally important, of getting the US Congress to accept what was agreed, was given to Robert Strauss, who thus became the US Special Trade Representative (now USTR). Strauss was one of the members of the Carter Administration who carried some political weight, which he employed to some effect in getting the GATT agreements through Congress. The status of the US Trade Representative is always enhanced by the exis- tence of trade negotiations, and the fact that great importance was placed on completion of the Tokyo Round, meant that Strauss had a relatively high standing in the Administration.

While the Carter Administration generally handled trade issues well, things were different in the field of monetary policy. As discussed above, Burns had used his position as Chairman of the Federal Reserve Bank to criticize the Admini- stration's policies. This clearly caused tensions between the White House and the Federal Reserve (the Fed), which senior economic officials and many Democrats saw as damaging the credibility of the Administration's policies. President Carter himself was probably less concerned about Burns than some of his officials and there was some debate about whether he would in fact keep Burns on when his four-year term came to an end in late 1977. In Congress a bill was introduced which would have empowered the President to appoint the Chairman of the Federal Reserve for a term of office to run concurrently with that of the President. This proposal was modified because of fears that it would encroach into the independence of the Federal Reserve in implementing US monetary policy, and in the end a compromise was reached in which the Chairman was to be appointed for a term of four years, commencing one year after the beginning of the presidential term.[12]

Arthur Burns was replaced by William Miller, another business-person like Blumenthal and Kreps, in January 1978. Following the tensions with Burns, there was some concern that the Administration would appoint someone who could be expected to follow instructions from the White House, and would there-fore fail to uphold the independence of the Fed. This fear was, however, soon dispelled and the financial community had reasonable confidence in Miller even if he was not a banker.

Faced with a continued lack of confidence in his economic policies, the President made some important changes in his economic team in the summer of 1979. Blumenthal, who had been hard-pressed to establish himself as the leading spokesman on economic issues, left the Administration and was replaced by Miller as Secretary of the Treasury. Paul Volker, who had been Chairman of the Reserve Bank of New York, was appointed to lead the Federal Reserve, and thus became the first banker to hold a leading post in the Carter Administration. These changes heralded the major shift in US monetary policy which came in October 1979, in response to a continued lack of confidence in the dollar and the ability of the Administration to control inflation.

Effectiveness of policies

The strength of the economy in the early stages of his Admini-stration helped President Carter make progress towards his general objectives, despite the apparent disarray in policy-making. By the end of 1978 unemployment had fallen from the 8 per cent of 1976, and was close to Carter's objective of full employment. It was estimated that an unemployment rate of 5.1 per cent was the full employment rate at that time.[13] In the last quarter of 1978 unemployment had fallen to 5.8 per cent.

The budget deficit was held at $44.8 billion in 1977, after a deficit of $45 billion in 1976 and President Carter was planning to reduce it to $37.4 billion in 1979. Therefore, although a balanced budget was still some way off, progress had been made towards the objective. There was also a reduction in the share of federal expenditure in GNP, which fell to about 22 per cent of GNP in 1979, from nearly 23 per cent in 1977. After some initial successes, however, things began to go wrong in 1978. Throughout 1978 Carter resisted pressure from his conservative critics, and foreign governments, to act to slow the growth in demand, in part, because of congressional elections in November 1978 and because he preferred a more long-term indicative approach to controlling inflation.

Much of the progress made towards reducing the budget deficit was due to the growth of the economy and inflation, both of which had the effect of increasing tax revenue. There were no significant reductions in any spending programmes even with the use of zero-based budgeting (ZBB).[14] Inflation was 9 per cent during 1978 and with the economy close to full employment President Carter switched to controlling inflation as his main priority at the end of 1978. In November both monetary and fiscal policies, were to be tightened.[15] Despite the fall in the budget deficit, $40 billion was still too high. In 1976 the deficit was countercyclical but in late 1978 a large deficit, projected at $37 billion for 1979, was procyclical; i.e. it was tending to add further stimulus to the economy.

In November 1978 interest rates were increased to 10 per cent, up from about 6 per cent at the beginning of the year and there was a shift towards controlling demand as a means of slowing the economy but it was a gradualist approach, which was to go hand-in-hand with voluntary wage and price controls. The objective was still to contain inflation without precipitating a recession. In early 1979 inflation accelerated and reached 13 per cent in March. There was a continued decline of the dollar, which threatened to develop into a currency crisis, and as the year proceeded, it became clear that

President Carter's anti-inflation policy was falling apart. Just as they had underestimated the strength of the economic recovery in late 1976, the Carter economic team also underestimated what it would take to slow the economy. Midway through 1979 it became clear that President Carter could not enter an election campaign in 1980 with double-digit inflation which, by this time, had become the number one political issue. It was also clear that only a recession could check the economic growth and thus inflation.

President Carter, therefore, chose to go for a short sharp recession which would still leave him a few months of economic expansion in the run-up to the election.[16] This attempt at fine tuning resulted in volatile interest rates and caused uncertainty at home and abroad. There was a short sharp recession, followed by a spurt of growth, but the overall result was an annual rate of inflation of 13 per cent in 1980. By precipitating the recession, President Carter lost favour among traditional Democrat voters, and his late conversion to a policy of controlling the money supply also failed to convince conservatives that he could control inflation. As a result, he entered the election without much support on the basis of his economic policies. Earlier important achievements in reducing unemployment, as well as in certain aspects of international economic policy, were pushed from electors' minds by the fear of inflation and the prospect of major tax reductions promised by Mr Reagan.

Fiscal policy

President Carter did not achieve his objective of a balanced budget by the end of his term of office. After a deficit of $66 billion in 1976 and about $45 billion in 1977 and 1978 the deficit rose to $60 billion again in 1980. On coming to office, President Carter had had to consider the 1977 budget proposals of his predecessor. As discussed above, Carter planned a stimulative tax concession of $15 billion in 1977, followed by a further $15 billion in increased spending in 1978. In view of the strength of the economy in 1977, the tax concession was dropped, which left only minor tax changes in 1977. Congress increased the spending from $15 billion to about $20 billion for the year 1978, but on balance Carter's 1977 budget was ultimately no more expansionary than that proposed by Ford.[17]

In the late 1978 budget, drawn up in 1977, there were no significant increases in spending in addition to those already set out as part of the 1977 economic stimulation package. As in previous years, however, Congress ensured that taxes were reduced to compensate for increased tax revenue due to inflation. With inflation, taxpayers are moved into· higher tax brackets and thus pay higher taxes. In order to compensate for this tax drift Congress has generally reduced taxes so as to hold individual contributions at about 11 per cent of income. In 1978 the Carter Administration also wished to see a reduction in taxes in order to stimulate the economy.

In the 1979 budget the Carter Administration also recommended tax reductions to compensate for tax drift. Tax reductions of $25 billion and increased spending of a further $8 billion, mainly on energy-related projects, youth unemployment and education, were therefore proposed to offset the deflationary effects of the $30 billion tax drift, and to ensure that the Administration's objective of a 4.75 per cent rate of economic growth was continued in 1979. The 1979 budget proposals were therefore expansionary.[18] In early 1978 inflation was only just beginning to accelerate from a rate of 6 per cent at the beginning of the year, so the Administration did not believe that the budget would be inflationary. It also believed that the economy would slow down if the $25 billion tax reduction was not made. On the spending side there was little or no evidence that the introduction of zero-based budgeting techniques had had any effect on the rate of growth of expenditure. As outlays were growing at a rate of more than 10 per cent, merely compensating for inflation meant that the target of a balanced budget was pushed further into the future.

When President Carter came to consider the 1980 budget he had already made inflation his first priority.[19] In late 1978 he committed himself to a budget deficit of less than $30 billion for the fiscal year 1980, as a means of showing his determination to do so. Combined with the dynamic of increased expenditure based on past programmes this meant that he had very little flexibility in drawing up what was a critical budget. There was no scope for any reduction in taxation, and thus no way of responding to the tax-cuts offensive of the Republicans, following the controversial vote in favour of the so-called Proposition 13 in California, which created a momentum for tax reductions in the whole country. At the same time, United States' commitments to increased defence spending meant that a greater burden of cuts would have to fall on non-defence expenditure.

In order to keep the deficit below $30 billion, spending on existing programmes had to be cut. The main reductions in expenditure were to focus on another attempt at reducing federal spending on health programmes by containing price rises in medical charges, and holding public-sector pay rises to 5.5 per cent. The pay policy was clearly seen by the Administration as showing the way for moderation in private-sector pay negotiations. Even in 1979 the chances of keeping the deficit below $30 billion were not seen as being very great, and the Congressional Budget Office, working on more realistic assumptions of growth and inflation, projected a deficit of more than $40 billion for 1980. In the end this figure turned out to be optimistic.

During his election campaign President Carter promised to make the tax system fairer by introducing major tax reforms. Given the difficulties encountered in past attempts at tax reform it was probably necessary to give such an objective a very high priority, and to introduce legislation at an early stage. This did not happen, and indeed even before the election Mr Carter had decided not to act immediately but to delay making proposals for one year.[20] In 1977 he again delayed, largely because of the fact that Congress was already burdened with a number of bills, such as the energy bill, which had important tax implications. When he finally introduced his modest reform proposals as part of the 1979 budget they were swept aside by Congress, which accepted tax reductions but was not interested in any changes in the structure of taxes, such as the controversial plans to end tax deductions for business lunches and entertainment.[21]

Unemployment

In the early stages of the Carter Administration significant progress was made towards reducing unemployment. By the beginning of 1978 unemployment was down to 5.7 per cent— its lowest level since 1974—and millions of new jobs had been created, with 3.5 million in one period of just twelve months.

This positive achievement of the Carter Administration was, however, forgotten by 1980.

Wage and price stability

By shifting his attention to inflation in the latter part of his term, Carter put his policies in tune with the trend in majority public opinion. But his past record on controlling inflation was not good, and many held his policies responsible for creating inflation in the first place. His anti-inflation policy was driven by, rather than in control of, inflation, so that as inflation quickened efforts were made to strengthen the policy. In April 1978 Robert Strauss was given the job of leading the President's anti-inflation task force, but despite rising inflation Carter clung to his belief in a voluntary approach to wage and price controls, augmented by the work of the Council on Wage and Price Stability.

In October 1978 there was another change in staff, when Alfred Kahn took over the job of leading the task force. At the same time an attempt was made to introduce a wage norm of 7 per cent with the backing of a real wage insurance policy. Under this scheme any group settling for a pay rise of 7 per cent or less who subsequently found that inflation reduced the increase in their real income to less than 7 per cent would be entitled to tax concessions which guaranteed an increase of 7 per cent. To limit the commitment on the part of the executive, real income was only to be guaranteed up to a limit set at an inflation rate of 10 per cent.

On prices, guidelines were laid down which were intended to keep price rises below the average of the previous two years. In October 1978 the Administration also proposed measures to back up these indicative guidelines with the threat of sanctions. The sanctions took the form of a potential denial of public procurement contracts for any company, with contracts valued at more than $5 million, which exceeded the price guidelines. In other words, the voluntary policy failed and had to be replaced by a progressively more interventionist one.

During 1979 the wage and price policy was challenged by organized labour. In a major test the Teamsters Union went on strike for wage increases in excess of the 7 per cent norm. Although the Administration modified its pay norm in an attempt to prevent a strike, a strike still took place which was only ended by a settlement which exceeded the pay norms. In the summer of 1979 President Carter became personally involved in 'jawboning', or using political muscle to persuade companies to moderate price increases, but the policy could not be rescued.

Monetary policy

To begin with, the Administration used interest rates as a target variable for its monetary policy rather than the growth in money supply. It was particularly keen to reduce interest rates in order to stimulate investment, and thus do something to improve the poor record on productivity. With a given target for interest rates the money supply was allowed to fluctuate in order to balance supply and demand for money. The more monetarist-orientated economists, such as Arthur Burns at the Federal Reserve, argued that the growth in the money supply should have been the target variable and should have been carefully controlled so as to prevent inflation but allow for non-inflationary growth.

After two years of trying to hold down interest rates the first change came in November 1978 when a move was made to tighten monetary control and increase interest rates. But the general orientation of policy remained basically unchanged. It was not until after Volker had taken over at the Federal Reserve that there was a major reversal of policy, in October 1979, when the money supply became the target variable. Interest rates were allowed to fluctuate, and there followed a period in which they varied dramatically, reaching a peak of 20 per cent. The change in monetary policy was mainly due to domestic concerns about inflation, but the policy change was also motivated by a desire to avert a currency crisis with the dollar suffering continued attacks in foreign exchange markets.

International economic policy

Unlike the previous, or subsequent administrations, the Carter Administration had a positive international economic policy. The intention was a world-wide economic recovery in order to reduce the risk of the multilateral economic order collapsing under the weight of protectionist pressures and the mounting burden of Third World debt. There was also a desire to strengthen the existing system by, in particular, concluding the Tokyo Round of trade negotiations.[22]

The more robust growth of the US economy certainly helped to stimulate the world economy at a time when growth was slowing in a number of countries. The United States was, however, not very successful in gaining support for its policy of co-ordinated economic expansion which it had promoted in the form of the locomotive theory. The locomotive concept was based on the view that growth in the United States, and some other surplus countries, such as the Federal Republic of Germany and Japan, would more effectively help bring about a world-wide recovery, if it was co-ordinated.

As discussed above, the failure to gain German and Japanese support was, in part, due to the unfortunate timing of the cancellation of the 1977 economic stimulation package. The main reason for failing to gain the support of the other countries was, however, that they simply were not particularly interested in expansion at that time. The Germans, for example, argued that the only way their economy had any further scope for non-inflationary growth was via export-led growth, and the German authorities were afraid that reflating domestic demand would result in inflation.

As early as March 1977 it became clear that the Carter Administration was getting less than full support from the United States' major economic allies. Nevertheless, US economic expansion continued; but without support from other countries the US trade deficit deteriorated as it imported more foreign products into its growing economy.

In 1978 some progress was made towards a co-ordinated approach during the Western economic summit in Bonn. In return for the agreement of the Federal Republic of Germany and Japan to specific targets for economic growth the United States was, however, obliged to agree to reduce oil imports. The other OECD countries were concerned that the rapid growth of US oil imports would push up the price of oil. President Carter was happy to go along with such a proposal because he too was keen to reduce oil imports. From the outset his Administration had recognized that the United States had to reduce its oil imports if it was to provide a constructive lead in the world economy. Pressure from other countries was particularly welcome if it could help President Carter persuade Congress to legislate on his energy policies. On the other hand, however, the lack of progress on energy did some damage to United States credibility in international economic relations.

The Carter Administration's commitment to maintaining an open trading system was also apparent from the beginning. After receiving confirmation from the other trading blocs on the need to speed up negotiations, President Carter made it clear to domestic lobbies, such as the automobile industry, that he was not prepared to give in to protectionist pressures. Carter maintained this position through almost all of his term in office. In the run-up to the Presidential election this position cost him some political support, and it was only in the period immediately before the election in 1980 that he appeared to adopt a less strident anti-protectionist position. For example, in response to calls for protection for the automobile industry Carter reminded the industry that when he had first come to office he had called on that industry to produce more fuel-efficient cars. Had they done so, he argued, they would have been more able to match import competition from Japan.[23]

In general terms therefore, the Carter Administration was prepared to accept some domestic costs in its efforts to maintain an open trading system. When it came to important trade policy decisions such as how to deal with the problems in the steel industry, the international slant in the Cabinet may well have been a determining factor in resisting protectionist pressures. By retaining control of trade policy within the executive, such as by means of the trigger price mechanism for steel, the Carter Administration was able to avoid the disruptive effects of numerous private petitions for remedies against imports. In this way it did much to defuse tensions in trade policy. During the Tokyo Round it was often the United States which dragged a somewhat reluctant European Community into the negotiations and in doing so helped sustain a relatively open international trading system.

In the field of international monetary relations it was a different picture. The Carter Administration got into difficulties early on when the strength of US economic growth, and a general uncertainty about US economic policies, led to a fall in the value of the dollar. Rather than seeking to reassure nervous exchange markets, Secretary Blumenthal suggested that the Carter Administration would be prepared to see the dollar float down still further. The view in the Administration was that a depreciation of the dollar would help to promote exports, and that one should in any case not intervene in floating exchange rate markets. The United States was then roundly accused of having talked down the dollar.

In what came to be known as a policy of 'benign neglect', or 'malign neglect', as many Europeans argued, the dollar was allowed to depreciate. When the decline continued throughout 1977 and 1978 concern grew in Europe, where the decline was seen as destabilizing. The main problem was that as the dollar declined other currencies and in particular the D-Mark became stronger. The appreciation of the mark, and of the yen, not only made it harder for these countries to export, it also tended to increase the rate of domestic money supply in the countries concerned as central banks intervened, buying dollars in order to check the appreciation of their currencies. More importantly, however, the appreciation of the Mark brought pressure on the weaker European currencies in the European currency snake. These weaker currencies then had the choice of either deflating their economies in order to defend their currencies, or of leaving the currency snake.

Towards the end of 1978 there was increased United States intervention in support of the dollar in currency markets, mainly because of the fear that a further decline would lead OPEC countries to increase the price of oil in order to compensate for the declining value of their dollar-denominated oil revenues. Swap agreements were reached with the German, Swiss and French central banks, which provided the Federal Reserve with funds to buy dollars. This intervention helped stabilize the markets a little but the value of the dollar remained volatile.

During 1978 European criticism of US economic policy intensified, and the policy was seen by some as being amateurish.[24] Finally, in late 1978 the Germans and French, frustrated with ineffective attempts to stabilize international money markets by focusing on the dollar, decided to create a European zone of currency stability in the form of the European Monetary System (EMS). The 'inability of Congress and President Carter to reach any meaningful economic policy decision',[25] was seen as an important reason for seeking such a European solution.

It would be wrong to overstate the problems caused by US

monetary policy. Given the continued dominance of the dollar in international monetary relations, the European economies have always been dependent on US economic policy. This asymmetry will almost always cause tensions. However, there can also be little doubt that the Carter Administration underestimated how important its domestic economic policies were in influencing what happened to the dollar.

Faced with the complexities of increasing international economic interdependence, the Carter Administration adopted an outward-looking approach, which sought to face up to the problems caused by such interdependence. Whilst it was not successful in everything it tried, its active foreign economic policy largely kept faith with the concept of constructive leadership of the international system by the United States. The trend since 1980 has been to insulate domestic economies from the implications of economic interdependence. Whilst this approach is undoubtedly more popular among domestic constituencies it remains to be seen what the effects of increased tensions in international trade and debt will have on the United States' and world economies.

Conclusions

The Carter Administration, therefore, had a mixed record on economic policy. After initial progress in the domestic economy the failure to devise an effective means of containing inflation led to an overheating of the economy. When President Carter was finally forced to act he was approaching the 1980 Presidential elections, and was put in a bad position politically by the lack of flexibility in his economic policies. He found himself in this position because of his earlier reluctance to restrict demand as a means of bringing the economy under control. In its international economy policy, however, the Carter Administration had some degree of success with its trade policies.

Notes

1. Joseph A. Pechman (ed.), *Setting National Priorities: The 1980 Budget*, The Brookings Institution, Washington, DC, 1979.
2. Joseph A. Pechman (ed.), *Setting National Priorities: The 1978 Budget*, The Brookings Institution, Washington, DC, 1977, p. 359.

3. Pechman, *The 1978 Budget*, p. 368.
4. *New York Times*, 18 June 1976.
5. For details see Pechman, *The 1978 Budget*, p. 43.
6. *Financial Times*, 15 April 1977.
7. *Financial Times*, 16 April 1977.
8. For a detailed description of the policy see Pechman, *The 1978 Budget*.
9. See *The Times*, 3 November 1977 and *Fortune*, June 1977.
10. *Financial Times*, 14 September 1977.
11. George Mellon, *The Carter Economy*, Wiley, New York, 1978, p. 76.
12. *Financial Times*, 24 June 1977.
13. Pechman, *The 1980 Budget*, p. 29.
14. The zero-based budget was a system Carter had introduced in Georgia. Its object was to ensure that existing expenditure competes with new expenditure for resources rather than simply basing a budget on the previous year, suitably increased to account for inflation.
15. *International Herald Tribune*, 2 November 1978.
16. *Financial Times*, 8 October 1979.
17. Pechman, *The 1978 Budget*, p. 3.
18. Joseph A. Pechman (ed.), *Setting National Priorities: The 1979 Budget*, The Brookings Institution, Washington, DC, 1978, Chapter 1.
19. Pechman, *The 1980 Budget*.
20. *International Herald Tribune*, 28 July 1976.
21. *Financial Times*, 12 August 1978.
22. See speech by Richard Cooper, the Deputy Assistant Secretary of State for Economic Affairs, outlining the US foreign economic policy of the time, *International Communication Agency*, 21 March 1977.
23. *The Times*, 18 May 1977.
24. *Financial Times*, 2 March 1978.
25. *The Times*, 7 September 1978.

4 The Carter Presidency and foreign policy

Raymond A. Moore

Carter and the Kissinger legacy

When Jimmy Carter of Plains, Georgia, became President of the United States on 20 January 1977, he was confronted by the foreign policy legacy of the Nixon and Ford administrations, called, not without reason, the Kissinger Era. As *The New York Times* remarked on his departure, 'Henry Kissinger has not been President of the United States for the past eight years: it only seemed that way much of the time'.[1]

This legacy, discussed at great length in Kissinger's memoirs as well as in those of Nixon and Ford and quite critically in Seymour Hersh's *The Price of Power*, was comprised not only of concrete policies but of philosophies and styles as well.[2] Looking at 'The Kissinger Legacy', Leslie Gelb suggests that it was composed of three periods.[3] The first, from 1969 to 1973, saw Kissinger organizing and running the National Security Council but functioning as a Secretary of State. During this period SALT I was ratified, helped along by back-channel negotiations which were also used to facilitate ping-pong diplomacy and the historic opening to China. Meetings with Le Duc Tho of North Vietnam led to the Paris Peace Accords and a ceasefire in Vietnam. *Détente* was emerging as the keystone of Soviet–American relations.

In the second period, Nixon was consumed by Watergate. Kissinger became Secretary of State as well as Special Assistant for National Security Affairs. It was time for shuttle diplomacy to settle the Yom Kippur War, bringing about troop disengagement in the Middle East and peace for the first time in twenty years. It saw the Soviet Union and the United States at loggerheads over the Middle East, the imposition of an oil embargo, the Turkish–Greek Cyprus dispute of 1974 and the crisis over the USSR Trade Bill caused by the Jackson Amendment, which mandated the Soviets to permit Jewish immigration, mostly to Israel. It also saw Nixon's resignation and the accession of Gerald Ford to the presidency.

The final period, lasting until Carter's inauguration, saw Kissinger having to surrender his National Security Adviser's hat, struggling with Congress over Angola and Rhodesia, and defending his record on wiretaps of his colleagues and CIA covert activities in Chile. Negotiations on SALT II faltered and second thoughts about *détente* arose, even to the extent of Ford's purging the word from his election campaign. Increasingly, attention was paid to global problems such as the world economy, energy, sea-beds, health and international law.

The Kissinger legacy included his grand design to build a new structure of peace based on a stable and enduring balance of power. This would avert nuclear disaster and pave the way toward the solution of global problems through a strategy of interdependence. *Détente* with the Soviets would be achieved through an admixture of power, persuasion, threat and the creation of a network of vested mutual interests. American credibility would be maintained not only by military power but by *realpolitik* diplomacy practised by a modern-day Bismarck or Castlereagh who could safely steer the ship of state between the rocks and reefs of troubled international waters. This diplomacy would require cunning, secrecy, manœuvring and back channels. Above all, it would require a knowledge of, respect for and judicious use of power to achieve the noble goals of international equilibrium and global order.

The Carter critique

During his presidential campaign Jimmy Carter offered his critique of these policies. Both the style and substance of the Nixon–Ford–Kissinger policies were attacked in his campaign speeches. Among the themes developed were the following:

1. That America's image had been tarnished by the use of machiavellian tactics—secret diplomacy, back channels, 'Lone Ranger' diplomacy, excessive concern with power politics and an accompanying neglect of principles and morality.
2. The United States had been out-traded by the Soviets on *détente* in agreeing to a SALT I treaty which allowed both

too-high and unequal numbers of missiles, permitted itself to become stalemated in the Middle East and remained overly passive regarding the aspirations of Africa and Latin America.

3. The United States became a status quo power, interested in preserving the prerogatives of the superpowers and maintaining a posture of historical pessimism.

4. SALT talks had stalled, instead of advancing, after SALT I. Nuclear proliferation continued to complicate arms control.

5. Human rights had been neglected for *realpolitik*, and Third World countries had been ignored in the pursuit of an East–West condominium.

6. Congress and the American people had been by-passed in the making of US policy. A 'closed' decision-making process had short-circuited input from a wider spectrum of American opinion.

It is true, as Brzezinski points out, that 'Every new administration feels it has a mandate for new foreign policy. This is especially the case when a new President comes from a different party than his predecessor'.[4] There is also, as Carter himself has admitted, 'driving pressure' on a challenger to 'dispute or contradict the President on the issues' in order to advance his political interests.[5] Nevertheless, this does not explain away Carter's genuine commitment to some new and different policies.

If one may be barbarously Barberesque for a moment and reflect on Carter's foreign policy image during the campaign and his first year in office, it is possible to say that his 'active positive' character exhibited a devout, 'born again' biblical soul and a tough, smart, hard-working, technocratic mind. His 'world view' was filled with the good intentions of neo-Wilsonianism and a missionary zeal for good works. His 'style' was keyed to bobbing and weaving with the polls and public opinion. He was supremely opportunistic, with an 'outer-directed' policy that took its cues from the latest configuration of Almond's foreign policy mood patterns. His 'power position' dictated that he be anti-Washington, anti-Watergate, anti-Nixon and Ford, anti-power politics, anti-secret diplomacy and the policies and style of Kissinger, and against traditional interest group politics. The 'climate of expectations' demanded that he should do something different from Nixon, Ford and Kissinger.[6]

What he did, out of a combination of politics, character and commitment, was to renounce the politics of power, embrace morality and elevate Third World problems to the level of high policy. As John Stoessinger remarks, Jimmy Carter was 'a born again Baptist and deeply religious person. The new president had decided to make a concern for human rights the cornerstone of his foreign policy'.[7] Carter believed that the United States had been damaged by Watergate, Vietnam and the CIA revelations and that the best thing the country could do to change its image as a nation with no moral values or with moral values that it had forgotten, would be to deal fairly with the world's downtrodden, persecuted and abused, under the aegis of freedom, democracy and human rights.[8]

Carter also felt that some long-standing issues needed resolving under a new administration. One was the passage of the Panama Canal Treaty which had been bedevilling presidents since 1964. Another was the normalization of relations with China, which had languished since the first spectacular China opening in 1971. A third thrust was to conclude the SALT negotiations which had been going on for five years under Ford and Nixon, and had produced SALT I and the Vladivostok agreement. Following these agreements, negotiations had dragged on and, according to Carter, had been put on the back burner because in the 1976 primaries, Ronald Reagan contested Ford for the Republican nomination. Carter was determined to rejuvenate SALT II and to conclude it by 1978 after the Panama Canal Treaty had been passed.[9]

The Carter Administration's image of the international system

According to Jerel Rosati,

During its tenure the Carter Administration developed an image of the international system which changed substantially over time. Furthermore, while the early image of the international system was initially shared by the three principal policy-makers involved [Carter, Vance, Brzezinski], intra-administration differences eventually emerged until consensus was revived during the final year.[10]

This image consisted of a quest for global community in a

complex world. Although the system was complex, it was not rigidly bipolar. Global change could take place. As President Carter said, 'It is a new world, but America should not fear it. It is a new world and we should help shape it. It is a new world that calls for a new American foreign policy'.[11] Carter hoped to build a new international system which contained 'a new world-wide mosaic of global, regional, and bilateral relations'.[12] Interdependence was the new international reality and neither the United States nor the Soviet Union could control the world's destiny. Mutual co-operation was not just a convenience, but a necessity.

The Old Order of the post-World War II era was thought to be over. New issues and actors were arriving on the international scene. The focus on East–West issues and the US–Soviet rivalry was considered anachronistic. As Rosati suggests, 'Human rights and democracy, normalization and improvement of relations, the resolution of conflict in Africa and the Middle East, arms control, the health of the global economy, and Third World development were all believed to be significant issues'.[13]

Clearly the Carter Administration thought it could improve the world by emphasizing the positive aspects of America with a new, different and better foreign policy. Fundamental to its pursuit of a global community was its perception of the Soviet Union. The Soviet Union was at first viewed optimistically as a country with limited capabilities, occasionally opportunistic but basically co-operative and peaceful in its intentions. Carter himself was especially sanguine about the Soviets' peaceful intentions; as a result, East–West and Soviet–American relations could be regarded in context with other world problems. As President Carter put it:

Our national security was often defined almost exclusively in terms of military competition with the Soviet Union. This competition is still critical because it does involve issues which could lead to war. But however important this relationship of military balance, it cannot be our sole preoccupation, to the exclusion of other world issues which also concern us both.[14]

In fact, according to Rosati's analysis of seven major issues (human rights, normalization of relations, arms control, Middle East, Africa, the international economy and Third World development) that 'were of principal concern throughout the first year, Carter Administration policy-makers believed that the Soviet Union had a major role to play only for arms control.'[15] This perception of the Soviets allowed the US to take the initiative in other areas.

One of those areas was concern for human rights, which became the early cornerstone of Carter's foreign policy, and clearly differentiated him from his predecessors.

What the Administration had in mind was to integrate human rights considerations into its bilateral and multilateral relationships as a key element in decision-making. A case-by-case approach was used to improve specific human rights situations. The policy, while concerned with progress on a full range of human rights, continued to recognize differences among countries. These 'differences' were later used to justify continued aid to the Shah of Iran in spite of his increasingly serious violations of human rights. Critics made much of these alleged double standards.

The Administration's definition of human rights was based on United States historical documents and diplomatic experience, the United Nations Charter and other international instruments, including the Universal Declaration of Human Rights approved by the UN General Assembly in 1948. Among the human rights pursued were:

1. Freedom from arbitrary arrest and imprisonment, torture, unfair trial, cruel and unusual punishment, and invasion of privacy.
2. Rights to food, shelter, health care and education.
3. Freedom of thought, speech, assembly, religion, press, movement and participation in government.

To implement this policy, an Assistant Secretary of State for Human Rights and Humanitarian Affairs was appointed along with human rights officers in each bureau of the Department of State. An inter-agency committee was created to review human rights and foreign assistance issues. Other actions included the reduction or halting of military and security assistance to serious offenders and monitoring economic aid to see that it reached those who needed it most.

This commitment to human rights 'reflected Carter's own religious beliefs, as well as his political acumen', according to Brzezinski.[16] The policy was applied to the Soviets and Eastern

Europe, to Latin America and to Africa and became increasingly controversial as many regimes reacted vigorously to the Administration's attempt to impose principle by power.

An overview of the Administration's policy was expressed by its two chief foreign policy architects, Secretary of State Cyrus Vance and National Security Adviser Zbigniew Brzezinski. Vance said that 'Global interdependence . . . had become a reality'[17] and Brzezinski described the 'general philosophical presentation' as 'constructive global engagement'.[18]

New policies, new actors

For Vance—Kissinger's choice to be the Secretary of State under Nixon in 1968—a new realistic American foreign policy should consist of four basic principles:

1. It should be understood and supported by the American people and Congress.
2. It should formulate a program for managing East-West relations, especially US-Soviet relations.
3. There should be a recognition of the changes taking place in global, political, economic and social conditions and the need to understand the process of change.
4. It should harness the basic values of the Founding Fathers to foreign policy . . . America would flourish in a world where freedom flourishes.[19]

For Brzezinski who, along with Henry Owen and Richard Gardner, wrote a long comprehensive foreign policy position paper for Carter, the ten major goals of the Administration were:

1. To engage Western Europe, Japan and other advanced democracies in a closer political co-operation.
2. To weave a world-wide web of bilateral, political and economic relations with the new emerging regional 'influentials'.
3. To develop more accommodating North-South relations, political as well as economic, so as to develop greater economic stability and growth in the Third World, diminish hostility toward the United States, lessen Soviet influence, and increase the stake those nations would have in the good relations with the North and West.
4. To push US-Soviet strategic arms limitation talks into strategic arms reduction talks . . . we wanted to match Soviet ideological expansion by a more affirmative American posture on global human

rights, while seeking consistently to make *détente* both more comprehensive and more reciprocal.
5. To normalize US–Chinese relations.
6. To obtain a comprehensive Middle East settlement.
7. To set in motion a progressive and peaceful transformation of South Africa toward a bi-racial democracy while in the meantime forging elsewhere a coalition of moderate black African leaders in order to stem continental radicalization and eliminate the Soviet–Cuban presence from the continent.
8. To restrict the level of global armaments, unilaterally and through international agreements.
9. To enhance a global sensitivity to human rights through actions designed to highlight US observance of such rights and through multilateral and bilateral initiatives meant to influence other governments to give higher priority to such human rights.
10. To maintain a defense posture capable of deterring the Soviet Union, both on the strategic and the conventional level, from hostile acts and from political pressure.[20]

President Carter formally incorporated many of these goals into his major foreign policy speech at the Notre Dame Commencement on 22 May 1977.

To carry out these policies, Carter relied primarily on his Secretary of State and National Security Adviser with heavy input from Vice-President Walter Mondale and Secretary of Defense Harold Brown. In addition, Ambassador Andrew Young at the United Nations, Assistant Secretary of State for Human Rights Patricia Derian, Paul C. Warnke, the Director of the Arms Control and Disarmament Agency, and Stansfield Turner of the Central Intelligence Agency played key roles, as did Vance's chief assistant, Warren Christopher.

Vance, who was a mainline centrist in foreign policy and who felt Jimmy Carter was one too, organized his department along those lines and appointed a large number of career officers to senior positions. He also brought in people from outside government, such as Anthony Lake in policy planning, Richard Holbrooke for East Asian and Pacific Affairs, Richard Morse for management, Leslie Gelb as director of political–military affairs, William Maynes for international organization, Hodding Carter Jr. for public affairs, Marshall Shulman as special adviser on the Soviet Union, and Richard Cooper for international economic affairs.

Brzezinski, a naturalized citizen of Polish origin and a brilliant intellectual specialist in communist affairs at Columbia University, proceeded to reorganize The National Security Council in a fashion compatible with the needs of the President who wanted a simple and responsive system that could initiate, co-ordinate and supervise the execution of policy. Carter wanted no 'Lone Rangers' making policy at NSC by chairing multiple committees, so Brzezinski was forced to simplify the structure and share the 'chairing' power. One main committee created was the Policy Review Committee, which handled foreign policy issues, defence policy issues and international economic issues. The chair was to be rotated between the Secretaries of State, Defense and Treasury. In practice, Vance usually presided. The second committee, called the Special Co-ordinations Committee, dealt with intelligence, arms control and crisis management. Brzezinski headed up this committee which dealt with specific 'cross-cutting' issues requiring 'co-ordination in the development of options and the implementation of Presidential decisions.'[21]

The new National Security Council

The NSC is by statute a co-ordinating committee comprised of the President, the Vice-President, the Secretary of State and the Secretary of Defense, plus others invited by the president, such as the Director of Central Intelligence, the Chairman of the Joint Chiefs of Staff, the President's assistant for National Security Affairs, the Secretary of the Treasury and the Chairman of the Council of Economic Advisers. Brzezinski's main task was to co-ordinate and record the views and recommendations emanating from the SCC and the PRC. If no conclusions were reached, Brzezinski would prepare a summary report for Carter. When recommendations for action were arrived at by the principals, the National Security Adviser would forward a PD (or presidential directive) to the President for his signature. The summaries or PDs were not circulated to the SCC or PRC participants for review before they were sent to the President. According to Vance, 'this meant that the national security adviser had the power to interpret the thrust of discussion or frame the policy recommendations of department principals'.[22]

The Secretary of State was opposed to this arrangement and admits now that he made a serious mistake 'in not going to the mat on insisting that the draft memoranda be sent to the principals before they went to the president, whatever the risk'.[23] The risk in this case, which prompted Carter to adopt the procedure, was the fear of press leakage. Vance even recommended to his successor, Edmund Muskie, that he should insist on the right to review NSC-prepared summaries and presidential directives in draft form before they went to Carter.[24]

The NSC reorganization under Carter gave Brzezinski cabinet status. It also made the President the chief crisis manager and gave Brzezinski major influence in setting policy in sensitive areas. As Brzezinski notes in his memoirs:

Under the new system, the PRC was to be responsible for setting broad and longer-term policy lines; at the same time, I did preserve NSC control over especially sensitive or potentially important matters. Through co-ordination of the SALT decision process, I would have a major input on our policy toward the Soviet Union, while retention of crisis control meant that in the event of major difficulties I would be in a position to share the agenda and thus influence the outcome of our deliberations. The role of the Secretaries was formally enhanced, but certain key levers were reserved for the President's Assistant.[25]

It is apparent that the seeds of later difficulties between Vance and Brzezinski were planted early on in the Administration. These small cracks in harmony revolving around the review procedures and the committee allocation of issues at NSC gradually widened as it became evident that substantial differences also existed in the foreign policy outlooks of Vance and Brzezinski. These diverse outlooks meant that the Big Two of Carter's foreign policy team responded to the impact of external events and crisis in different ways.

The Soviet problem and changing images

While Carter, Vance and Brzezinski all shared an optimistic image of the Soviet Union at the outset, there were subtle differences between them. Carter and Vance were basically highly optimistic about a co-operative relationship with the Soviet Union, while Brzezinski was merely 'hopeful'.

I can say this, we are challenging the Soviets to co-operate with us or run the risk of becoming historically irrelevant to the great issues of our time. We are not being naive in the sense of expecting an instant accommodation. I think we're reasonably vigilant to the fact that the competition goes on and therefore we have to compete. But we are also very much aware of the fact that in this shrinking world the imperative of co-operation has become more urgent.[26]

Brzezinski was also sceptical about Soviet intentions and warned early on:

To be perfectly blunt . . . given the fact we still live in a world in which there is competition between the United States and the Soviet Union, given the fact that the Soviet Union has a different view of global change than we do in many significant respects, the Soviet Union may be tempted to adopt policies and then take action which would exacerbate and fuel conflicts.[27]

For Brzezinski, the Soviets were 'still on the upswing of the historical cycle—of assertiveness, of expectations. I think it would like to be number one. I don't think it feels comfortable being number two militarily and a much lower number in many other areas'.[28]

These subtle differences in outlook were outweighed by the degree of consensus among the three policy-makers as the second year of the Administration unfolded. Still high on the agenda were such items as the peaceful resolution of the Arab–Israeli conflict, the problems in Rhodesia, Namibia and South Africa, the SALT II negotiations, the normalization of the China relationship and the passage of the Panama Canal treaties. Concern for human rights continued unabated even though Argentina, Brazil, El Salvador and Guatemala all rejected US military aid in reaction to US attacks on their human rights practices.

This consensus began to show strain when Somalia invaded Ethiopia. The invasion was successfully repulsed after Ethiopia received large-scale military assistance from the Soviet Union and Cuba, including the use of Cuban troops. At about the same time Zaïre's copper-rich Katanga province was invaded by a force from Angola. These events caused Administration officials to re-evaluate their assumptions about the Soviet Union, whose actions in Africa were considered to be a breach of good faith. The President observed:

To the Soviet Union, *détente* seems to mean a continuing aggressive struggle for political advantage and increased influence in a variety of ways. The Soviet Union apparently sees military power and military assistance as the best means of expanding its influence abroad. Obviously areas of instability in the world produce a tempting target for this effort and all too often they seem ready to exploit any such opportunities.[29]

At the same time, the President challenged the Soviets to choose between a path of confrontation or co-operation. Brzezinski was distressed that the Soviets were engaging in a 'sustained and massive effort' to build up their conventional forces in Europe, further concentrating forces on China's frontiers, maintaining a vitriolic world-wide propaganda campaign against the United States, encircling and penetrating the Middle East and stirring up racial trouble in Africa.[30]

In spite of growing concern about Soviet behaviour, Carter and Vance remained committed to their original image of the Soviet Union and saw the Soviets as opportunistic but ultimately failing. Brzezinski on the other hand proceeded to grow increasingly pessimistic and emphasized that an 'arc of crisis' existed in the Persian Gulf, in Iran and along a line extending into southern Africa.[31] Chaos and instability would result if the Soviet Union were able to successfully exploit the situation. He began to stress more and more the need for strong national defence and defence of the West. As Rosati perceptively observes, 'One still heard about the importance of promoting international co-operation and pursuing a global community, but those themes were overshadowed by Brzezinski's perception of an increasingly fragmented and unstable international system.'[32]

More and more Brzezinski came to believe that the Soviet Union was at the bottom of the problem of global instability. The Soviet Union was not only becoming strong, but it was exercising less and less restraint. Vance and Carter continued to believe the international system offered hopes of positive change, although Carter periodically had moments of pessimism and showed greater sympathy with Brzezinski's views as the Administration concluded its third year in office. The year 1980 proved to be the end of the Administration's search for global community. Two events which overwhelmed the Administration, and especially Carter and Brzezinski, were the taking of the American hostages in Iran and the Soviet military intervention in Afghanistan. As the President noted, 'these two acts—one of international terrorism and one of military aggression—present a serious challenge, to the United

States of America and indeed to all the nations of the world.'[33] Carter and Brzezinski now focused on the Soviet threat in the Persian Gulf and south-west Asia. Carter said that the Soviet invasion of Afghanistan 'could pose the most serious threat to peace since the Second World War'.[34] He admitted that he had learned more about Soviet behaviour in two weeks than he had in the previous two and a half years. Carter had become convinced, with Brzezinski, that the Soviets were aggressors and expansionistic in outlook. Vance's views were eclipsed by events. He left office when Carter authorized a military raid to rescue the American hostages. As Harold Brown once remarked, 'Secretary Vance was persuaded anything that involved the risk of force was a mistake.'[35] He was succeeded by Edmund Muskie whose views were more in accord with those of Carter and Brzezinski. However, Muskie did espouse many of Vance's beliefs, which were seldom discussed in 1980, such as human rights, Third World development, improvement of bilateral relations and the importance of arms control.

From liberal idealism to political realism

The Carter Administration evolved from an initial philosophy of foreign policy which embraced liberal idealism to one of political realism in its final year in office. Rosati describes this as follows:

Three fundamental patterns occurred in the Carter image of the international system. Originally . . . Carter Administration policy makers perceived a very complex international system made up of a multitude of important issues and actors. The Carter team attempted to maximize international peace and co-operation in an effort to build a global community. In, the second and third years as the Carter Administration's image of the international system was subject to increasing challenges, its perception of a complex world was modified and intra-administration differences became greater. By 1980 the Carter Administration's image of the international system had completely altered. The original image of a complex global system was disavowed and supplanted with an image of a fragmented international system in which the pursuit of global security became dominant.[36]

Brzezinski has suggested that Carter's foreign policy embraced power and principle and that it tried to blend idealism and realism into what Anthony Lake called 'principled pragmatism'.

While both traditions were clearly present, it is questionable whether both were pursued at the same time. It may be that the 'Carter Administration's image of the international system was the first truly moral and idealistic vision in US foreign policy since the end of World War II',[37] but its early failure to accord a 'higher recognition of the centrality of force in world affairs', as Brzezinski phrased it, was a severe handicap in its dealings with the Soviet Union and with many of the intractable problems of international politics. This included human rights, where Stoessinger's judgement is, 'If result, rather than intent, is the criterion of effectiveness in human rights, Kissinger had more success than Carter. The balancer had done better than the evangelist.'[38]

The role of the President

In an evaluation of the Administration's foreign policy, it is clear that the key player was the President. He set the tone, established the themes, appointed the principal advisers, played a decisive role in the Camp David, Panama Canal and Iran hostages negotiations and made the crucial decisions when they had to be made. As he said in 1980, 'There have been Presidents in the past, maybe not too distant past, that let their Secretaries of State make foreign policy. I did not.'[39]

From the memoirs of Carter, Vance and Brzezinski and Hamilton Jordan's *Crisis, The Last Year of the Carter Presidency*, it appears that Carter was at the centre of the decision-making process in spite of the fact that he spent roughly 75 per cent of his time on domestic politics. He had a clear idea of the roles he wanted Vance and Brzezinski to play. Jordan observes:

In organizing his foreign policy team, Carter saw no inherent conflict between the men and institutions they represented. Zbig would sit at his side, stimulating new ideas, creating long range plans, and sifting through the mountains of foreign policy papers that regularly came to the White House for the President.

Vance would be the diplomat, meeting with ambassadors and foreign dignitaries: the manager, trying to control the sprawling State Department bureaucracy; and the implementer, responsible for making policies work.

The president-elect was not worried about conflicts, and relished their different ideas and lively debate. The roles were clear to him. Zbig would be the thinker. Cy would be the doer, and Jimmy Carter would be the decider.[40]

Jordan also remarks that the two men represented the different sides of the President's mind and personality. Brzezinski represented Carter's bold side, the side that challenged the party hierarchy and won, the side that by-passed conventional wisdom and brought Sadat and Begin to Camp David and would later lead him to go to the Middle East and salvage the agreement when it appeared to be falling apart. Vance represented Carter's more traditional and methodical side, which worked eighteen and twenty hours a day over the language of the Camp David settlement, always seeking a way to overcome the most difficult of problems. Vance, like the President, laboured long and hard at the State Department, wading through endless cables and problems, attending innumerable meetings, testifying before Congress and ending his long days at foreign embassy receptions.[41]

If Jimmy Carter was his own Secretary of State, he was not immune to taking advice and listening to all sides of an argument. This led to the frequent charge that he was indecisive and inundated with details, unable to see the forest for the trees. However, he sensed that he could act more on his own in foreign than in domestic affairs where tedious bargaining with Congress usually led to compromise on controversial issues. He told this author that the most interesting, intriguing and gratifying elements in his Administration were those dealing with foreign policy because he could act as he thought, subject only to reversal by Congress. Most Americans underestimate the authority the President has in foreign policy while overestimating the authority he has in domestic affairs.[42]

President Carter did not begin his presidency as an expert on foreign policy but as early as 1972 he sought experience and credentials in this field and accepted an invitation to serve on the Trilateral Commission—a group of Japanese, European and American leaders interested in improving relations among their peoples. Later he recalled, 'Those Trilateral Commission meetings for me were like classes in foreign policy—reading papers produced on every conceivable subject, hearing experienced leaders debate international issues and problems and meeting the big names like Cy Vance and Harold Brown and Zbig.'[43] Brzezinski became his teacher and supplied Carter with a steady stream of books and articles on foreign policy. Carter was a fast learner and with his passion for detail soon became knowledgeable about the great issues of the day. He relied heavily on the acknowledged expertise of Vance, Brzezinski and Brown, but when it came to addressing the larger issues involved in human rights, SALT II, the Panama Canal treaties, the Middle East settlement, China normalization and the hostage issue, Carter, during his time in office followed his own beliefs about what had to be done.

Accomplishments

The Carter Administration accomplished some notable achievements in foreign policy during its four years. In fact, Stuart Eizenstat, Carter's chief domestic policy adviser, concedes that 'most of the lasting accomplishments are probably in the foreign arena rather than in the domestic'.[44] Certainly the Camp David Accords which Carter personally mediated between Egypt and Israel must rank near the top of his successes. Although subject to widespread criticism for being too narrow and isolated from an overall Middle East settlement, it remains the framework for what peace does exist in the troubled area. The Panama Canal treaties defused a sensitive controversy of long standing in Central America. A careful reading of Carter's memoirs on this point convinces this author that Carter was at his best on this delicate problem. His efforts to convince Congress to accept the treaties were a notable achievement. As he observes, 'Some fine members of Congress had to pay with their political careers for their votes during these long and difficult months.'[45] Would the United States have gone to war with Panama if the treaties had not been ratified? Carter says that he honestly does not know, but if a massive military confrontation had occurred, the US 'could have prevailed against this tiny country, but in the bloody process all of us would have suffered, and the Canal would have been closed.'[46]

The Administration's long, arduous efforts to bring the SALT II Treaty to fruition deserve recognition also. In spite of the fact that it was shelved after the Soviet Union invaded Afghanistan, its agreement for limiting long-range nuclear weapons is still being observed while the Reagan Administration's initiatives in arms control and reduction are pursued. President Carter painfully admits, 'our failure to ratify the SALT II treaty and to secure even more far-reaching agreements on nuclear arms control was the most profound disappointment of my Presidency.'[47]

On human rights the Administration raised the banner of American concern and showed the world that America was not solely occupied with superpower relations. It scored some notable success in Africa, Latin America and Third World countries, but it fared less well in areas under communist authoritarian governments. Its efforts towards normalization of relations with China continued the process begun under Nixon. Certainly the establishment of formal diplomatic relations and the extraordinary visit of Vice-Chairman Deng Xiaoping did much to advance United States relations with the world's most populous nation. In spite of rhetoric to the contrary, the Reagan Administration has not downgraded United States relations with China or re-established formal ties with Taiwan.

The Carter Doctrine, warning that 'Any attempt by any outside force to gain control of the Persian Gulf region will be regarded as an assault on the vital interests of the United States of America and such an assault will be repelled by any means necessary, including military force', has not as yet taken on the historic importance of the Truman Doctrine. However, considering the high stakes involved in Persian Gulf politics and the volatility of the Middle East generally, the day may come when President Carter's pronouncement will take on more than symbolic importance. It recognizes publicly a new area of United States concern and perhaps permanent commitment.

Three other aspects of Carter's foreign policy deserve a few kind words. One is the calibre of the people he recruited for service in his Administration. Vance was an experienced, able, hardworking man of decent instincts who sought not glory, but the opportunity to serve his country. It may be, as Brzezinski writes:

Cy would have made an extraordinarily successful Secretary of State in a more tranquil age. There his strongest qualities would have stood out, reinforcing this country's basic decency and commitments to fundamental principle. He was at his best when negotiating with decent parties in the world: the British over Zimbabwe, the Israelis and Egyptians regarding

Middle East peace; he was at his worst in dealing with the thugs of this world. His deep aversion to the use of force was a most significant limitation on his stewardship in an age in which American power was being threatened on a very broad front.

Brzezinski played well the role Carter assigned him as ideas man and co-ordinator. He was bright, competent and hardworking. He was also at times brash, erratic and self-promoting. Hamilton Jordan comments, 'And if Cy Vance didn't have an ounce of the self-promoter in him, Zbig has several pounds.'[49] He then adds:

Zbig's intelligence was intense and raw, and when added to his tough-guy image, it made many people uncomfortable. On the private side, however, he was as charming as Kissinger was abrasive. Zbig may have worked his staff hard, but they liked him and cared for him and he developed an esprit de corps at the NSC that was lacking during the Kissinger years.[50]

Vance had serious reservations about Brzezinski's propensity to take on the role of foreign policy spokesman and asserts, 'Brzezinski's practice became a serious impediment to the conduct of our foreign policy.'[51] He also found the National Security Adviser's activities in the Iranian crisis mischievous when he opposed direct contacts with the Ayatollah,[52] urged the President and General Robert Huyser, on special assignment to Iran, to push the Iranian military into a coup attempt,[53] and when he allegedly opened his own back-channel communications with Teheran without informing the State Department.[54] After the invasion of Afghanistan, Vance judiciously sums up the impact which that event had on the President's foreign policy team:

Any American administration is a coalition of individuals with diverse viewpoints, and the Carter administration was no exception. Before Afghanistan, the differences, though sharp at times, were containable at the cost of not having a truly coherent policy. Afterward, however, it became increasingly difficult to hold the coalition together.[55]

The third major player, Harold Brown, was by all accounts an experienced hand in security matters and a brilliant defence intellectual. At first he sided with Vance on most issues, but came closer to Brzezinski's harder line as the term wore on. Brzezinski came to regard him as 'my closest partner'.[56] Jimmy Carter was unstinting in his praise and in 1983 expressed the wish that Brown were still Secretary of Defense and would remain there for twenty years.[57] Brown's technical expertise was such that he could more than hold his own in arguments with the military and Paul Warnke at the Arms Control and Disarmament Agency.

In addition to the Big Three, the Administration could rightly be proud of such outstanding people as Warren Christopher and Marshall Shulman at State, David Aaron and Henry Owen at the NSC, Charles Duncan at Defense and Paul Warnke at ACDA. Andrew Young and Pat Derian both appear better in retrospect than they did at the time, and Vice-President Mondale must be rated as an able, intelligent and sensible junior partner to the President.

Beside the number of outstanding and able appointees, the Carter Administration must be credited with a willingness to face and even embrace change, even if it didn't always turn out to be a blessing. Few administrations in the post-World War II period have been willing to make change a virtue. Accompanying this and closely related was the Administration's, and especially Carter's and Vance's, dedication to 'good works'. When Fritz Mondale summed up the four years of the Carter Presidency, he said, 'we told the truth, we obeyed the law. We kept the peace. And that ain't bad.'[58] While this may not be the whole story, it none the less conveys the sense of decency and purpose that represented the main thrust of the Carter Presidency in the conduct of US foreign policy.

Shortfalls in policy

If good intentions and a willingness to innovate were attractive attributes of Carter's foreign policy, then lack of realism and inconsistency may have been the shortcomings of this Administration. From the beginning it tended to repudiate much of what previous administrations had done. When it turned its back on *realpolitik*, decried the 'inordinate fear of communism', reduced the defence budget, curtailed arms sales, planned to pull troops out of Korea, pursued normalization with Cuba and Vietnam and put conservative regimes at arms length, it overreacted to the presumed sins of the Kissinger legacy. As Winston Lord suggests, 'A more vigorous assertion of American values was in order. But Carter policies ran into the realities of geopolitics—Moscow's relentless military buildup, Third World adventures and invasion of Afghanistan.'[59] The failure to perceive the 'centrality of power' in international politics at the outset meant that costly lessons had to be learned the hard way. A misreading of Soviet intentions was corrected only after Somalia and Afghanistan. The human rights campaign had to be downgraded because it proved to exacerbate more problems than it solved and even proved counter-productive with the communists. Moreover, Charles W. Kegley Jr. and Eugene R. Wittkopf observe, as two friendly critics:

Talk of reform is not the same as actualized reform, experimentation is not a substitute for a grand design, comprehensive concern for new issues is not the same as new doctrine . . . intentions do not constitute new programs . . .

Indeed, much criticism of Carter's early endeavours centred on his attempts to solve too many problems at once, and his promise to provide solutions for problems that perhaps cannot be solved.[60]

Brzezinski believes the assertion that the Administration had no central strategy is incorrect, but does admit that 'we were overly ambitious and that we failed in our efforts to project effectively to the public the degree to which we were motivated by a coherent and well thought-out viewpoint.'[61]

However, as coherent and well thought-out the policy may have been, major reversals did take place, much to the chagrin of Carter's European allies, especially the West Germans, who found these inconsistencies both confusing and irritating. Helmut Schmidt was particularly upset at Carter's decision to defer production of the ERW (enhanced radiation weapons) or neutron bombs. It permanantly soured relations between Schmidt and Carter. The planned troop withdrawals from Korea were dropped, policy was reversed on the neutron bomb, defence cuts were reinstated and added to, the CIA was revived, arms sales were relaxed and the Soviet Union was restored as the great disturber of international equilibrium. It is difficult to say to what extent this was due to faulty judgement, lack of coherence in policy-making, the intrusion of external events and the great intervening variable of crisis. No doubt all entered in.

It seems clear in retrospect that the Carter image of the international system was seriously flawed. Mounting divisions within the policy coalition contributed to the inconsistencies. Carter's own leadership, or lack of it, was almost certainly contributory. Yet it cannot be denied that the impact of external events added greatly to the inability of the Carter Presidency to achieve the architectonic policies it enunciated at the outset. The fall of the Shah of Iran, the intrusions of the Russians and Cubans in Ethiopia, the Soviet invasion of Afghanistan and the seizure of the American hostages were all beyond the control and perhaps even the decisive influence of the United States. These events created emergencies which distorted the agenda and forced the Administration to spend much of its time, energy and resources on crisis management. It has even been suggested that Carter's Presidency was the victim of bad luck, exemplified by soaring oil and food prices, high interest rates and the aborted hostage rescue.[62] Be that as it may, Carter ended his Presidency himself a hostage to the crisis in Teheran—a crisis which contributed to his defeat in the presidential election of 1980. By failing to retrieve the hostages by diplomacy, by voluntarily sequestering himself in the White House during much of the campaign and by the decision to try, and then to abort, the rescue mission, the President only added to the widespread impression that he was unable to manage the country, its foreign policy and ultimately the presidency.

Assessment

Most presidents have to cope with the unexpected and their best-laid plans can go awry under the pressure of events. In describing a typical presidential term, Stephen Hess has noted in his book *Organizing the Presidency*:

By the end of his first year the President should have learned two important lessons: first, that the unexpected is likely to happen; second, that his plans are unlikely to work out as he had hoped. The Soviet Union launches Sputnik. A U-2 is shot down. There is an uprising in Hungary, a riot in Watts, a demonstration in Berkeley. US missiles that he thought had been removed from Turkey were not removed. The Chinese explode a nuclear device earlier than his intelligence forecasts had predicted. The president finds much of his time spent reacting to events over which he has no control or trying to correct the errors of others.[63]

Surely Jimmy Carter could empathize with this analysis, but the Carter Aministration itself was hardly an historical aberration.

It may have had more than its share from the fickle finger of fate, but it also made more than its share of mistakes. From the beginning, as Winston Lord correctly notes, 'Carter was too trusting' and deviated too far from a centrist course.[64] In the second half of his term, Carter moved erratically toward the centre and began scoring some successes. NATO's conventional forces were strengthened, SALT II negotiations progressed, ambassadors were exchanged with China, Camp David succeeded beyond expectations, defence budgets were increased and a base agreement with the Philippines concluded. 'But the Carter administration never shook its early image', says Lord, and 'America seemed on the defensive, our impotence symbolized by the Iranian hostages. National frustration ushered in the Reagan Administration.'[65]

If Carter was too trusting in foreign policy, then the Reagan Administration may have overreacted by becoming too truculent. If it does not move toward more centrist policies as the Carter Administration did (although from a different direction), then it is possible that the longer Reagan conducts foreign policy, the better Carter will look. Most presidents overreact to the mistakes of their predecessors and in so doing, begin a series of their own. Frequently they end up doing no better, and sometimes worse, than the man they succeeded. Carter thought he could improve on the foreign policy of Nixon, Ford and Kissinger. It is doubtful that he did. Reagan thought he could improve on Carter's. It is doubtful that he will. It is still too soon to judge. While most of Carter's domestic policies have been discarded, many of his foreign policies are still being followed by Reagan's Administration, which even announced on 26 July 1983 that it was reaffirming the Carter Doctrine in response to Iranian threats to close the Persian Gulf.

The 'idealism' of Carter's early policies will continue to appeal to the liberal wing of the Democratic Party for years to come. The 'realism' of later policies will no doubt be attractive to the 'neo-liberals' on the Democratic right. An experienced Fritz Mondale or a retired astronaut like John Glenn may be in a position to more effectively wed the two in the future than Carter was able to do in the past.

In the final analysis the successes and failure of Jimmy Carter's foreign policies depended upon Jimmy Carter. Ben Heineman, who left the Administration when Joseph Califano was fired as Secretary of Health, Education and Welfare, asserts that 'his legacy would have to be confusion and failure because he never learned how to run the office.'[66] Sol Linowitz, a former OAS Ambassador, diplomatic troubleshooter and negotiator of the Panama Canal treaties, believes Carter 'could have been great if he had managed the presidency better'. But he says, in appreciation of his performance at Camp David, 'Carter showed himself to be a man of extra-ordinary courage, of real commitment, of willingness to swim upstream, to follow his own drummer rather than the advice that came to him from people concerned with the political fallout, with the implications for his own career if he didn't succeed.'[67] A similar paradoxical conclusion is reached by John Stoessinger in his study of 'Movers of Modern American Foreign Policy'. Here he judiciously and perceptively summarizes the strengths and weakness of the Carter approach to foreign affairs.

Jimmy Carter . . . falls somewhere between the crusader and the pragmatist. His religious conviction, while profound, did not have the rigidity of Wilson's or of Dulles'. His tenacity and perseverance did not lock him into an obsession. Unlike the crusader's zeal, his faith did not become a dogma. It always remained a quest. And it inspired him in 1979 to mediate a peace between Israel and Egypt. On the other hand, his global human rights campaign was often ineffectual and even boomeranged when it collided with the realities of power . . . The president's faith . . . lacked a practical dimension and thus his foreign policy especially in the human rights arena, had some aspects of the amateur. But then, perhaps even the most sophisticated statesman would be bound to fail if he bases his foreign policy on the cornerstone of human rights. Such an attempt might always come to grief on the rocks of national interest and power. Perhaps it cannot be done.[68]

Jimmy Carter tried, and if he did not always succeed, he did not always fail. Churchill once said, 'The further back you look, the farther forward you can see'. The further back we look at Carter's foreign policy, the better it may look in the future.

Notes

1. *The New York Times*, 'The Era of Kissinger', 16 January 1977.
2. Gerald R. Ford, *A Time to Heal*, New York, Harper and Row, 1979. Seymour M. Hersh, *The Price of Power: Kissinger In the Nixon White House*, New York, Summit Books, 1983. Henry A. Kissinger, *White*

House Years, Boston, Little, Brown & Co., 1979; *Years of Upheaval*, Boston, Little, Brown & Co., 1982. Richard M. Nixon, *RN: The Memoirs of Richard Nixon*, New York, Grosset and Dunlap, 1978.

3. Leslie Gelb, 'The Kissinger Legacy', *The New York Times Magazine*, 31 October 1978.
4. Zbigniew Brzezinski, *Power and Principle: Memoirs of the National Security Advisor 1977–1981*, New York, Farrar, Straus, Giroux, 1983, p. 81.
5. Tom Wicker, 'Six Years For the President', *The New York Times Magazine*, 26 June 1983, p. 19.
6. See James David Barber, *The Presidential Character*, second edn., Englewood Cliffs, NJ, Prentice Hall, 1977, Chapters 1 and 16, and Gabriel A. Almond, *The American People and Foreign Policy*, New York, Harcourt, Brace & Co., 1950, Chapters 4 and 5.
7. John Stoessinger, *Crusaders and Pragmatists: Movers of Modern American Foreign Policy*, New York, W. W. Norton & Co., 1979, p. 262.
8. Interview with President Jimmy Carter, Plains, Georgia, 18 April 1983.
9. Ibid.
10. Jerel Rosati, 'The Impact of Belief on Behavior: The Foreign Policy of the Carter Administration', Chapter in Donald A. Sylvan and Steve Chan, eds, *Foreign Policy Decision-Making: Perception, Cognition, and Artificial Intelligence*, New York, Praeger, 1984.
11. Jimmy Carter, 'A Foreign Policy Based on America's Essential Character', Notre Dame University, South Bend, Ind., 22 May 1977, *Department of State Bulletin*, 13 June 1977, p. 622.
12. Ibid., p. 625.
13. Rosati, op. cit.
14. Jimmy Carter, 'The US–Soviet Relationship' (remarks made before the Southern Legislative Conference at Charleston, SC, on 21 July 1977), *Department of State Bulletin*, 15 August 1977, pp. 193–7.
15. Jerel Rosati, 'The Carter Administration's Image of the International System: The Development and Application of a Belief System Framework', unpublished Ph.D. dissertation, American University, 1983, Chapter 6.
16. Brzezinski, op. cit., p. 49.
17. Cyrus Vance, *Hard Choices: Critical Years in America's Foreign Policy*, New York, Simon and Schuster, 1983, p. 27.
18. Brzezinski, op. cit., p. 53.
19. Vance, op. cit., pp. 27–8.
20. Adapted from Brzezinski, op. cit., pp. 53–6.
21. Vance, op. cit., p. 36.
22. Ibid., p. 37.

23. Ibid.
24. Ibid.
25. Brzezinski, op. cit., p. 63.
26. Zbigniew Brzezinski, Interview with *US News and World Report*, 30 May 1977. Also in *DOD Selected Statements, June 1, 1977.*
27. Zbigniew Brzezinski, Interview on 'Face the Nation', 30 October 1977, *Department of State Bulletin*, 5 December 1977, pp. 800–5.
28. Ibid., p. 802.
29. Jimmy Carter, 'The United States and the Soviet Union', address made at the US Naval Academy's commencement exercises, 7 July 1978, *Department of State Bulletin*, July 1978, pp. 14–16.
30. Zbigniew Brzezinski, Interview on 'Meet the Press', 28 May 1978, *Department of State Bulletin*, July 1978, pp. 26–8.
31. Zbigniew Brzezinski, Interview with James Reston of *The New York Times*, 31 December 1978, *DOD Selected Documents, January 1, 1979.*
32. Rosati, 'The Carter Administration's Image of the International System: The Development and Application of A Belief System Framework', op. cit., p. 181.
33. Jimmy Carter, State of the Union Address, 1980, *Department of State Bulletin*, February 1980.
34. Ibid.
35. Harold Brown, *The New York Times*, 7 December 1980.
36. Rosati, 'The Carter Administration's Image of the International System', op. cit., p. 196.
37. Ibid., p. 199.
38. Stoessinger, op. cit., p. 268.
39. Quoted in Brzezinski, op. cit., p. 513.
40. Hamilton Jordan, *Crisis: The Last Year of the Carter Presidency*, New York, G. P. Putnam's Sons, 1983, pp. 46–7.
41. Ibid., p. 47.
42. Carter Interview, 18 April 1983.
43. Quoted in Jordan, op. cit., p. 45.
44. Michael Putzel, 'Carter's Legacy', Associated Press Dispatch, 3 July 1983.
45. Carter, op. cit., p. 185.
46. Ibid.
47. Ibid., p. 265.
48. Brzezinski, op. cit., pp. 43–4.
49. Jordan, op. cit., p. 49.
50. Ibid., p. 50.
51. Vance, op. cit., pp. 35–6.
52. Ibid., p. 340.
53. Ibid., pp. 340–1.

54. Ibid., p. 328.
55. Ibid., p. 394.
56. Brzezinski, op. cit., p. 47.
57. Carter Interview, 18 April 1983.
58. Putzel, op. cit.
59. Winston Lord, 'Our Careening Foreign Policy', *Newsweek*, 25 April 1983.
60. Charles W. Kegley, Jr. and Eugene R. Wittkopf, *American Foreign Policy: Pattern and Progress*, New York, St. Martins Press, 1979, p. 428.
61. Brzezinski, op. cit., pp. 56-7.
62. Putzel, op. cit.
63. Stephen Hess, *Organizing the Presidency*, Washington, DC, The Brookings Institution, 1976, p. 21.
64. Lord, op. cit.
65. Ibid.
66. Putzel, op. cit.
67. Ibid.
68. Stoessinger, op. cit., p. 284.

Chronology

1977   Carter becomes thirty-ninth President of the United States

Carter honours campaign pledge and grants pardon to Vietnam War draft evaders and military deserters

Carter pledges a phased withdrawal of US troops from South Korea

UN Ambassador Andrew Young tours black Africa for ten-day diplomatic consultations

Carter greets Soviet activist Bukovsky; Soviets warn that US objections to their treatment of dissidents could endanger arms control agreements

President Carter writes open letter to Sakharov, foremost Soviet dissenter

Argentina, Brazil, El Salvador and Guatemala reject US foreign aid in reaction to US attacks on their human rights practices

Fighting breaks out in Zaïre; 2,000 troops invade from neighbouring Angola

United States sends aid to Zaïre to assist in resistance to Angolan invasion

Soviet Union rejects two US proposals for resuming stalled SALT talks

Moscow charges that United States' human rights stance constitutes interference in Soviet internal affairs

Begin wins election in Israel, pledges never to negotiate liberated territory

Secretary of State Vance and Soviet Foreign Minister Gromyko confer in Geneva on arms talks; agree to set up United States–Soviet world-issues study groups

Carter announces plan to stop production of B-1 supersonic bomber; recommends development of cruise missiles instead

Carter reaffirms US defence of South Korea in event of an attack by North Korea

United States and Soviet Union sign Convention prohibiting hostile uses of environmental modification techniques

US diplomats take up residence in Cuba for first time in sixteen years

Carter and Panamanian President General Torrijos sign Panama Canal Treaty at headquarters of OAS in Washington

Vietnam is admitted to the United Nations

Soviet Union agrees to join United States in adhering to existing SALT pact while negotiations continue on a new one

United States and Soviet Union issue joint declaration urging Israel to recognize 'legitimate rights of the Palestinian people', to grant negotiating role at Middle East peace talks to Palestinian 'representatives', and to withdraw from occupied territory

Carter withdraws United States from International Labor Organization—first US withdrawal from UN organization since UN founding in 1945

United States prohibits export of military and police equipment to South Africa and attacks South Africa's crackdown on dissent

Somalia breaks relations with Cuba, expels all Soviet advisers, and renounces 1974 friendship treaty with Moscow

Egyptian President Sadat makes historic two-day visit to Israel for meetings with Israeli Prime Minister Begin and a speech before the Israeli Parliament; other Arab states oppose the visit

Begin meets with Carter to outline new Israeli peace proposal which includes the return of almost all of the Sinai to Egypt and limited autonomy for the West Bank

Peace talks with representatives from Egypt, United States, Israel and United Nations begin in Cairo; Christmas Day meeting takes place between Sadat and Begin in Egypt

1978 Executive order broadens powers of CIA director over entire US intelligence community and reorganizes the latter

Sadat makes six-day visit to United States to discuss Middle East with Carter

White House announces plans to sell sophisticated weapons in 'package deal' to Egypt, Saudi Arabia and Israel

Ethiopian army, with Soviet and Cuban aid, captures Somali stronghold of Jijiga

In retaliation for PLO terrorist raid, Israeli armed forces invade Lebanon and take control of almost all of southern Lebanon

First of Panama Canal Treaties guaranteeing Canal's neutrality passed by US Senate

Carter announces postponement of production of neutron bomb

Senate passes second Panama Canal Treaty to turn over the Canal to the Panamanians by year 2000

Coup in Afghanistan brings communist-leaning government to power

Senate approves sale of jet planes to Israel, Egypt and Saudi Arabia

Camp David Summit reaches 'Framework for a Peace Treaty' between Egypt and Israel

Vietnam withdraws request to United States for war reparations; United States announces intention to establish full diplomatic relations with Vietnam

Syrian peacekeeping force launches an assault on Christian areas of Beirut, Lebanon

John Paul II of Poland assumes papacy, initiates communications between the church and East European leaders

United States offers to help mainland China develop its energy reserves in a joint economic venture

Shah of Iran orders military take-over amidst widespread protests against his regime

Carter ends three-year US arms embargo against Turkey; arms shipments resumed

Soviet Union announces testing of neutron bomb as well as decision against putting it into production

Carter announces that the United States will extend full diplomatic relations to the People's Republic of China on 1 January 1979, while at the same time severing formal ties with Nationalist China, including termination of the mutual defence treaty with Taiwan

1979   Shah leaves Iran; Ayatollah Ruhollah Khomeini returns from exile and seizes power from Prime Minister Shahpur Bakhtiar within two weeks

United States and Soviet Union hold talks in Berne on banning hunter-killer satellites

Communist China invades Vietnam as 'punishment' for the presence of Vietnamese troops in Cambodia

Pakistan and Turkey withdraw from CENTO

Begin and Sadat sign peace treaty in Washington; Organization of Arab Petroleum Exporting Countries (OAPEC) imposes oil embargo on Egypt

Carter–Brezhnev summit in Vienna leads to signing of SALT II

Andrew Young, US ambassador to United Nations, resigns following disclosure of secret meeting with PLO's UN aide

Carter announces decision to deploy MX missile system in the western United States

Iranian students seize over sixty hostages in US embassy; demand Shah's return as condition of release

Soviet troops enter Afghanistan, engineer coup against Amin, and install Babrak Karmal as prime minister

1980   Carter asks Senate to table consideration of SALT II in light of Afghan intervention

Carter outlines retaliatory measures for Afghan invasion, including suspension of high-technology sales, grain embargo and boycott of summer Olympics in Moscow; Brezhnev calls such measures attempts to 'poison' relations

Carter says United States will defend Persian Gulf oil fields (Carter Doctrine); calls for draft registration

Canada's embassy in Iran smuggles six hidden US embassy employees out of Iran

United States obtains access to military facilities in Oman, Kenya and Somalia

Carter breaks diplomatic relations with Iran

American mission to rescue hostages in Iran aborted, as eight die; Secretary of State Vance resigns in disagreement over mission

United States and fifty-nine nations boycott Moscow Olympics over Soviet presence in Afghanistan

Shah of Iran dies while in exile in Egypt

Presidential Directive 59 gives Soviet military targets priority over cities in case of nuclear attack

Polish strikes win workers right to form independent unions; Soviet Union threatens military intervention to end Polish liberation

Iraq–Iran war begins as Iraq invades ninety square miles of Iran in controversy over Shatt al Arab waterway

Boatlift brings 125,000 Cuban refugees to United States

Ronald Reagan wins electoral landslide to become fortieth president

United States rejects Brezhnev proposal for joint non-intervention in Persian Gulf

NATO warns Soviet Union against Polish intervention

1981   United States promises military assistance to combat insurgency
          in El Salvador
        United States presses allies to improve military forces
        United States and Iran sign hostage accord

5 Carter's defence policy

Phil Williams

Any attempt to assess the defence policy of a particular president encounters enormous problems. The president is only one actor in a complex process and attempts by him to impose his own preferences on the size, shape, equipment and deployment of the armed forces may encounter powerful and deeply entrenched bureaucratic and industrial interests. Although the president as Commander-in-Chief has ultimate responsibility for the preparedness and the use of these forces, his influence on them is, in many ways, rather limited. The military services themselves specify what they deem to be their requirements, and even if the president does not approve, can often find support in the Congress which wields enormous influence through the appropriations process. Indeed,

the President is not the only actor even when he is the one who finally chooses. His calculations will turn out the way they do, as will his choice, in large part because of the way the bureaucratic-political apparatus has defined the situation and his options, and because interests besides his own and the nation's, will have advocates that he will not want to ignore. The President, partial creator of the system that serves him, is also constrained by it and may become to some degree the victim of it.[1]

There are also difficulties in establishing criteria on which to base an assessment. Threats to national security are often uncertain and ambiguous to say the least. Consequently, what some observers may see as neglect may be regarded by others as excess.

This problem of perspective looms particularly large in any attempt to evaluate Jimmy Carter's record on defence. So much depends on one's ideological perspective. The accepted wisdom among conservative commentators and officials is that Carter seriously neglected America's defences, that he was soft on the Soviet Union, and that he did not take measures commensurate with the threat to US security posed by Moscow. Although some of the critics accept that after Afghanistan Carter redeemed himself to some extent by adopting a tougher line, even this is often dismissed as an inevitable response to public and Congressional pressures in a presidential election year. In this assessment, the measures of 1979 and 1980 were too little too late. For many liberals, on the other hand, Carter's record represents something of a betrayal: coming to power committed to cuts in the United States defence budget, the President appeared to bow to expediency and abandon his ideals by beginning the massive rearmament programme which has been further accelerated by the Reagan Administration.

The present analysis endeavours to avoid this rather facile pigeon-holing of Carter's defence policy. It looks briefly at the inheritance from the Nixon and Ford Administrations, and examines the trends in the defence budget (in terms both of its overall size and its composition) under Carter, as well as specific decisions made by the President. At the outset, however, it has to be acknowledged that Carter's record in office is in many respects rather ironic. The President came to the White House with deeply-held views not only about the need for a more moralistic and less militaristic approach to foreign policy but also with the intention of ending the preoccupation with the Soviet Union (which, he believed, was distorting national priorities) and replacing it with a more pluralistic approach to global problems. During his campaign for the presidency he pledged to reduce defence spending by up to $7 billion, while his commitment to strategic arms control was genuine and abiding. Yet during the four years of Carter's presidency the competition with the Soviet Union was as important and as intrusive as ever, and despite his efforts to maintain a modicum of the *détente* relationship, Carter found himself presiding over what was in many respects a reversion to the Cold War policies of some of his predecessors. His aspirations for lower spending on defence were replaced by a reluctant acceptance of the necessity for significantly increased defence budgets. And probably most disappointing of all for the President personally, he left office with a Strategic Arms Limitation Treaty (SALT II) signed but not ratified.

The legacy

The effect of the legacy of the Ford and Nixon Administrations on national security matters was rather mixed. The Nixon

Administration had emphasized the need to maintain strength while simultaneously proclaiming that the 'era of confrontation' had been replaced by an 'era of negotiation' with America's adversaries. Despite the rhetoric of strength, however, the Nixon Presidency was a period of substantial military retrenchment which went well beyond the withdrawal from South Vietnam. Defence spending was reduced very considerably and military planning was predicated on the assumption that the United States might have to fight only one and a half wars simultaneously (i.e., a major and a minor conflict) rather than two and a half wars, which had been the benchmark through most of the 1960s. Yet there was little criticism of these changes. Part of the reason was, of course, the widespread disillusionment with the Vietnam War and the popularity of the 'peace dividend'. The major criticisms of the Administration were not that it had gone too far in dismantling American military might but that it had not gone far enough in demilitarizing American foreign policy. An additional reason why the main attacks on Nixon's defence policies came from the liberals rather than the conservatives was the President's credentials as a Cold Warrior, which, coupled with the declaratory emphasis on strength, helped to obscure the real thrust of his policies. And even where the implications were apparent it did not seem to matter because of superpower *détente*, which was sold as a fundamental change in superpower relations when, in fact, it was little more than an attempt to ensure that the Soviet Union did not exploit American weakness. The SALT Agreements of 1972 in particular gave credence to the idea that a major transformation had occurred in superpower relations.

The reaction, however, was not long in coming. The Ford Administration, despite the continuity with its predecessor, symbolized by the continuing role of Henry Kissinger, began to reverse the process of declining defence budgets. The realization that during the previous ten years American defence spending had declined by about 7 per cent, while that of the Soviet Union had continued to increase by about 3 or 4 per cent each year, prompted what one analyst has described as a 'remarkable consensus' that the trend had to be halted and American military spending substantially increased.[2] Indeed, the defence budget itself came to be regarded as a symbol of American will and determination. In the aftermath of the withdrawal from Vietnam, it was argued that an augmented budget would signal to both the Soviet Union and America's allies that the United States was still prepared to meet its commitments. There were also substantive weaknesses to be repaired. American naval forces in particular had undergone a startling reduction, with the number of general purpose ships (excluding aircraft carriers and strategic nuclear submarines) falling from 840 in 1968 to 450 in 1975. Although the size of the fleet declined further during fiscal year 1976 the Administration's projections envisaged spending increases of over 6 per cent a year in real terms on naval procurement, resulting in a 540-ship navy by the mid 1980s. Ground forces were also to be upgraded with the creation of three extra divisions and a reorganization programme designed to augment combat capability at the expense of support forces. Furthermore, stategic nuclear forces were to be modernized with the continuation of the Trident SLBM programme, the production of the B1 bomber and the development of a new land-based missile, the MX.

In other words, the Carter Administration inherited a fairly comprehensive programme to modernize and strengthen both conventional and nuclear forces. Another legacy of the Ford Administration was the Vladivostok Accord of 1974, which established guidelines for a second SALT agreement. The Accord set a limit of 2,400 launchers for Soviet and American strategic forces, of which 1,320 could be MIRVed missiles (i.e., missiles with multiple and independently-targeted warheads). The provisions of the agreement also allowed some 'freedom to mix' between the different systems. There was some criticism of the accord on the grounds that the ceilings envisaged were too high and would not constrain the strategic forces of either side to the extent that many observers had hoped. Nevertheless, Vladivostok did appear to promise a continuation of the arms control process at a time when, partly because of the Soviet Union's unremitting force modernization and partly because of Moscow's actions during the Yom Kippur War, there was increasing antipathy in the United States towards *détente*. In a foretaste of things to come Gerald Ford, facing opposition from Ronald Reagan for the Republican nomination, banned the word *détente* from his political vocabulary. It was against this background of increasing doubt, anxiety and uncertainty about the nature of the relationship with the

Soviet Union that Jimmy Carter was faced with the task of formulating a coherent and consistent defence policy for the United States. 'How much is enough?' is never an easy question. During the Carter years it was to prove particularly troublesome. And the President's answer was very different in the last year of his incumbency than it was at the outset.

The Carter defence policy

It is possible to identify at least three different phases in the evolution of President Carter's defence policy. The first phase was one in which the President's own preferences were very much to the fore and lasted from January 1977 through to the early part of 1979. The second phase, which went through 1979, was one in which Carter made compromises regarding higher defence spending in an attempt to obtain the consent of the Senate to the ratification of SALT II. The third and final phase followed the Soviet invasion of Afghanistan and was one in which the President adopted the tougher approach that his critics had long been demanding.

Although Carter had had no experience in national security matters before becoming President, he had been a member of the Trilateral Commission and had also attended a number of meetings on foreign and defence policies at the Brookings Institution. The discussions on these occasions combined with his broader world view to suggest a number of guidelines for the new Administration's defence policy:

1. Priority amongst America's commitments was to be given to Western Europe. This required new initiatives in NATO and the strengthening of both United States and allied forces in Europe in an attempt to offset the military superiority of the Warsaw Pact.
2. Although the commitment to Japan was also important, United States ground forces in Korea could safely be withdrawn, thereby completing a process begun by President Nixon in 1971. Not only would this help to save money but it would also ensure that the United States would not be drawn into hostilities on the Korean peninsula merely by dint of the presence of the Second Infantry Division.
3. Defence spending had to be examined very carefully to identify areas for the kind of savings that candidate Carter had

promised. This was not simply a matter of following through on election promises though. Carter had a profound distrust of the military industrial complex which, he believed, was constantly attempting to inflate the defence budget far beyond the requirements of American security. This concern was manifested in frequent injunctions to his National Security Adviser, Zbigniew Brzezinski, to exert more control over the Pentagon's budgetary process. His experience in office did little to reassure him about the problem, and in his memoirs he complains about the dominant role of the weapons manufacturers and 'their natural allies in the Pentagon'. As he put it, 'The resulting purchase of necessary military equipment is undoubtedly the most wasteful element in American government'.[3] At the same time the President quickly became aware that America's defences had been neglected and that the overall trend in spending had been going down until the Ford Administration's recent changes. The President's position, therefore, was inevitably somewhat ambiguous and he can perhaps best be characterized as wanting a defence budget which was as large as necessary and as small as possible.

4. A high priority had to be given to arms control with the Soviet Union. Indeed, one of the President's aides suggested that Carter had an almost 'theological belief' in both non-proliferation and superpower arms control.

It is hardly surprising, therefore, that Carter's early actions in office raised serious doubts among many observers both inside and outside government about the President's approach to national security problems. Even before his inauguration the President-elect requested that the Joint Chiefs of Staff initiate studies relating to a minimum deterrent posture based around 200 to 250 submarine-launched ballistic missiles—a request which apparently appalled both the outgoing President and his Secretary of State, Henry Kissinger. Although ideas for radical measures of this kind were not pursued very far, Carter's initial proposals for the SALT II Treaty reflected his desire for 'deep cuts' in strategic forces. Because this departed abruptly from the previous American position in the negotiations it led inevitably to an immediate Soviet rejection. In retrospect, this initiative was enormously counter-productive as it helped to delay a SALT agreement. Yet it is important to remember that

Carter was simultaneously attempting to demonstrate to the Soviet Union that he preferred an early agreement to pressing ahead with the strategic modernization programme he had inherited. The defence budget for fiscal year 1978 had been prepared by the Ford Administration, and the budgetary calendar afforded the new President scant opportunity to impose his own preferences or make anything more than marginal changes. Nevertheless, Carter slowed the development of both the MX missile and the B1 bomber. Furthermore, in testimony before Congress, Carter's Secretary of Defense, Harold Brown suggested that there was 'no reason for immediate or grave alarm about our ability to deter major military actions by the Soviet Union'.[4]

The impression that the new Administration was more sanguine than its predecessor about the Soviet threat was reinforced by the announcement on 30 June 1977 that the President did not intend to proceed further with the development of the B1 bomber: the slow-down had become a cancellation. Although the rationale for this decision was based on the difficulties that any manned bomber would face in attempting to penetrate Soviet air defences, on the greater cost-effectiveness of B-52s armed with air-launched cruise missiles, and on the potential of new technologies which would make radar detection of American planes much more difficult to achieve, it was still heavily criticized. And because the 'stealth' technologies as they were known, were still highly secret, they could not be used in the President's attempts to persuade critics that his decision was right. Even if this argument had been deployed, however, it would hardly have placated an Air Force which saw the cancellation of the B1 as a challenge to its *raison d'être*. Maintaining existing roles and missions with existing technologies tends to be more attractive to the military services than relying on potential and far from certain technological breakthroughs.

If Carter angered the Air Force, however, he also upset the Navy by making reductions in the ship construction programme outlined by Ford. And although Carter was particularly concerned with strengthening American ground forces he also alienated sections of the Army by what seemed to be an emphasis on NATO at the expense of America's commitment in the Pacific. In March 1977 the President announced that he intended to fulfil his campaign promise to withdraw American ground forces from South Korea during the next four to five years.

Although this decision was highly controversial, it reflected the new Administration's strategic priorities. The main concern was NATO's Central Front and considerable effort was to be devoted to augmenting the conventional forces available to the Alliance to ensure that they would not be immediately overrun in the event of a Warsaw Pact attack. How much effort was required was itself a source of some disagreement in the Carter Administration's first year and was reflected in the bureaucratic battles over PRM 10. On coming to office President Carter almost immediately initiated a series of policy reviews, the most important of which was the comprehensive review known as PRM 10. This study was under the direction of Samuel Huntington, who was a close friend and former colleague of Carter's National Security Adviser, and who had a reputation as a hard-liner. Although it was hoped by some members of the Administration that the review would lead to a more sober view of the Soviet threat, this proved more difficult than had been anticipated. From the outset the study was bedevilled by bureaucratic battles. The Department of Defense succeeded in splitting the study so that all issues relating to force structure were under its jurisdiction, and then found rather ironically that the force packages developed by the Deputy Assistant Secretary of Defense for International Security Affairs was not acceptable to the Joint Chiefs of Staff. The other part of the analysis also encountered problems. As a result of State Department objections that Hungtington's assessment was too pessimistic, the conclusions of the net assessment were revised to reflect a more moderate approach—a development which created further concern over the Administration's intentions on defence.

A study which had involved 175 people and taken six months degenerated into what has been described as an 'exercise in confusion'.[5] The resulting Presidential Directive, PD18, was of less use in establishing guidelines for policy than had been hoped. There was, for example, considerable ambiguity in the document regarding the level of defence expenditure for the following year. Although PD18 began with the proposition that there should be a real increase in defence spending of 3 per cent (in accordance with the agreement that had been reached at the NATO Heads of Government meeting in the Spring of 1977) the base on which such an increase was to be calculated was not specified. Inevitably, therefore, there were arguments between the Department of Defense and the Office of Management and Budget about whether the 3 per cent figure applied only to NATO-related spending or applied right across the board.

The lack of clear direction was not the only problem though. By the end of 1977 there was considerable dissatisfaction in the Pentagon with what appeared to be a willingness on the part of the President and his main advisers to disregard military judgements. The overall defence philosophy of the Administration seemed to stem from the President and several members of the National Security Council staff, while the close relationship between Carter and Secretary Brown accentuated concerns that military advice was being disregarded. Brown, it was frequently alleged, conceived of his role as an agent of the White House rather than as a defender of the services, and although the Joint Chiefs were given unprecedented access to both the Secretary and the President, it quickly became apparent that this was no guarantee of influence. When the Secretary of Defense re-organized both management and budget procedures to facilitate early Presidential participation in the budgetary and decision-making process there was considerable resentment among the military. It was argued that political considerations were intruding into defence planning in a way which made it impossible for the military services to provide unencumbered statements of their requirements. Nor was this the only complaint. As well as giving the President greater influence, the changes also consolidated the authority of both Brown himself and the civilian analysts who worked for him. Consequently, there were allegations that defence planning and policy-making had become reminiscent of the McNamara years when the Pentagon had been dominated by the civilian 'whiz kids' and the power of the military severely curtailed—a complaint which was intensified by Brown's attempt to provide what was called Consolidated Budget Guidance.

These changes were of considerable importance in relation to the preparation of the defence budget for fiscal year 1979 and made possible the extensive involvement of the President. 'Because he recognised that it would be his first full statement of priorities, policies, and proposals, the chief executive spent literally hundreds of hours focusing on the size and distribution of the defence budget which was unveiled on January 23, 1978.' In addition, 'the Secretary of Defense personally reviewed about 300 program packages and 2,000 decision elements in formulating the budget'.[6]

Nor were the results of all this effort of much comfort. The budget for fiscal year 1979 merely reinforced the existing concerns of many conservatives about the Carter defence effort while also alienating many liberals. Part of the problem was that the President tried to be all things to all men. Carter wanted to be seen to be redeeming his campaign promises to cut the budget and actually did cut the projections of the Ford Administration for fiscal year 1979. At the same time there was a significant increase over the defence budget of the previous year. Rather than satisfying the various constituencies, however, the budget served merely to antagonize them. The liberals in the Democratic Party regarded defence spending as far too high, arguing that the President had chosen guns rather than butter at a time when the United States could not have both. The major challenge to the Carter defence budget, however, came from those who regarded it as a weakening of the remedial steps initiated by President Ford. In their view the 1977 package had suggested that the Carter Administration might not be as 'reliable' on defence as they wished. The package unveiled in early 1978 for the next fiscal year confirmed these fears.

The Carter defence budget for fiscal year 1979 increased defence spending beyond the previous year but was about 5 per cent below the levels projected by the Ford Administration. Furthermore, the cutback was not uniform. As one analyst has pointed out, it was achieved primarily by reducing the strategic force programmes of the Air Force—through a slowdown in the development of the MX—and Navy general purpose forces. Army procurement programmes in contrast emerged unscathed while there was an increased emphasis on the readiness of conventional forces, especially those on the Central Front in Europe. The Navy's ship-building programme was hit particularly hard, with something like a 20 per cent drop in funds below that of the previous year.[7] Although the Navy completed a major review of its future structure and force goals in March 1978, entitled Sea Plan 2000, this did not prevent the Carter projections of future naval strength being well below what the review characterized as a high-risk option and some 80 to 90 ships less than had been envisaged by Ford.[8] In addition, there were cutbacks in naval aviation capabilities, thereby underlining the fact that the Navy was the main loser in a posture which was predominantly orientated towards the NATO commitment.

It was not entirely surprising, therefore, that there were rumblings of protest in Congress, and when the House Committee on Armed Services added funds for a fifth nuclear-powered carrier (the fourth in the Nimitz class) this was endorsed not only by a majority in the House but also by the Senate (albeit with the proviso that future carriers would be smaller and less costly). As a result of this the President vetoed the bill on 17 August, a decision he justified on the grounds that in order to fund the new carrier Congress had cut into other capabilities. He emphasized that it was not a question of money but of how the available money was to be spent—and, by turning around 41 House Democrats who had voted for the carrier—upheld the veto despite an attempt to override it.[9] At this stage Carter was still able to manage the Congress on defence issues, something which he would find much more difficult the following year when the SALT II Treaty came up for consideration in the Senate.

If the shape and size of the American Navy was a controversial issue in 1978, it was far from being the only problem. More damaging to Carter's reputation was the announcement on 8 April 1978 that the President had decided to defer production of the Enhanced Radiation Weapon or, as it was more commonly known, the neutron bomb. Although it is not possible to recount the details of this episode, it seems fairly clear that there were misunderstandings not only between the Administration and its European allies—especially the Schmidt government—but also between Carter and his advisers. Almost from the outset Carter was reluctant to go ahead with the system and in the Summer of 1977 suggested to his advisers that unless the Europeans were prepared to make a firm commitment to deploy the weapons, the United States should not proceed further. This was intended to provide a rationale for cancellation but was interpreted instead by Brzezinski in particular as an injunction to persuade the allies that they should come out in support of the weapon. When this firm commitment was not forthcoming Carter, against the advice of his National Security Adviser, the Secretary of State and the Secretary of Defense, decided to defer production. This undercut the position of Chancellor Schmidt who had been working towards a compromise formula to make deployment acceptable and appeared to be far more of a reversal in Carter's own position than it really was. In the final analysis the most fundamental misunderstandings seem to have been those between the President and Brzezinski. Indeed, Brzezinski himself has admitted that he misread Carter's feelings on the subject. As he put it: 'When the bureaucratic train was set in motion, I had assumed that we were fulfilling the President's requirements, paving the way toward an eventual decision to produce and deploy the ERW. I had underestimated the degree of Carter's reluctance to deploy this weapon and as a result the President was clearly caught unprepared' by how far the process had gone by March 1978.[10] Although Carter may not have deserved the charges of vacillation and inconsistency which were levelled at him in the aftermath of the deferment decision, the fact that his National Security Adviser could so misread the President's preferences suggests that there were weaknesses in both communication and decision-making in the White House itself.

Brzezinski was correct, however, in his prediction of the political consequences of what appeared to be a complete reversal by the President. The doubts about the President's capacity to manage national security issues which had existed in 1977, albeit in rather muted form, now became both more widespread and more explicit. What made this all the more damaging to the Administration was that it coincided with growing public and congressional concern over American steadfastness and capability in the face of what was widely construed as an increasingly assertive and powerful Soviet Union. It is not surprising, therefore, that the rise of single-issue pressure groups on domestic policy issues was accompanied by the emergence of a number of groups whose primary concern was with strengthening American military preparedness and who were enormously suspicious of an Administration which seemed willing to eschew development of weapons such as the neutron bomb without any attempt to obtain a quid pro quo from the Soviet Union. The Committee on the Present Danger was perhaps the most important of these groups, consisting as it did not only of Republicans but also of leading Democrats, such as Eugene Rostow and Paul Nitze, who were worried about the direction of American defence policy under Carter. With the support of other organizations such as the American Security Council and the National

Strategy Information Centre, the Committee on the Present Danger helped to create a political climate which was more disposed towards higher levels of defence spending than the President, with his concern to limit the overall budget deficit, seemed willing to contemplate. By the end of 1978 there were also indications in the opinion polls that a majority of those questioned favoured an increase in defence spending. As well as facing pressure from outside his Administration to do more for defence, Carter also faced considerable pressure from within. From the outset Brzezinski had been an advocate of greater increases in defence spending than the President regarded as necessary or desirable, and from mid or late 1978 onwards seems to have been joined by Secretary of Defense Harold Brown who became much more assertive and helped counter the arguments of Vice-President Mondale, Stuart Eizenstat of the Domestic Policy Staff, and others who wanted to give priority to domestic social programmes over defence.[11]

As a result of all this, 1979 can be understood as a year of transition in which the President's own preferences were subordinated to those of his advisers and to political expediency. This is not to argue that there was a fundamental change in the Carter defence budget for fiscal year 1980. On the contrary, the priorities which had been established the previous year remained intact. Nevertheless, there were several decisions during this period which suggest that the Administration was attempting to reverse its image and convince its critics that it was not neglecting the needs of national security. The decision, just prior to Carter's summit meeting with President Brezhnev in Vienna, to deploy the MX in a mobile-basing mode, can be understood in this context. This is not to deny that there were very real, if considerably exaggerated, concerns over the vulnerability of US land-based missiles. It does appear though that this decision ran against all Carter's instincts and in his diary of 4 June 1979 he described MX deployment as 'a nauseating prospect to confront, with the gross waste of money going into nuclear weapons of all kinds'.[12] In opting for deployment, however, Carter almost certainly recognized that it was a prerequisite for Senate consent to the ratification of the SALT II Treaty which would be signed at Vienna a few weeks later.

Indeed, the attempt to obtain Senate approval for SALT II became the dominant issue in American defence policy during the latter half of 1979. The Treaty itself had taken considerable time and effort to negotiate even though the Administration, in the aftermath of the Soviet rejection of its deep cuts proposal, had reverted to the approach outlined by its predecessors and enshrined in the Vladivostok Accords. This was partly because the substantive issues had become much more complex than they had been prior to the SALT I Agreement of 1972—with particular problems arising over the Soviet Backfire bomber and American cruise missiles. This complexity was reflected in the SALT II package, which consisted of the Treaty itself which was to run until 1985, an interim protocol to run until 1981, and a statement of principles for SALT III. Among its more important provisions the Treaty set a ceiling of 2,400 missiles and bombers (a number which was to be reduced to 2,250 after 1982), while the Protocol prohibited the deployment of ground and sea-launched cruise missiles with a range over 600 kilometres. The debate over SALT II both in the Senate and in the nation went far beyond the precise terms of the agreement, however, and became instead a far-reaching discussion of the strategic balance and the Soviet threat. Although anxiety was expressed about particular provisions and the resulting asymmetries, such as Soviet possession of over 300 'heavy' missiles for which there was no counterpart on the American side, much of the debate reflected a more general resentment with the fact that Moscow had attained strategic parity and on some indicators was actually ahead of the United States. It was also symptomatic of the disillusionment with *détente* which had been apparent in 1976 but had become much stronger during Carter's tenure.

Soviet actions in the Third World, and especially their involvement, along with that of the Cubans, in the Horn of Africa had contributed to a pervasive climate of mistrust which spilled over and influenced attitudes to SALT. In one sense this vindicated the position of Brzezinski who all along had argued that SALT should be linked to Soviet good behaviour in the Third World but had never succeeded in convincing Secretary of State Vance or the President of this. Although it is difficult to quarrel with Vance's contention that if SALT was in America's interests, then it should not be dependent on Soviet restraint elsewhere, politically this was naïve. Linkage was not adopted as a strategy by the Carter Administration, but the SALT debate revealed that it had become a fact of political life. If some of the critics of SALT were really passing judgement on Soviet behaviour, others were passing judgement on the Carter Administration itself. Even the Joint Chiefs of Staff emphasized that their support for SALT II was conditional upon the Treaty not having a tranquilliser affect on American military preparations. Harold Brown also took a hard-nosed position, arguing that if the Treaty required him to trust the Soviet Union he would not be willing to support it. These views emerged in the Hearings on SALT II over the summer of 1979, and the Administration, by adopting a more hawkish attitude, appeared to be mobilizing support more successfully than had been anticipated. This trend was reversed by the controversy over a Soviet combat brigade in Cuba. Although this was a fabricated issue—used by the opponents of SALT to sabotage the prospects of the Treaty in the Senate and by some SALT supporters to demonstrate that they too could be tough on the Russians—it highlighted the state of American opinion. It also delayed the Treaty in the committee stage, a delay which proved of critical importance in relation to developments in Iran and Afghanistan. Even before these developments SALT was in trouble. Nevertheless, an attempt was being made to work out a package whereby the Senate accepted SALT along with an increase in the defence budget of around 5 per cent—a combination advocated by Senator Sam Nunn, one of the Senate's leading authorities on defence, and by Henry Kissinger. Such a deal was very attractive to Brown and Brzezinski with Carter's National Security Adviser being particularly pleased that 'SALT, rather than being the vehicle for acquiescent accommodation with the Soviet Union was becoming the catalyst for a more assertive posture'.[13]

On December 12 Carter announced that his budget request for fiscal year 1981 would be 5 per cent higher than his request for fiscal year 1980 and that the average increase in the programme projected for the next five years would be above $4\frac{1}{2}$ per cent. Despite such concessions by the President, it seems unlikely that the Treaty would have been approved without the addition of several 'killer' amendments. At the very least, these would have required a return to the negotiating table. As it was, SALT was overtaken by events and in the aftermath of the Soviet invasion of Afghanistan the President had little alternative other than to ask the Senate to defer further consideration of the Treaty.

If higher defence spending was the most important manifesta-
tion of the Carter Administration's changing approach to
defence in 1979, it was not the only one. On July 20 Brzezinski
announced that Carter had suspended the withdrawal of US
ground troops from South Korea—a process the President had
initially hoped to complete by 1982. This decision was apparently made with considerable reluctance and reflected the
strength of the opposition to the withdrawal plan as well as new
intelligence estimates which suggested that North Korean
military strength was far greater than had been supposed. From
the outset the withdrawal plan encountered opposition from
American military commanders in Asia, and Major-General
Singlaub, the third ranking officer in Korea, was removed from
his post as a result of his open criticism of the President's policy.
This did not succeed in stifling the opposition, however, and the
military opponents of the disengagement were joined by important civilian officials in the State Department and on the staff
of the National Security Council. The American ambassadors to
China and Japan also warned of the consequences of the withdrawal for American allies in North-east Asia. These doubts
about the wisdom of the President's plan from within the
executive branch were amplified by Congress and further reinforced by the Japanese government. Yet Carter himself must
ultimately bear the brunt of the responsibility for the reversal
of a policy to which he had been strongly committed but for
which he did very little. There was no real constituency for the
troop withdrawal plan in either the Congress or the public, and
Carter made no attempt to build one.[14] Having made his initial
withdrawal announcement, the President gave little attention to
the issue, an oversight which suggests that he had a limited
understanding of the limits of presidential power, especially
when it came to matters of implementation.

If the decision to suspend the withdrawal of American troops
from Korea was a reversal of the President's previous stance,
another major decision made in 1979 can be understood as the
culmination of a study initiated during Carter's first year. It
became clear in June that Carter's Policy Review Committee
was examining options for a new American policy in the Persian
Gulf and the Middle East in the aftermath of the fall of the
Shah of Iran—a development which had robbed Washington of
its 'surrogate gendarme' and spelled the failure of the Nixon

Doctrine in an area of considerable strategic importance. In deciding that America needed a capacity to intervene rapidly and to fight what was known as a 'half-war' in the region, however, the Administration was picking up a theme which dated back to PRM 10 in 1977. This analysis had acknowledged the need to create light and highly mobile forces with a capacity for intervention outside the NATO area, although little had been done to make this a reality. In 1979 though there was a much stronger impetus behind the plan and by December the joint force which was being set up was becoming known as the Rapid Deployment Force. Although the RDF was to be composed of existing units the Administration acknowledged the need to acquire a greater air-lift and sea-lift capability—a task which became even more urgent after the Soviet intervention in Afghanistan.

A few weeks prior to this intervention NATO had announced plans to deploy 464 ground-launched cruise missiles and 108 Pershing 2s in Western Europe. Once again this decision can be traced back to the first year of the Administration and to Carter's concern with reaffirming the American security commitment to Western Europe. The issue had also become bound up with the desire not to repeat the fiasco of the neutron bomb. This made it imperative for NATO to demonstrate that it did after all have a capacity for taking hard decisions on force modernization, especially in view of the Soviet modernization of its missiles targeted against Western Europe. Together with concerns over maintaining the American nuclear guarantee to Western Europe and the desire to demonstrate that the allies would not be compromised by the terms of SALT II, the desire to avoid another débâcle helps to explain why NATO in December 1979 embarked on a course of action which precipitated intense opposition throughout Western Europe. Although the deployment decision was accompanied by an 'arms control track' this was seen by many American officials as simply a way of legitimizing the deployment.

In other words, by the end of 1979 American policy had moved a long way from the concerns of 1977 when an early agreement on arms control had been one of the major objectives of the new Administration. This trend was taken even further in 1980 and the Soviet intervention in Afghanistan finally ended any remaining ambiguity in the Administration's stance towards

Moscow. The problem of how to deal with the Soviet Union, which had increasingly divided Brzezinski and Vance, and caused the President to appear confused and inconsistent, was finally decided in favour of Brzezinski. The President himself admitted that he had been wrong about the Soviet Union and in the early months of 1980—almost certainly with one eye on his re-election prospects—adopted a much tougher policy.

This concern over the Soviet threat was reflected partly in further increases in the defence budget for fiscal year 1981. Equally important though was the change in the composition of the budget: there was less of a preoccupation with spending for NATO and more concern with the role of conventional forces elsewhere. The hard line approach to the Soviet Union was also evident in Carter's State of the Union message of 23 January 1980 in which he made clear that the Persian Gulf was a vital interest of the United States and one that it was prepared to uphold by force. Although the rhetoric outran the capability in that there were serious question marks about the capacity of the Rapid Deployment Force to provide anything more than the barest of trip-wires in the event of major Soviet aggression, what became known as the Carter Doctrine was still an important development. The State of the Union message effectively marked the end of what many critics regarded as an excessive preoccupation with the military balance in Central Europe and the adoption of the broader geostrategic perspective that had long been urged upon the President by his National Security Adviser.

Another development which added to the perception of the Carter Administration as adopting a much more vigorous defence posture was the revision of nuclear strategy which culminated in Presidential Directive 59, signed in July 1980. This revision had been going on since the first year of the Administration and in many ways was merely a further refinement of the targeting options that had been outlined by Secretary of Defense Schlesinger during the Nixon and Ford Administrations. In certain respects, however, PD59—together with several other Presidential directives on nuclear strategy—represented a significant departure from past policies. Unprecedented emphasis was placed on the possibility of a protracted nuclear conflict and Soviet political control targets were given a higher priority than Soviet recovery resources. In addition, considerable efforts were to be devoted to minimizing the vulnerability of American command, control and communication systems. The purpose of this, and indeed of what became known as the countervailing strategy, was to make clear to the Soviet Union that, whatever the circumstances, Moscow could not expect to win a nuclear war.

These changes in America's strategic posture prepared the way for the Reagan Administration's adoption of a nuclear warfighting strategy designed to ensure that the United States prevailed in any conflict with the Soviet Union. Nevertheless, the steps taken by the Carter Administration in 1980 to project an image of toughness were undermined by the abortive attempt to rescue the American hostages in Iran. The Carter Administration was much more reticent about the use of force than either its predecessors or its immediate successor. And the one occasion on which force was used was a fiasco. The failure of the rescue attempt is sometimes attributed to Presidential interference in the operational details of the mission. Yet this is unfair to Carter. He can be criticized for undertaking a mission which was bold in conception but at best was a high-risk venture which required a lot of luck to succeed. The problems which arose in its implementation, however, were problems which it was difficult to foresee and for which the services themselves have to bear the brunt of the responsibility. It was the President though who had to face the domestic consequences and his failure to resolve the hostage crisis by force or by any other means played a major part in his election defeat. The toughening-up of defence policy had not convinced the electorate that Carter could provide the kind of leadership on national security matters that was required as America moved into the 1980s. In the light of this, and with the caveats mentioned at the outset in mind, an attempt must now be made to provide an overall assessment of President Carter's defence policy.

Conclusion

Even on the basis of a superficial survey of Carter's defence policy several conclusions stand out.

1. During the first two years of his Administration, Carter attempted to impose his own personal preferences on defence policy in a way which created considerable opposition. His

thinking on defence was very close to that of the liberal Democrats who in the early 1970s had challenged the Nixon Administration and attempted to secure a more substantial peace dividend as American involvement in Vietnam was brought to a close. The mood of the Congress and of the public was changing, however, and becoming increasingly concerned about American weakness and Soviet strength. This juxtaposition ensured that Carter's defence policies in his first two years were subjected to considerable criticism. Indeed, it is difficult to escape the conclusion that Carter so damaged his reputation on defence in 1977 and 1978 that nothing he did thereafter was sufficient to redeem him. Throughout 1979, which was a pivotal year, Carter made decisions on defence which he almost certainly found abhorrent. In the aftermath of Afghanistan, however, he embraced a hard-line policy with a degree of conviction which had hitherto been lacking. But by then he could do little to alter the image of himself as a President who was fundamentally unsound on defence.

2. While some of Carter's policies during his first two years were a departure from the more cautious approach of his predecessors, the problem was, in part, one of public relations. Nixon had reduced the defence budget while adopting the rhetoric of strength; Carter increased the defence budget but without the rhetoric. As a result, he failed to convince his critics that he was serious about maintaining American military power. To some extent this problem also resulted from Carter's attempts to convince his liberal supporters that he was fulfilling his campaign pledge to reduce defence expenditure. By emphasizing different baselines to different audiences Carter hoped to satisfy those who wanted less spent on defence and those who wanted more. He succeeded in satisfying neither.

3. Some of Carter's problems were procedural. He never appeared to grasp the realities of bureaucratic politics and in particular failed to realize not only that Presidential power was no more than the power to persuade but that if policies were to be implemented successfully this power had to be exercised to the full. It was partly because he lacked a concept of policy implementation that the President frequently appeared indecisive. This was particularly the case with the neutron bomb. Yet the problem was less one of indecision than of

ambiguity. Carter failed to convey to Brzezinski his distaste for a weapon system that his National Security Adviser was keen to deploy. The result was a serious rift in Atlantic relations and a blow to the President's prestige from which he never fully recovered.

4. Despite suggestions to the contrary, Carter did have a clear set of priorities for American defence policy. The problem was that these priorities—the emphasis on European defence and on arms control—were not as widely shared as the President might have hoped. Indeed, the Reagan Administration has not only reordered national priorities to give more to defence but has altered the emphasis within defence itself. The Navy has been accorded a much more significant role by Reagan than it was by Carter, while the preoccupation with Europe has been replaced by a more global approach. Although Carter began to move in this direction in 1980 the process has been taken much further by his successor.

5. If the Carter Administration had a clear set of priorities, it lacked a strategic vision or overarching strategic concept. Consequently, it conveyed an image of constant improvization or what Stanley Hoffmann has described as an addiction to erratic tactics.[15] Without a clear decision about the nature of the relationship with the Soviet Union there was no way of avoiding this. And such a decision was enormously difficult given Carter's choice of advisers. Although Carter may have seen advantages in having a National Security Adviser and a Secretary of State who had fundamentally different prescriptions for dealing with the Soviet Union, this merely institutionalized a schizophrenic approach to American foreign and defence policy. As Hoffmann has pointed out, institutionalized diversity can be useful if the President nevertheless imposes his own views and makes his own synthesis.[16] Jimmy Carter was able to do neither of these things. Nor was he able to force his advisers to reconcile their contradictory approaches—a managerial failure which had far-reaching consequences for his ability to influence Congress, the electorate, and the Russians, and one which helps to explain why his defence policy alienated both conservatives and liberals. With a defence policy based on conceptual confusion and managerial incompetence, it could hardly have been otherwise.

Notes

1. R. Gallucci, quoted in S. Sarkesian (ed.), *Defence Policy and the Presidency: Carter's First Years*, Boulder, Colorado, Westview Press, 1979, p. 12.
2. L. Korb, 'The Policy Impacts of the Carter Defense Program', in ibid., p. 139.
3. J. Carter, *Keeping Faith: Memoirs of a President*, New York, Bantam Books, 1982, p. 80.
4. See G. C. Wilson, 'Brown Convincing Congress Soviet Threat is Overstated', *International Herald Tribune*, 16 March, 1977.
5. The argument here draws heavily on the analysis of L. Korb, 'National Security Organisation and Process in the Carter Administration', in Sarkesian, op. cit., especially p. 125.
6. Korb, 'The Policy Impacts of the Carter Defense Program', op. cit., p. 139.
7. Ibid., p. 160.
8. Ibid., p. 160.
9. See *US Defence Policy: Weapons Strategy, Commitments*, second edn, Washington, *Congressional Quarterly*, 1980, p. 51.
10. Z. Brzezinski, *Power and Principle*, New York, Farrar, Straus, Giroux, 1983, p. 306.
11. Ibid., p. 45.
12. Carter, op. cit., p. 241.
13. Brzezinski, op. cit., p. 345.
14. See L. A. Niksch, 'US Troop Withdrawal From South Korea: Past Shortcomings and Future Prospects', *Asian Survey*, Vol. 21, No. 3, March 1981, pp. 325-41.
15. S. Hoffmann, 'Requiem', *Foreign Policy* No. 42, Spring 1981, pp. 3-26, at p. 9.
16. Ibid.

6 The Carter Administration and domestic civil rights

M. Glenn Abernathy

The topic of President Carter and civil rights almost invariably evokes recollections of Carter's strong and repeated statements with regard to human rights in the international community, and less attention has been paid to his activity in the areas of domestic civil rights. This is at least partially a result of his own conception of his role in that area. In discussing his domestic civil rights initiatives, Carter stated, 'I looked on them as kind of a continuum of what had been initiated under Lyndon Johnson and talked about under President Kennedy . . . And so I didn't look upon those achievements as notable in nature. I just felt as if they were my duty.'[1] The President's preoccupation with several major foreign policy problems—the Panama Canal treaty, the hostage crisis, and the Soviet invasion of Afghanistan —and the deteriorating economic situation could well have led him to accord his civil rights contributions less weight than they probably deserve. They may not have been exceptional, but they were surely of greater importance than anything in the Nixon or Ford Administrations. In this chapter the various aspects of Carter's civil rights activity will be examined and, in addition, the success rate and the factors contributing to the success or failure of the proposals.

Appointments

President Carter appears to feel that his record of appointment of women and minority representatives to executive and judicial positions is among his most satisfying accomplishments in the civil rights area. And many of these persons were civil rights activists. In a 1977 article Florence Isbell stated:

No other president has appointed so many avowed civil libertarians to high office. Among them are Eleanor Holmes Norton, former ACLU Assistant Legal Director, as director of the Equal Employment Opportunities Commission; Patricia Wald, former Litigation Director of the ACLU-sponsored

Mental Health Law Project, as Assistant Attorney General for Legislative Affairs; Pat Derian of the ACLU National Board as a State Department senior staff member on international human rights; Barbara Babcock, former National Capital Area ACLU Board member as head of the Civil Division of the Justice Department; Togo West, member of the National Capital Area Litigation Committee as General Counsel of the Navy; and Marilyn Haft, former director of the ACLU's Sexual Rights Project, as Associate Director of the White House Office of Public Liaison.[2]

Carter's appointments that had, and will have, the greatest impact, however, were his appointments to the federal bench.[3] Although he had only one term in office he named more people to lifetime positions on the federal district and appeals courts than any other President in history, primarily because Congress created 152 new lower court judgeships in 1978. Two hundred and two of these were to district courts and fifty-six to courts of appeal. Nearly 40 per cent of the federal bench in 1981 were Carter appointees. During the campaign for the presidency Carter made commitments to appoint more women and minority candidates and to institute merit selection. In an interview President Carter stated:

Right after I was elected, we had a meeting in the Roosevelt room of Hispanic women and black civil rights workers. Both my attorney general at the time, Griffin Bell, and I sat in with them, and we listened to all the problems that they described to us. There was not a single United States Attorney, for instance, who was a woman. I think that there had been only one in history. It is a ridiculous thing; I couldn't believe it. And in all the southeastern states, as you well know, there was a dearth of black judges. Since there is a heavy concentration of blacks in this region, I thought that there ought to be not only district court judges, but also circuit judges who were black. So I promised them that I would set this as a major goal—in the presence of Griffin Bell. Griffin was not nearly so enthusiastic about that as I was, nor was he as enthusiastic as other people in the White House. Bob Lipshutz, Stu Eizenstat, Vice-President Mondale, all of us were very eager to see these commitments carried out, not just stingily, but enthusiastically, with open recruitments of highly qualified blacks and women and Hispanics for judges. I'm not saying this as any criticism of him, but Griffin was a product of the silk-stocking law firms (King and Spalding) and he was a product of the federal judiciary, and he was very active in the American Bar Association. So his ties were with the white, male, highly competent, very distinguished members of the bar, and whenever there was a circuit court opening, then Griffin could give me a list of twenty outstanding district court judges who were qualified to be promoted. But what we were looking for was a qualified black or qualified woman, or Hispanic—in some cases, I don't mean in every case—so that was the initiative. It came from those who supported me for President, it came from those who knew about my own civil rights background and from those who were my natural political allies.

With regard to judicial appointments, Carter clearly made good on his promises. In total he appointed twenty-eight blacks, twenty-nine women (including six black women), and fourteen persons of Hispanic origin (including one woman) to the federal courts. By the end of his Administration the proportion of women judges had risen from 1 per cent to nearly 7 per cent, and for blacks, from 4 per cent to nearly 9 per cent. It should be noted that three out of four of the Carter appointees to the courts of appeal were rated either 'well qualified' or 'exceptionally well qualified' by the American Bar Association Standing Committee on Federal Judiciary, and none was rated 'not qualified'.

Privacy

Carter's concern for privacy interests led him to announce on 2 April 1979 a sweeping proposal calling for legislation to protect the privacy of individuals.[4] The proposal focused on four well-defined areas that he considered needed attention: extension of the right of individual access to one's medical or financial records, greater privacy protection from outside access to the individual's records, a slight expansion of opportunities for prosecution for illegal wiretapping, and restrictions on police searches for materials held by the media.

The 'Privacy of Medical Information Act' and the 'Fair Financial Information Practices Act' were submitted to address the first two areas of privacy concern. With regard to the medical records proposal, the message stated that the Act would give individuals the right to see their own medical records, but if direct access might harm the patient, the Act provided that access might be provided through an intermediary. 'This legislation allows the individual to ensure that the information maintained as part of his medical care relationship is accurate, timely, and relevant to that care. Such accuracy is of increasing importance because medical information is used to affect employment and collection of insurance and other social benefits.'[5] The Act would also limit the disclosure of medical information and make it illegal to collect medical information under false pretences.

The 'Fair Financial Information Practices Act' was designed to 'expand the laws on consumer credit and banking records to provide full fair information protections. It will ensure that consumers are informed about firms' record-keeping practices and thereby help them decide which firm to patronize.'[6] Consumer-credit reporting agencies would be required to give consumers the right to see and copy credit reports about them. Firms granting credit, including retail stores as well as banks, would be required to inform individuals of the reasons for any adverse decisions made about them. Insurance companies would be required to allow individuals to see, copy and correct insurance records about themselves. In addition, it would restrict disclosure of data from electronic funds transfer systems. 'Such systems are efficient, but they pose major privacy problems. Not only do they contain extensive personal data on individuals, but they can be used to keep track of people's movements and activities.'[7] Carter also said that he endorsed a Senate bill to restrict the use of polygraphs or lie detectors in the hiring of employees.

An additional proposal, the 'Privacy of Research Records Act', was also submitted to ensure that personal information collected or maintained for a research purpose would not be used or disclosed in individually identifiable form for an action that adversely affected the individual. Carter pointed out in his message to Congress that researchers often promise confidentiality to persons who participate in studies, but added that no legal basis for that promise existed. The legislation would require the researcher to tell study participants of the possibility, if any, that information about them would be disclosed. It would also establish criminal fines for unauthorized disclosure of research information.

On the matter of government access to the files of the news media, the Carter message noted that the Supreme Court's decision in 1978 in the case of *Zurcher* v. *Stanford Daily* posed 'dangers to the effective functioning of our free press'. The President submitted legislation to restrict police searches for documentary materials held by the press and by others involved in the dissemination of information to the public. With limited exceptions, the bill prohibited a search for or seizure of 'work product'—such as notes, interview files and film. For documents which did not constitute work product, the bill required that the police first obtain a subpoena rather than a search warrant. This would ensure that police would not 'rummage through the files of people preparing materials for publication and that those subject to the subpoena have the opportunity to contest the government's need for the information.'[8] The two exceptions under Carter's bill in which search warrants could be used were: (1) when authorities wanted a hostage note or other material whose seizure might prevent harm to a person, and (2) when the journalist or writer was suspected of a crime. The second exception generally would not apply if the only suspected crime was possession of stolen documents, but if the documents related to national defence or contained classified information, then they could be subject to seizure under a warrant, rather than a subpoena. The bill did not provide criminal sanctions. Instead, it allowed a person who was unlawfully searched to seek civil damages against the government or the employee who committed the search.

Carter also expressed his views on the 1976 report of the National Commission for the Review of Federal and State Laws Relating to Wiretapping and Electronic Surveillance, agreeing with some of the recommendations and disagreeing with others. He supported the Commission's recommendation that misdemeanor and civil penalties be added to existing felony penalties for the punishment of privately conducted electronic eavesdropping. The Commission reported that the prosecution record against illegal eavesdroppers was disappointing, and in no jurisdiction did it find a bold affirmative action programme against such illegal action. It found that between 1969 and 1976 the Department of Justice had successfully prosecuted only seventy-five persons for eavesdropping violations. It prosecuted forty-six others whose cases ended in dismissal or acquittal. The Commission concluded that there were several factors which accounted for this state of affairs, including hostility of judges and jurors where the illegal surveillance was conducted with intent to expose marital infidelity or other wrongdoing by a member of a family. The Commission suggested that it might be easier to enlist the support of the judge and the jury in punishing illegal eavesdroppers, regardless of motive, if criminal penalties for nonprofessionals were lowered, so that such persons need not face the present felony penalties.

Carter also endorsed the proposed amendment to federal law explicitly allowing the disclosure of illegal interceptions 'when relevant in a prosecution for illegal interceptions'. The Commission had concluded that it might be easier to encourage victims to complain to law enforcement departments if the law explicitly made it clear that the contents of illegal wiretaps were admissible in evidence to prove the case against an illegal wiretapper, but that the judge should retain discretion to deny use of the evidence 'where relevance is outweighed by undue loss of privacy to the victims of the interception'.[9] Carter did not support the Commission's recommendation, however, that the law be amended to permit the Attorney General to designate any United States Attorney or federal strike force chief to authorize applications for court-ordered wiretapping. He felt that the existing requirement that delegation could be made only to an Assistant Attorney General was a necessary privacy protection.

In addition to legislative proposals, Carter also stated that he would take administrative steps to ensure the better protection of privacy in the use of records maintained by the Federal government. The message stated, 'While the Privacy Act is working reasonably well and is too new to decide on major revisions, I have ordered a number of administrative actions to improve its operation.' He pointed out that the Federal government holds almost four billion records on individuals, most of them stored in thousands of computers, and modern technology makes it possible to turn this store into a dangerous surveillance system. The specific problem which concerned him was the use of 'matching programs', that compared computerized lists of individuals to detect fraud or other abuses. And while such programmes were making an important contribution to reducing abuse of federal programmes, he felt that safeguards were needed to protect the privacy of the innocent.

Carter also directed that action be taken to: extend Privacy Act protections to certain data systems operated by recipients of federal grants; strengthen administration of the 'routine use' provision of the Privacy Act, which governs disclosures of personal information by federal agencies; ensure that each federal agency has an office responsible for privacy issues raised by the agency's activities; and limit the amount of information the government requires private groups and individuals to report.

Housing

In his legislative message to Congress on 21 January 1980, Carter gave strong emphasis to the need for amendment of the Fair Housing Act of 1968 (PL 60–284). He stated:

I will continue to press for enactment of this important civil rights initiative; it will enable the government to enforce our fair housing laws effectively and promptly. It is the most critical civil rights legislation before the Congress in years. The promise of equal housing opportunity has been far too long an empty promise. This bill will help make that promise a reality.[10]

The 1968 law prohibited discrimination in the sale or rental of housing on the basis of race, colour, religion or national origin. A 1974 amendment prohibited discrimination based on sex. The law did not, however, give the Department of Housing and Urban Development authority to enforce the law. HUD can only attempt conciliation between an aggrieved person and an alleged violator. If the dispute is not resolved by conciliation, the complainant must bring his own lawsuit. The Justice Department is permitted to take legal action only if it finds a *pattern or practice* of housing discrimination. The Carter proposal urged legislation to provide the Department of Housing and Urban Development with the power to hold administrative hearings and to issue 'cease and desist' orders in cases where illegal discrimination was found. The President stated that 'Its enactment will continue to be my highest legislative priority in the civil rights area.'

Racial equality

With the exception of the housing proposal just discussed, President Carter's activities to promote racial equality were primarily through executive and agency action rather than legislative initiatives. It has already been noted that he substantially increased the number of black federal judges. Carter stated in an interview that one of his goals was to strengthen the

Equal Employment Opportunity Commission and to help it overcome a 30,000 case backlog. Another was the channelling of government contracts to minority firms. He stated that his administration had set a goal for themselves to triple such government contracts in one year. Although that goal was not reached, such contracts increased nearly two and a half times. He also set a goal of $100,000,000 of federal deposits in minority-owned banks. The actual total by 1980 was less than that figure, but such deposits had nearly doubled. His administration was also quite successful in its efforts to increase minority ownership of radio and television stations. In his 1980 message to Congress he stated that this ownership had increased by 65 per cent. Almost 15 per cent of the funds spent under the Local Public Works Act of 1977 went to minority-owned firms. His 1981 budget reflected an effort to expand management, technical and training assistance for minority firms and to provide substantial funding increases for minority capital development under the Small Business Administration's minority enterprise small business investment company programme. Carter stated that 'those were the kinds of things that we tried to do in a more mundane way to provide jobs, investments and ownership of the media among the black people.'

Carter was personally involved in the move to strengthen black colleges in America. He was honorary chairman of the drive to raise $50,000,000 for the United Negro College Fund. He was a very active honorary chairman—he called meetings in the Roosevelt Room in the White House; he made radio and television tapes to encourage people to contribute; he recruited Tom Murphy (then chief executive officer of General Motors) to be the active chairman; and the result was that some $62,000,000 was raised for the Fund.

Carter stated, 'Whenever the blacks had a problem with a particular local or state government, they quite often felt at ease to come to see me and say, "Mr. President, we've got a problem. Will you help us with it?" ' He indicated that his policies with respect to blacks often derived from his close association with a cadre of supporters who originated around Atlanta—Andrew Young, Danny King, Coretta King, Maynard Jackson, Vernon Jordan, the Atlanta University group and associates with the major churches in Atlanta. Much less effective, apparently, were the tactics of the Black Caucus in Congress.

Carter said that he would always give them an attentive ear, understanding always that they were never satisfied. 'Their main method of operation was public condemnation of the incumbent president and the congress because they didn't get 100% of what they demanded.'

In an article examining the Carter Administration's civil liberties activity in his first year in office, John H. F. Shattuck is generally critical of the accomplishments.[11] He did give the Carter Administration a favourable rating, however, in its moves to achieve racial equality. In particular, 'The administration's record on employment discrimination has been generally good.' In a Supreme Court case, *Hazelwood* v. *United States* [433 U.S. 299 (1977)] the Justice Department strongly supported the constitutionality of an interpretation of Title VII of the Civil Rights Act of 1964 which would prohibit employment practices that have a discriminatory *effect*, rather than only barring actions with a discriminatory *intent*. In another action, the Justice Department sued the Los Angeles Police Department for using non job-related testing procedures that discriminated against minorities.

The Administration's position on affirmative action in employment, as indicated in the Justice Department's brief in the *Bakke* case, was that race may be taken into account as an affirmative factor in employment (or education) decisions so long as the decision is not tied to firm numerical quotas. And in two important desegregation cases (involving Dayton, Ohio and Wilmington, Delaware) the Justice Department filed *amicus* briefs generally supporting the plaintiffs. The briefs actually argued in favour of system-wide remedies, which in Wilmington meant a metropolitan remedy—a sharp departure from the position of the Justice Department under President Ford. Near the close of his term Carter vetoed an appropriations bill (HR 7584) that would have barred the executive branch from any expenditure to initiate suits to require busing to achieve school desegregation. The primary thrust of his veto message, however, was that the prohibition was an infringement on the Article II powers of the President:

I have often stated my belief that busing should only be used as a last resort in school desegregation cases. But busing even as a last resort is not the real issue here. The real issue is whether it is proper for the Congress to prevent the President from carrying out his constitutional responsibility under Article II to enforce the Constitution and other laws of the United States.[12]

Civil justice reform

On 27 February 1979 Carter submitted a message to Congress outlining his programme to reform the federal civil justice system. Not all of the proposals directly related to matters of civil rights, but several of them were designed to improve access to the courts, reduce delay and reduce the costs of litigation. The message stated:

> The courts cannot perform their traditional and essential function if they are required to operate with inadequate resources, saddled with outmoded procedures, and burdened with more business than they can fairly dispose of within a reasonable time. Nor can our citizens avail themselves of their 'day in court' if, as is too often true in these days of rising litigation expenses, the price of participation in litigation is beyond their means.
>
> Delay and expense play a part in our civil justice system. We have long recognized that justice delayed is justice denied. For many injured parties, having to wait a year or two to obtain legal relief in the courts is extremely harmful.
>
> The benefits of a legal victory are sometimes outweighed by the costs of achieving it. As litigation expenses and the size of court dockets increase, this seems to be happening with increasing frequency. Legal redress should not consume years of time and thousands of dollars.[13]

One of the proposals would have promoted the use of arbitration, rather than full court adjudication, in certain types of cases. The arbitration proposal 'would provide an innovative means for resolving speedily, fairly, and at reduced cost certain types of civil cases in which the main dispute is over the amount of money that one person owes to another.' It would allow federal district courts to adopt a procedure requiring that tort and contract cases involving less than $100,000 be submitted to arbitration, in order to resolve cases faster and with significantly less expense to the parties than with full court resolution. In order further to speed up disposition of cases in federal courts, another proposal contemplated the total abolition of the federal courts' diversity jurisdiction so that their jurisdiction would be confined to cases involving federal questions. (At present, if bankruptcy cases are excluded, diversity cases comprise some 35–40 per cent of the caseload in the federal district courts.)

A further proposal was designed to improve the means available to the people for 'resolving everyday disputes, such as complaints by neighbors, customers, tenants, and family members.' This legislation, entitled the Dispute Resolution Act, would provide federal assistance to the states to improve the institutions that deal with these programmes—small claims courts and more widespread use of Neighborhood Justice Centers, then being tested by the Department of Justice in selected metropolitan centres. Carter urged that the passage of these various bills 'would be a major step in eliminating excessive delays, red tape, and exorbitant costs within the civil justice system.'

Women's rights

Although the Carter Administration was strongly criticized in some quarters for its opposition to freedom of choice with regard to abortion, it was generally given high marks for its strong support of women's rights. Carter's conscious effort to appoint more women to governmental positions, particularly judgeships, has already been noted. He was a strong supporter of the Equal Rights Amendment, and when Congress debated the matter of extension of the time for ratification of that Amendment, he opposed the view that such extension required a two-thirds vote rather than a simple majority. He stated in an interview that he always felt that some of the strongest and most vocal supporters of the Equal Rights Amendment spelled its death knell:

I'm from Georgia, and I understand Georgia, South Carolina, Alabama and North Carolina—states that didn't ratify the Equal Rights Amendment. And for these brassiere-burning firebrands to come down here and try to ram the Equal Rights Amendment down the throats of a conservative Georgia Senate was the worst possible thing that they could have done.

Carter employed a different strategy. He tried, primarily with the help of Rosalynn Carter, Betty Ford and others, to put together a responsible group of women who did not have the Equal Rights Amendment as their only goal, but who also wanted corrective action taken by state legislatures and by the Congress in private sectors where there was obvious discrimination against women concerning retirement benefits and other areas.

The Carter Administration also supported legislative action to amend the Equal Employment Opportunity Act to extend employment disability benefits to cover pregnancy. This would reverse a 1976 Supreme Court decision which held that the Act did not require that pregnancy must be treated in the same manner as other medical disabilities affecting working men and women.

Carter suggested that the future of the all-volunteer armed forces might depend on expanding the role of women in military service. It appears that several lawsuits attacking sex discrimination in military employment were settled because the armed forces agreed to take steps to extend opportunities for women.

Carter's opposition to federal action to expand the availability of abortion subjected him to strong criticism from the freedom-of-choice advocates and some ACLU officials. In a 1978 article, John Shattuck, then Director of the Washington office of the ACLU, had some especially trenchant comments concerning the Carter Administration's stance on abortion:

> The administration has given lip service to finding alternatives to abortion, but as yet has had nothing to offer the one million teenagers who get pregnant each year, a substantial number of whom are welfare recipients dependent upon Medicaid. To make matters worse, some of the administration's welfare reform proposals would exclude teenage mothers.
>
> HEW Secretary Califano's solution to the problem of what to do with the unwanted children of women who are denied abortions is for the government to subsidize their adoption by 'minority and rural families who might want to adopt children but can't afford to.' Whatever the merits of this notion as an independent program, as an alternative to abortion, it is outrageous. It would force women to bear children so that other families could adopt them, thus making poor women government brood mares.[14]

The abortion issue is one about which both sides obviously feel very deeply, and the right-to-life proponents would feel that Shattuck's criticisms are both excessive and misdirected. It is clear that Carter's position stems from a strong religious conviction on the subject.

Voting rights and elections

On 22 March 1977 Carter submitted to Congress a five-part package of election reform proposals, including a new federal voter registration plan and a proposal for public financing of congressional elections. Universal voter registration was one of Carter's major campaign pledges, and this part of his recommendations has been characterized as the most innovative portion. Under this proposal the states would be required to sign up voters at the polls on election day when federal elections were being held. State and local officials would continue to administer voter registration and elections, and would still register as many voters as possible prior to election day in the usual manner, in order to avoid congestion at the polls, but registration could not be cut off in advance of election day. Proof of identity and residence, such as a driver's licence, would still be required. Carter proposed that the states be given financial assistance to employ additional registrars and to help pay the cost of registration by mail, travelling registrars, or any other pre-election registration efforts the states might choose. In House hearings on the legislation, Attorney General Bell, testifying on behalf of the Administration, cited studies that showed that registration complexities were responsible for keeping 20 to 25 per cent of non-voters from voting. When some members of the Committee expressed fears that vote fraud might be increased if the proposal were adopted, Bell responded that he thought present provisions were adequate for controlling the problem and, further, that most fraud was committed by election officials, not voters.

Carter also proposed public financing of congressional campaigns by means of the same income tax check-off method now used to finance presidential campaigns. He favoured 'the broadest possible application of public financing', and would apply it to primaries as well as general elections.

A third proposal would allow presidential candidates to designate one committee in each state to raise and spend a limited amount of money for campaign activities within the state—two cents per eligible voter. The purpose was to promote more grassroots participation in presidential races.

The fourth recommendation was that Congress adopt a Constitutional amendment to provide for direct popular election of the President. Such an amendment, which would abolish the Electoral College, would ensure that the candidate chosen by the voters would actually become President. He did not submit a specific amendment, however, but left it with Congress to work out the preferred language.

The fifth recommendation concerned the political rights of federal employees. The message stated:

> Over 2.8 million federal employees, including postal workers and workers for the District of Columbia, are now denied a full opportunity to partici-pate in the electoral process. Unlike other Americans, they cannot run as a partisan candidate for any public office, cannot hold party office, and can-not even do volunteer work in a partisan political campaign.
>
> I favor revising the Hatch Act to free those federal employees not in sensitive positions from these restrictions. . . . Acting on standards pre-scribed by Congress, the Civil Service Commission should determine which positions would be treated as sensitive in all relevant government agencies.
>
> Under such a Hatch Act revision, the vast majority of federal employees would be able to participate in federal, state and local elections and other political functions.[15]

Budget proposals

The Carter Administration's recommended budget for fiscal 1981 included estimated expenditures of $585 million for various civil rights activities in more than sixteen federal agencies. According to a special budget analysis prepared by the Office of Manage-ment and Budget, this represented an 8.3 per cent increase over the anticipated expenditure for fiscal 1980. The programmes receiving the largest increase were those designed to ensure equal employment opportunities in both the government and the private sector. The Equal Employment Opportunity Com-mission, for example, was budgeted for an estimated $290 million for fiscal 1980, and the estimate for fiscal 1981 was $322 mil-lion. The main thrust of programmes within the private sector was to promote the policies requiring federal contractors and subcontractors to give equal opportunities to job applicants and to develop affirmative action programmes.

Conclusions

The Carter Administration's proposals in the domestic civil rights area were not widely publicized and, with the exception of Carter's judicial appointments and his activity in support of the ERA, they have been almost ignored in the literature on the Carter Administration. In his memoirs, *Keeping Faith*, Carter himself totally omits any discussion of these proposals. But the foregoing account of his recommendations would seem to justify a conclusion that Carter deserves considerably more credit for his civil rights initiatives than has been accorded to him. The problem, of course, is that so few of these recommendations made their way successfully through the Congress, and a high failure rate in a domestic policy area tends to result in its relegation to obscurity.

In examining the various legislative proposals one must be struck with their sweeping coverage—from privacy concerns to civil justice reform to broad changes in the election laws. But almost none of them was adopted. The Fair Housing Act amendments passed the House but failed by a narrow margin in the Senate late in 1980. None of the five election law changes were passed. Only two of the varied recommendations concerning civil justice reform were adopted before Carter's term expired. One was the Federal Magistrate Act of 1979 (PL 96-82) that expanded the jurisdiction of the United States Magistrates to permit the trial of jury or non-jury civil matters with the consent of the parties and to permit the trial of misdemeanours if the defendant waived trial in the District Court. The other was the Dispute Resolution Act of 1980 (PL 96-190) to encourage the development of less formal dispute resolution mechanisms (such as arbitration centres) which would be less expensive and faster than court decisions and would assist the states financially in establishing such programmes. (It may be noted that at least some of Carter's proposals on civil justice reform were incorporated in the Federal Court Improvement Act of 1982 (PL 97-164) which was passed by the Reagan Administration.)

A major piece of legislation was the Privacy Protection Act of 1980 (PL 96-440) designed to limit governmental search and seizure of documentary materials possessed by persons involved in dissemination of communications to the public—employees of newspapers, publishers or broadcasters. While Carter supported such a proposal, a substantial move was already under way in both houses of Congress, and the Act would probably have gone through the Congress without his public endorsement. Another aspect of privacy protection, however, was proposed by the Carter Administration and passed the Congress. This was the Right to Financial Privacy Act of 1978 (Title XI of the 1978 Acts Affecting Financial Institutions—PL 95-630) that was designed to protect the confidentiality of customer records held by financial institutions.

The conclusion is clear that Carter's success rate in getting his domestic civil rights proposals adopted by the Congress was extremely low. With the possible exception of his request for legislation to institute universal voter registration, most of his legislative initiatives would not be characterized as radical or particularly novel. So why his low batting average? The answer is probably twofold. First, Carter submitted massive numbers of bills for action, many of which involved complex and controversial matters, and he seemingly established no priorities to guide the Congress in their selection of the most important bills for consideration. The attrition rate is almost inevitably high in these circumstances. Second, there is no indication that the White House made any concerted effort to lobby for the passage of these bills or to gather outside interest groups to concentrate their lobbying efforts on behalf of passage. When the Panama Canal Treaty was being considered Carter personally telephoned almost all the Senators to garner support. The civil rights proposals, on the other hand, were submitted to Congress and simply left to run their course, unless hearings were held by the various committees and administration spokesmen invited to appear. Without any sustained pressure from the White House, the Congress chose not to devote time and energy to most of the recommendations.

Where Carter could act on his own authority, however, he did achieve some gains. His appointments, particularly to judicial positions, resulted in major increases in the number of minorities and women in high positions in the Federal government. And many of these appointees were prominent in activist civil rights organizations. By executive order Carter attempted to improve privacy protection in federal agencies by limiting cross-agency exchange of personal information on Americans and the release of such information to outside groups. The area in which Carter achieved the highest marks would be that of promoting racial equality. Not only with respect to judicial and other appointments, but also through a variety of economic aids to blacks and Hispanics, Carter left a substantial record of support. Probably his most dramatic move, however, was his grant of amnesty to draft-evaders of the Vietnam War. This was a clear promise made during his campaign, and he fulfilled it shortly after his inauguration in 1977.

In summary, the Carter Administration did present a

substantial and varied programme of civil rights initiatives. Some gains were made through direct application of the executive power, but very little was accomplished through congressional action. There was a virtual absence of leadership from the White House, and the Congress, which was already leaning to a more conservative position, simply devoted its energies to other matters (particularly economic and energy problems) which it considered to be more pressing. Despite his lack of success, however, Carter should be credited with having proposed a number of far-reaching measures in the domestic civil rights area.

Notes

1. Interview with President Carter in Plains, Georgia, 18 April 1983.
2. 'Carter's Civil Libertarians', *The Civil Liberties Review*, Vol. 4, July/August 1977, pp. 55-6. (ACLU—the American Civil Liberties Union.)
3. For an excellent analysis of Carter's judicial appointments, see: Sheldon Goldman, 'Carter's Judicial Appointments: a Lasting Legacy', *Judicature*, Vol. 64, 1981, p. 344.
4. For the text of the message, see *Congressional Quarterly Weekly Report*, 7 April 1979, pp. 656-8.
5. Ibid., p. 656.
6. Ibid., p. 656.
7. Ibid., p. 657.
8. Ibid., p. 657.
9. 'Electronic Surveillance', *Report* of the National Commission for the Review of Federal and State Laws Relating to Wiretapping and Electronic Surveillance, April 1976, p. 26.
10. See *Congressional Quarterly Weekly Report*, 26 January 1980, p. 204.
11. 'You Can't Depend On It', *Civil Liberties Review*, Vol. 4, January/February 1978, p. 10.
12. For the text of the veto message, see *Congressional Quarterly Weekly Report*, 20 December 1980, p. 3633.
13. For the text of the message, see *Congressional Quarterly Weekly Report*, 3 March 1979, pp. 383-4.
14. 'You Can't Depend On It', *Civil Liberties Review*, Vol. 4, January/February 1978, p. 10, p. 23.
15. For the text of the election law proposals, see *Congressional Quarterly Weekly Report*, 26 March 1977, pp. 566-7.

Part II
Constraints and Consequences

7 Jimmy Carter and the Democratic Party

Clifton McCleskey and Pierce McCleskey

One cannot accurately assess the record of Jimmy Carter as President of the United States without taking into account the nature of his relationship with the Democratic Party. That relationship, in turn, cannot be properly appreciated unless one also keeps in mind certain salient characteristics of the American party system. The make-up of a political party in representative democracies always includes three distinct elements: the activists who comprise the party organization; the public officials who identify with the party; and the voters who support it. The linkages between these three sets of partisans have for a long time been weaker in American parties than in most of those in Western Europe, a trend that has accelerated in recent years. Candidates for public office in the United States increasingly gain party nominations with little help from—and sometimes over the opposition of—the party cadres. Those who win public office, and the persons whom they select for appointive positions, often feel little obligation to the party organization, or to other officials elected on the same party ticket.

However, although it is indisputably true that candidates can win election to major public offices, including the presidency, without having to have the assistance of a strong party organization, it remains to be demonstrated that they can successfully govern without such aid. Indeed, the structure and processes of the American political system virtually guarantee failure for those political leaders unable or unwilling to effectively link their party in the government, in the electorate and in the organization. In this context, the relationship of a president to his party's cadres depends heavily on his own perspective and approach. Presidents who are comfortable with party cadres and who wish to maintain close ties can do so, as we know from Lyndon Johnson and Ronald Reagan. Conversely, we know from the Nixon years that a president may be able to exploit the party organization without sacrificing much of his own discretionary power over policy and personnel. The record of the

Carter Administration suggests still another approach, one in which a president neither courts his party's cadres nor yields much to them. Stated in that way, most of the blame for the relationship implicitly falls on Jimmy Carter. As we try to show below, he undoubtedly could have done more to promote a harmonious and fruitful relationship with the Democratic Party. Nevertheless, one must in fairness recognize that the Democratic Party has for a long time been a fractious, quarrelsome lot, characterized by incongruous elements, conflicting goals, and a notable lack of discipline. Thus, in the early 1970s the Democratic Party was confused, divided and disoriented. The excesses and mistakes of the Nixon Administration gave Democrats new electoral opportunities, but they could not heal their self-inflicted wounds.

As Jimmy Carter and his close advisers recognized, this disarray in the Democratic Party created the opportunity for him to win the Democratic nomination. In the campaign for the nomination, and later in the general election, Carter skillfully sidestepped the internal conflicts of the party in a way that the other major contenders for the Democratic nomination could not. But sidestepping problems does not solve them, and the continuing schisms within the Democratic Party all but guaranteed that, once in the presidency, Carter would have difficulty in governing. Thus, what does require explanation is the magnitude of his failure.

The quest for the presidency in 1976

One of the several anomalies in Jimmy Carter's election to the presidency was his origin in a one-party state. At least since the present party system took shape in the latter part of the nineteenth century, every successful candidate initially elected to the presidency (as distinct from those who succeeded to the office from the vice-presidency) has come from a competitive two-party state, as have most of the unsuccessful ones as well. Carter, in contrast, grew up in a political environment in which party politics hardly existed. Carter, like other Democratic governors of Georgia, was the nominal head of his party, but in reality there was little to lead. The Democratic Party in Georgia, as in the rest of the South, was in effect a public utility, forced by law and custom to share its name and miniscule resources with all candidates who sought them. Voter attachment to the party was (and is) real enough, but it had little meaning for elected public officials, and the party organization was largely irrelevant to the governing process.

The first opportunity for Carter to play a leadership role within the Democratic Party came when Democratic National Committee Chairman Robert Strauss visited Georgia in March 1973 and spent an afternoon talking politics with Carter and his political mentor Charles Kirbo. By the end of the meeting Carter was well on his way to serving as Chairman of the DNC's 'Campaigns '74' project, intended to strengthen the party's efforts in the approaching mid-term election.[1] The chairmanship of the 'Campaigns '74' project offered little public visibility and even less power. Carter, however, with no particular constituency to serve when he took the position, was able to throw himself wholeheartedly into the work. Carter's chairmanship of 'Campaigns '74' also gave valuable experience to Hamilton Jordan, who left his post as executive assistant to Governor Carter to become the research director for the mid-term elections project. A Jordan memorandum to Carter dated 4 August 1974 points up the alienation the two felt toward the Democratic Party as it discussed their relationship with Robert Strauss and the Democratic National Committee he chaired.[2] Not much later, the two decided that pursuit of the party regulars was both futile and unnecessary.

By the time Carter formally announced his candidacy on 12 December 1974, three weeks after Ted Kennedy declined to become a candidate and almost two full years before the election, the 'outsider' theme had been firmly settled. Being outside the circle from which presidential candidates are usually drawn (the Senate, the vice-presidency, the governorship of a large, two-party state), Carter was able to mould an image for the electorate that was free of preconceptions. It cannot be too strongly stressed that Carter's 'outsider' approach to the nomination was much more than a campaign ploy or a reflection of his political experience in Georgia.[3] His own personality and political values moved him in the same direction. Carter embodied to an extraordinary extent the old Progressive distaste for 'party politics'. In that tradition, the tendency is to regard parties and political organizations sceptically. Public policy, viewed from a thoroughgoing Progressive standpoint, should reflect not a vector of political forces but careful analysis of substantive problems and thoughtful, public-spirited solutions to them. The task of leaders is thus to devise or adopt such solutions and to educate others on their merits. The Progressive approach to political life is deeply-rooted, well-established, and widely shared.[4]

We stress the importance of Carter's political temperament and background because more than any other single factor they shaped his quest for, and handling of, the presidency. Jimmy Carter could only have won the Democratic Party's nomination and the ensuing general election by pursuing as he did the strategy of an 'outsider'. But others who have won office by that strategy have often found it possible to become an 'insider' after taking office. Carter would not—probably could not— re-orient himself in the same way; his experience and temperament precluded it.

Carter's unorthodox approach to the Democratic nomination struggle is illustrated by the campaign staffing arrangements. He put together a small campaign organization noted for its youth, idealism, commitment to the candidate, and distance from traditional Democratic circles. True to his colours, Carter launched the campaign by disregarding advice from party regulars. He entered the Iowa caucuses as a decided underdog ('In fact, we were told by the state party chairman that we had a nice guy, but that it wasn't his kind of place and he shouldn't go in there', Powell later related) but worked furiously to draw attention and to build support in all quarters. Carter's win in Iowa caught the eye of the media, and suddenly attention began to focus on 'Jimmy Who?'

In the primaries and caucuses that followed Iowa, Carter worked diligently and successfully to distinguish himself from the other Democratic contenders. His moderately liberal stance on issues put him near the Democratic centre in a way that antagonized no major bloc of voters. However, Carter did not emphasize his stand on issues but his personal qualities and his status as an untainted outsider willing to break away from the 'politics as usual' syndrome of the Washington politicians. For the most part, Carter did not bother much with those regarded as the power brokers in the Democratic Party—the interest group and party leaders accustomed to being courted. Instead, he appealed directly to their rank-and-file members and constituents, personally as well as through direct mail and mass media appeals.

That he struck a responsive chord is clear from the record. In the first presidential primary, New Hampshire, he led the field of Democratic hopefuls with 28 per cent of the vote. A poor showing for Carter (fourth place, with 14 per cent of the vote) in Massachusetts a week later was offset the following week by his 34.5 per cent plurality of the vote in Florida. The Florida victory, and that in North Carolina soon after, were particularly helpful, for they effectively eliminated George Wallace from the race. By the time of the Pennsylvania primary in late April, Carter had established himself as the choice of the South and of a plurality of Democratic voters in such diverse states as New Hampshire, Vermont, Illinois and Wisconsin. To that point, his cumulative share of all votes in the primaries was about 38 per cent, and his standing in national cross-sectional surveys of Democratic voters had climbed to about the same level.

For Carter, Pennsylvania was the acid test. As the *New York Times* later observed, it was a state 'where power blocs that like to run Democratic conventions (stood) shoulder to shoulder against Carter'.[5] But, though agreed on the necessity of stopping Carter, they could not unite in support of any one alternative candidate. Carter confounded everyone by winning a 29 per cent plurality, well ahead of both Jackson and the uncommitted slates, each with about 17 per cent of the vote. Part of the reason for Carter's victory, as Carter advance man Tim Kraft later explained, was the work done by 'guerrillas' imported from Wisconsin, Georgia and Florida. Their contribution is exemplified by the estimated 300,000 telephone calls they made: 'something you can't get local county chairmen to do', observed Kraft.[6] A fuller explanation of the Carter victory came from the Philadelphia Democratic Party Chairman, who saw the Carter victory as 'a clear sign that they (the organization leadership) had better start listening to the people'—which was exactly what Carter had been saying all along.[7] A few days after the win in Pennsylvania, Hamilton Jordan held out the olive branch, saying that it was 'time for us to make our peace with all the elements in the Party'.[8] Carter began to devote more time to winning his party's support, and less to primary campaigning, and in turn the Party began to open its arms to him. Hundreds of 'phone calls came from governors, mayors, congressmen, labour leaders and party officials ready to pledge their support now that this most irregular candidate seemed likely to win the nomination. As the pieces began to fall into place, Democratic Chairman Strauss spoke of the most united Democratic front since 1964.

The final month before the convention was not completely smooth sailing for the Carter team, however. Convulsive efforts were being made to 'Stop Carter', led by an assortment of high-level Democrats who had yet to endorse Carter and secretly prayed for a saviour's intervention. With no visible candidate of their own, united only by their dissatisfaction with Carter, the remnants of opposition pursued different strategies in each state. But it was a classic case of too little, too late. The convention itself was anticlimactic. Carter delivered a conciliatory, placatory acceptance speech. There were skirmishes with party liberals over the platform but in the end it emerged much as the candidate desired.

The lack of open intra-party conflict at the Democratic convention añd in the general election campaign led some observers to the conclusion that presidential primaries had at last demonstrated a potential to strengthen rather than weaken the party. But what was as clear then as it is now was that Carter's 1976 Democratic nomination was a triumph over the party regulars. *Congressional Quarterly*'s post-convention report opened by dwelling on that point: 'Jimmy Carter, whose brilliantly executed presidential primary campaign flouted Democratic Party regulars, brought the party's diverse elements together again . . . in a show of unaccustomed unity.'[9] Carter had also triumphed over the reformist and ultra-liberal elements of the party, a victory no doubt facilitated by the crushing defeat of their candidate (McGovern) in 1972. But, though Carter stood between those two wings whose conflicts had so badly damaged the party in 1968 and 1972, he was in no sense their compromise choice; he had beaten both factions, fairly and decisively, but he had not brought them to accept his perspective on the issues.

In accounting for his success, it is not enough to see that he won by pulling together the elements of the forty-year old Democratic coalition: blacks and other minorities, rural residents, the poor and the working class, and the South. Though the electoral components resembled the traditional New Deal coalition, the channels of support were radically different. Carter drew directly upon the victors in each group, rather than depending upon the assistance of labour union officials, urban party leaders, farmers' organizations, or the courthouse politicians of the South. That, too, was obvious at the time.[10] In short, the way Carter won the nomination had important implications for his conduct of the presidency.

Although the general election campaign was launched in Warm Springs in a calculated evocation of the memory of FDR and the coalition he helped to create, it was clear from the beginning that it would be the new politician's race. The national headquarters was established in Atlanta and the general election campaign staff built primarily around the personnel from the nomination phase, with the Democratic National Committee relegated to its (by then customary) secondary role. One of the most significant breaks with political convention was Carter's decision to appoint someone from out of state to head the various state campaign organizations. As with many of his iconoclastic decisions, it sprang from a genuine belief that such an arrangement would improve a system mired in tradition and scarred by countless conflicts. The supposition was that importing neutral outsiders to lead the state campaigns would minimize intra-party feuding. More often than not, however, it deeply antagonized the state party officials, long intimate with the inner workings of their territories and rightly resentful of the intrusion of naïve, if well-meaning, Carter appointees.

In spite of his late-primary and convention statements suggesting the contrary, Carter began the general campaign seeking to distance himself from interest groups and professional politicians, sounding the same note of 'getting back to the people'. He complained about scheduled appearances with California Democratic Senator John Tunney, up for re-election, and in general was loath to make all the fundraising stops he had earlier promised.[11] The point is not that the Carter general election campaign was handled ineptly. In spite of an unorthodox approach and some miscues, the campaign did more things right than wrong, measured by what is ultimately the only valid yardstick—the outcome. Our point, rather, is that the way in which Carter won the election, like the way in which he won the nomination, had important consequences for his handling of the presidency. This was clearly seen by Elizabeth Drew in a startlingly prescient assessment based on firsthand observation of the campaign. As the campaign neared its end, she noted 'a continuing tightness to the Carter circle, based on an understandable feeling that they did it, by God—a sense that they showed 'em in the primaries and they'd show 'em again . . . If these patterns are followed when the Carter group governs, if it does, there could be trouble.'[12]

The task of governing was greatly complicated for Carter by his narrow margin of victory in 1976; he won only 50.1 per cent of the popular vote to Ford's 48.0 per cent. Likewise, the electoral college vote was close, with Carter getting 297 to Ford's 241. Carter carried ten of the eleven states of the Confederacy (Virginia alone went Republican); they provided 40 per cent of his electoral votes. He won also in the border states of Delaware, Maryland, Kentucky and Missouri, and in Mondale's home state of Minnesota and in adjacent Wisconsin. He also carried New York, Massachusetts, Pennsylvania and Ohio, plus Rhode Island and the District of Columbia. But the Democratic ticket carried no state west of the Mississippi other than Missouri, three former Confederate states and Hawaii. The closeness of the vote and its distribution, as well as the terms of the campaign, made it an inconclusive election so far as signalling the nation's preferred direction on a wide range of issues. In short, the Carter nomination and general election victory in 1976 were not based on any substantive consensus within the Democratic Party or the nation's electorate. Rather than heralding the re-establishment of the New Deal Democratic coalition or the onset of a populist renaissance, his victory signalled the further personalization of American elections, and the continuing dissolution of the institutions known as political parties.

The Carter Administration and the Democratic Party

The displacement of political parties is nowhere more apparent than in the staffing of a new administration; a new form of carpetbagging from campaign organizations is replacing the party. The resulting loss of political expertise became painfully apparent during the Carter years.[13] The first year in office in particular was one of recurring conflict with the establishment of which the president was now a part. As Austin Ranney put it, 'the unfortunate reciprocal of the direct relationship with the people which Carter so cherished was poor relationships with Congress and the Washington "insiders" '.[14] Two incidents from the first year illustrate the problem. The first occurred even before the Inauguration, and involved Speaker of the House 'Tip' O'Neill. As O'Neill tells it, he received seats for the inaugural fête in the last two rows of the orchestra section at the Kennedy Center. Somewhat miffed, he reached Hamilton Jordan: 'I said to Jordan, "When a guy is Speaker of the House and gets tickets like this, he figures there's a reason behind it." Jordan replied, "If you don't like it, I'll send back the dollars" '.[15] Jordan firmly disputes this account, but what is important is the widespread acceptance of the O'Neill version, signifying as it does an early willingness even on the part of Democrats to believe in the political ineptitude of the President and his staff. A second example of self-inflicted political damage early in the first year involved Carter's declaration of intent to veto nineteen water projects—traditionally regarded as sacrosanct. The reaction of the Democrats in Congress reflected displeasure not only with Carter's substantive posture but also with the lack of consultation and private notice. The problem, as Powell later admitted, was that the President 'enjoys building a consensus with the public more than with the legislature'.[16]

Carter's approach to politics was especially debilitating to party relations with respect to the issue of patronage. Like pork-barrel public works projects, patronage was anathema to Jimmy Carter, although critics were quick to point to the plethora of Georgians he had brought with him to Washington. 'We won the election, but you'd never know it', O'Neill grumbled at a mid-July 1977 meeting of some fifty House members with Jordan, Frank Moore (another of the Georgian newcomers responsible for liaison with Congress) and Jim King, the titular head of patronage dispensing. Tales were exchanged of telephone calls ignored, of Republican holdovers, and in general of the undermining effect it was all having on Democratic morale and discipline. But the conference brought little change.[17]

At the same time that Carter was antagonizing Democrats in Congress, the Democratic National Committee was suffering from abysmal relations as well. After ten months of strained interaction, Chairman Kenneth Curtis of Maine resigned his post: 'we've been in the peculiar situation of having to (reconcile) what some have identified as two groups of Democrats: Carter Democrats and traditional Democrats'. The central dispute was again patronage. At the time of Curtis' resignation over 11,000 federal jobs were unfilled or still occupied by Ford appointees, and many of these positions are customarily awarded to state chairmen and other party functionaries. 'That's the sort of thing that drives the state chairs crazy', observed Ann Campbell, then head of the Association of Democratic State Chairmen.[18] The difficulties began to appear in the very first months of the Administration, and on 2 April, in a completely unprecedented move, the Democratic National Committee voted 353–0 to rebuke the President for neglecting to consult Democratic state officials on federal appointments, for delaying patronage doles, and for dispatching fundraisers to states without notifying local officials of his actions.[19]

Carter's first year was also marked by an uneasy relationship with interest groups important to the Democratic Party: with civil rights leaders over urban problems and the *Bakke* case; with organized labour grumbling that workers were no better off under Carter than under Ford. Liberals were worried that Carter wanted to slow down social welfare programmes, while feminists complained about 'foot-dragging' on appointments for women, about the insensitive dismissal of Bella Abzug and about the derisory fifteen minutes which had been allocated for the meeting with the Presidential National Advisory Committee for Women. Fortunately, however, the President and his advisers then began to see the need to improve relations with Congress and with groups, and conciliatory gestures began emanating from the White House in January 1978. 'The outsider has finally come home', said one National Committeeman.[20] The new Democratic Party National Chairman, John C. White, announced that Carter would appear at no fewer than five major fundraising dinners in the coming year (in contrast with two the previous year); would campaign on behalf of Democrats seeking to gain or hold office; and would go to the Cook County Democratic dinner in Chicago which he had spurned the year before.

No fundamental transformation took place, however, though a genuine effort was made to improve relations on all fronts. Anne Wexler, a talented veteran of Democratic politics in Connecticut, became a member of the senior White House staff, in charge of building political support with relevant groups for the Administration's policy initiatives. Carter invited the entire Democratic National Committee to the White House on 8 June, the first such gesture since the inauguration eighteen months earlier, and met with the Democratic State Chairmen the following day. He established the office of political co-ordinator, headed by Tim Kraft (who had engineered the victory in Iowa) to handle patronage, among other chores. It all reflected, Jordan understated, 'a recognition that we didn't handle our contacts with the party as well as we should have last year'.[21] By December Carter was well on his way to reversing the first year's political failures and the mid-term convention was clearly in his hands before it even began. He enjoyed relatively trouble-free relations in the months between the mid-term election and the beginning of the 1980 primaries, but continued to find it difficult to re-orient either the Democratic Party or the government he headed.

The quest for re-election

The calm that followed the mid-term convention did not lull the President's advisers into inaction. In an important memorandum of 17 January 1979 Jordan warned the President that fragmentation of the Democratic Party threatened the tradition that an incumbent president can expect re-nomination. Expressing greater fear of losing the nomination than the election, Jordan laid out a plan. Included in his renomination strategy was the pairing of 'troublesome' primaries with 'safe' ones. He also sought to move the selection of delegates from Southern primaries higher up on the timetable before facing primary voters and party caucuses in the heavily-populated, Kennedy-inclined Northern states.[22] Some measure of success was achieved. The biggest problem, however, was not delegate selection schedules but Carter's declining popularity. By October only 30 per cent of the electorate expressed approval of the way Carter was handling the presidency—over the energy crisis, and in face of the widespread criticism not only from Republicans and the 'Washington Observers'—the media, academic and political establishment—but from within his own party and Administration. The critics were joined by those groups traditionally aligned with the Democratic Party such as organized labour, blacks and feminists. In 1979 the name of the game seemed to be 'Dump on Carter', at which some of the players became exceedingly proficient.

Substantive difficulties and disparagement from opinion-leaders kept the Carter Administration on the defensive throughout 1979. This appeared to lessen when, returning from a trip to the Far East, Carter and his staff gathered at Camp David for an extraordinary period of self-examination and wider consultation. The major telecast that followed combined self-criticism with an appeal for more dedication and sacrifice from all. The speech was well-received, but the boost to the Administration was quickly dissipated when the President sacked several members of his Cabinet and shuffled other posts.

Carter's difficulties increased the likelihood that he would be challenged for the Democratic nomination.[23] From February through October 1979 opinion polls consistently showed that Democratic voters would prefer Senator Kennedy over Carter, sometimes by margins of 2-1 or better. Finally, in early November Kennedy announced that he would challenge the incumbent President for his party's nomination. The next day Governor Brown of California announced his own candidacy. Kennedy's presence in the race made it unlikely that the opposition to Carter would combine to back Brown as it had in 1976; the Governor's poor showing in the New Hampshire and Wisconsin primaries led him to an early withdrawal, having won only one delegate to the national convention. Thus the contest for the 1980 nomination effectively involved only two people, each with formidable resources—and liabilities. Kennedy was the recognized leader of the liberal wing of the Democratic Party; his name, wealth, family ties and political creed gave him a tremendous headstart in any campaign. But what had never been satisfactorily tested before was the weight of Kennedy's political liberalism and personal liabilities.

President Carter, too, had liabilities. Though the achievements of his Administration were not insubstantial its general image was nevertheless an unflattering one. Similarly, the positive image of the man had lost some of its lustre. Even so, the President had very substantial assets to draw upon in the nomination contest. His centrist policy objectives were clearly closer to those of rank-and-file Democrats than were Kennedy's. Party cadres now included many Carter supporters, and Carter had appointed Robert Strauss, Chairman of the Democratic National Committee from 1973 to 1977, as head of his campaign.

The tradition that it was improper to challenge one's own party incumbent also worked in his favour.

Three years in office had given Carter visibility and identity which no challenger could hope to match. The use of presidential patronage and preferments to boost re-election prospects is a well-established tradition, and the Carter Administration continued it. The process of balancing out the rival claims of the two candidates was also markedly affected by two international developments—the seizing of the American hostages in Iran, and the Soviet invasion of Afghanistan. As is usual in such cases, the result was a short-term increase in popular support for President Carter (the 'rally round the flag' syndrome). Furthermore, these two developments came at an otherwise inauspicious time for Carter's renomination drive—the hostage seizure just a few days before, and the Soviet invasion just a few weeks after, Kennedy's announcement that he would be a presidential candidate. Kennedy's campaign was also adversely affected by a weak start that reinforced doubts about his personal qualities. A televised interview with CBS correspondent Roger Mudd was particularly devastating. Again, Kennedy's candidacy revived discussion of the tragedy at Chappaquidick. The open discussion of Kennedy's personal qualities was paralleled by broader attention to his liberal stand on many public policy issues. Coupled with the international developments, this focus on the man and his politics brought a most extraordinary shift in support. What had been for Kennedy in October 1979 a 2–1 margin of support among Democrats for the party's nomination was by February 1980 a 2–1 margin of support for Carter![24]

It was to be expected that Carter's strategy for renomination would be built around the fact of his incumbency, in terms not only of the resources marshalled but also of the President's participation in the campaign. Declaring that the hostage crisis demanded his undivided attention and continuous presence in the capital, Carter announced that he would not campaign in person until it was resolved. This 'rose garden strategy' as it came to be called by reporters who remembered Nixon's similar conduct in 1972, probably benefited Carter initially, but as the hostage crisis dragged on, the President's absence from the campaign trail turned into a major handicap. Eventually, after the failure of the effort to free the hostages in a commando-style operation, Carter was forced to announce the abandonment of his self-imposed confinement. The decision not to campaign personally did not preclude the use of the telephone, and a torrent of calls poured from the White House to Iowa and the states that followed it in delegate selection.

The first challenge in a primary came in New Hampshire, and there too Carter led the field with 47 per cent of the vote (Governor Brown was still in the race at that point). Kennedy's handy win in Massachusetts was offset a week later by strong Carter victories in Alabama, Georgia and Florida. By the time of the Illinois primary on 18 March Kennedy had won only one of the eight primaries, and hence Illinois came to be regarded as critical for his candidacy. Carter won a smashing 2-1 majority there in the popular vote, and over 90 per cent of the Illinois delegates.   From that point, the outcome was never really in doubt. Later Kennedy victories in such states as New York, Connecticut and California were offset by Carter's victories in the South and Midwest. Oddly enough, once it was established that Carter would be renominated, Kennedy began to poll more primary votes, in part because of improvements in his campaign, but also because he became a focus for the expression of discontent with the Administration. As a result of Kennedy's stronger showing in the later contests, Carter ended up with only 52.7 per cent of the popular votes cast in all Democratic primaries. His stronger position *vis-à-vis* the Democratic Party organization is reflected in his 2-1 margin of delegates chosen in states using the caucus or convention system of delegate selection.[25] Still, Carter had had to wage a vigorous battle for a nomination that was his by 'right', and even as he was besting Kennedy an uneasiness with Carter spread within the party, fuelled no doubt by polls showing a sizeable Republican lead in the general election.[26] Unfortunately for the opposition, the only alternative to Carter was even less acceptable. A last-minute effort by Kennedy and others to allow delegates to disregard their commitments to candidates made in primaries and conventions failed by a substantial margin, and the renomination of Carter was ensured.

The 1980 Democratic national convention left no doubt that the fragile peace of 1976 had come unstuck. The struggle between Kennedy and Carter involved ideology as well as personality. The triumphant Carter sought to salve the loser's wounds by kind words to Kennedy and by accepting a number of liberal provisions in the party platform. Those efforts met with only limited success. Given the opportunity to address the convention, Kennedy used it not to try to rally his defeated troops behind the party's nominee but in effect to reassert his claim to be the authentic voice of the (liberal) Democratic Party.

Carter's general election strategy was necessarily shaped by geographical arithmetic. He would have to win again in the South and border states; he would have to add to their electoral votes those of enough Northern and Midwestern states of traditional Democratic strength, for the West was mostly a hopeless cause. But Carter's efforts in the South were hampered by Reagan's well-established appeal there to white conservatives. On the other hand, in crucial New York, the Liberal Party nominated John Anderson, the first time in its thirty-six year history that it had not endorsed the Democratic candidate for president. In Illinois the Carter effort was complicated by conflicts within the Democratic organization in Cook County, and by the lingering stiffness between Carter and Chicago Mayor Jane Byrne (a Kennedy supporter). And so it went everywhere, with the Carter campaign forces striving to contain defections, overcome resentment and lethargy, to call in political debts, counter disillusionment and scepticism. Public opinion polls taken at various points during the campaign show unusual volatility in voter preferences, with first Reagan, then Carter, and Reagan again in the lead.[27]

When the ballots were counted on 4 November Carter's scant (50.1 per cent) majority of 1976 had been reduced to a losing 41.7 per cent. The Republican presidential vote had increased only modestly, from 48.0 per cent in 1976 to 51.6 per cent in 1980; most of the remaining vote went to John Anderson (6.6 per cent). The drop of approximately 9 per cent in the Democratic total was relatively evenly distributed across the nation's geographical regions, but was unevenly distributed across important demographical categories.[28] For example, the decline in the Democratic vote was twice as high among liberals (from 70 to 57 per cent) as among conservatives (29 to 23 per cent) and even greater among men as compared to women. Similarly, the Democratic decline was greatest among Jews (from 64 to 23 per cent), and least among Protestants, with

Catholics in between. The percentage of Democratic votes held steady among blacks (82 per cent), but declined sharply among Hispanics (from 75 to 54 per cent). Somewhat surprisingly, the ebb in the Democratic strength was roughly the same across broad categories of income and education.

The geographical distribution of the popular vote transformed Reagan's solid electoral victory into a landslide in the electoral college (489 to 49). In the South, Carter carried only Georgia, though a shift of 2 per cent or less of the vote would also have given him victory in six other Southern states. In addition to Georgia, Carter carried Maryland, Minnesota, West Virginia, Rhode Island, Hawaii and the District of Columbia, and came within a whisker of carrying Massachusetts. The Democratic ticket lost respectably in New York, Maine, Wisconsin and in the border states of Delaware and Kentucky. Elsewhere, Carter's defeats were by margins ranging from substantial to devastating. Thus he received from 30.0 to 39.9 per cent of the total vote in fourteen states, and less than 30.0 per cent in another nine (mostly thinly-populated Western states). Significantly, Carter's best showings came in those states with a history of strongly Democratic voting. In defeat, as in victory, Jimmy Carter's biggest asset was the Democratic Party. And yet, three months after leaving the presidency, Carter told a group of Princeton students that during the re-election period he had come to view the Democratic Party as 'an albatross around my neck'.[29]

Conclusion

From the Civil War to 1980 five incumbent presidents lost their re-election campaigns.[30] Four do not concern us—three were lost by very close margins and the fourth was Herbert Hoover's overwhelming defeat in the depth of the depression in 1932. However, the fifth case is pertinent. In 1912 the incumbent Republican, William Howard Taft, polled only 23.2 per cent of the total vote, a result brought about by the split within his party that led the Progressive faction to break away and form the Bull Moose Party behind the candidacy of Theodore Roosevelt. No such dramatic split occurred in 1980, though John Anderson's candidacy was an invitation to it. Nevertheless, in the case of

Carter as of Taft, the re-election defeat is a sign of great stress in the party and of failure to manage it effectively. As chief executive Jimmy Carter turned in a creditable performance: his legislative record was better than was recognized at the time, and some of his foreign affairs achievements (the Panama Canal Treaties and the Camp David Accords between Egypt and Israel) were substantial.

Where Carter failed signally was in his role as party leader. His personality and style, plus his conception of the political process, made it extremely difficult for him to lead other Democratic public officials and activists. Gifted at substantive problem-solving, Carter found it difficult to engage in 'selling' his solutions to other officials and to the attentive public, at least in the time-honoured ways of politics. Highly effective in small groups and informal settings, and accustomed to taking his case directly to 'the people', he could not see the importance of revitalizing the party organization and otherwise building institutional support. Seeing clearly that the Democratic Party had to be reorientated to more centrist policies, he could not find the means of doing so. The conditions necessitated a different kind of leader.

But, for there to be leaders, there must be followers, and the ideology, structure and processes of the contemporary Democratic Party do not even encourage, much less mandate, followership. While the nation foundered, Democratic Party leaders fought their own schismatic battles. As the Party continued to disintegrate, its constituent groups manœuvred harder for advantage. In the face of the continuing atrophy of local party organizations, activists pressed for reforms in structure and process that could only exacerbate the problem. And when an 'outsider' became their elected leader, some in the upper levels of the Democratic Party sulked, others challenged, but only a few pitched in to help him.

And so we ended up with the classic mismatch: a highly intelligent, hard-working, dedicated President who could not build the necessary political support to achieve his policy goals or to win re-election; a party that had contributed immensely to the improvement and democratization of American life but that had also become confused, divided and increasingly unwilling to be led, especially in directions it needed to take. Each deserved better.

Notes

In addition to the sources cited, we wish to acknowledge our indebtedness to Professor James Sterling Young and to the Miller Center for Public Affairs at the University of Virginia for the opportunity to be involved in, and to utilize the resources of, the Carter Presidency project.

1. Martin Schram, *Running for President, 1976: The Carter Campaign*, New York, Stein & Day, 1977, p. 61.
2. Ibid., p. 378.
3. Carter's antipathy to political organizations may have been reinforced by the circumstances of his first significant election. Carter was able to take office as a Georgia state Senator only by virtue of a judicial order, the culmination of an investigation into charges of electoral fraud against his 'insider' opponent, backed by the courthouse cliques that figured so importantly in the area's politics.
4. The approach to politics attributed here to Carter resembles that said to characterize the 'amateurs' (i.e., the purists), analyzed in James Q. Wilson, *The Amateur Democrat*, Chicago, University of Chicago Press, 1962, pp. 2-12. For a concise statement of the consequences for both parties of the growth of 'purist' thinking, see James L. Sundquist and Richard M. Scammon, 'The 1980 Election: Profile and Historical Perspective', in Ellis Sandoz and Cecil V. Crabb, Jr. (eds), *A Tide of Discontent: The 1980 Elections and Their Meaning*, Washington, Congressional Quarterly Books, 1981, pp. 31-2.
5. *New York Times*, 22 August 1976, p. 1.
6. Kathy Stroud, *How Jimmy Won: The Victory Campaign from Plains to the White House*, New York, William Morrow & Co., 1977, p. 289.
7. *New York Times*, 29 April 1976, p. 27.
8. *New York Times*, 4 May 1976, p. 1.
9. *Congressional Quarterly Weekly Report*, 17 July 1976, p. 1867.
10. Ibid.
11. Elizabeth Drew, *American Journal: The Events of 1976*, New York, Random House, 1977, p. 414.
12. Ibid., p. 490.
13. Gerald Pomper, 'The Decline of the Party in Elections', 92, *Political Science Quarterly*, 21, spring 1977, p. 27.
14. Austin Ranney, 'The Carter Administration', in A. Ranney (ed.), *The American Elections of 1980*, Washington, DC, American Enterprise Institute, 1981, p. 7.
15. Martin Tolchin, 'An Old Pro Takes on the New President', *New York Times Magazine*, 24 July 1977, pp. 6 and 43.
16. Ibid., p. 43.
17. Ibid., p. 9.
18. *New York Times*, 11 December 1977, Section IV, p. 3.
19. Ibid.

20. *New York Times*, 28 January 1978, p. 6.
21. *New York Times*, 7 June 1978, p. 1.
22. Jonathan Moore (ed.), *The Campaign for President*, Cambridge, Ballinger Publishing Co., 1981, p. 47.
23. For a summary of Democratic nominating politics in 1980, Paul R. Abramson, John W. Aldrich and David W. Rohde, *Change and Continuity in the 1980 Elections*, Washington, DC, Congressional Quarterly Press, 1982, pp. 16–25; and Gerald Pomper and colleagues, *The Election of 1980*, Chatham, NJ, Chatham House, 1981, pp. 1–12 and 20–32.
24. This amazing shift is charted in Abramson, op. cit., Figure 1.1, p. 20.
25. Pomper, op. cit., pp. 25–6.
26. The July Gallup Poll (preceding the Democratic National Convention in August) reported that only 21 per cent of the respondents in the national survey approved of Carter's handling of the presidency. It was the lowest approval rating in the forty-year history of the survey. Sundquist and Scammon, loc. cit., p. 21.
27. Abramson, op. cit., pp. 38–40; Pomper *et al.*, *The Election of 1980*, pp. 70–4, especially Table 3.2.
28. The following summary is based on Pomper, op. cit., pp. 70–4, and especially Table 3.2.
29. *New York Times*, 19 March 1981, p. 20.
30. Not included in this set is Chester A. Arthur's failure to win renomination by the Republican Party in 1884, after his accession to the presidency to replace the assassinated Garfield.

8 The Carter White House staff

Q. Whitfield Ayres

A curious contradiction exists in the evaluations of President Carter's White House staff. On the one hand, some individual aides are praised and admired for their intelligence and competence. 'The consensus among most White House reporters', wrote one presidential scholar, 'was that (Jody) Powell was the best press secretary since James Hagerty (during Eisenhower's Administration).'[1] Hamilton Jordan earned widespread admiration as a political strategist: 'It is hard to find anyone who has worked with Jordan—even those who criticize other parts of his performance—who will denigrate his political judgement.'[2] Stuart Eizenstat's broad knowledge and keen intelligence were widely respected, and Jack Watson enjoyed a reputation as a fine administrator and excellent speaker.

On the other hand, evaluations of the White House staff as a whole are overwhelmingly negative, with numerous stinging indictments. From a presidential scholar:

By the end of the President's first year in office . . . it had become clear to everyone that his aides had failed—and failed miserably. Despite more publicity than any other White House staff in memory, despite the hiring of 140 new full time employees to supplement the more than 500 already in place when Ford left office, despite the frequent discussions of the President's unique approach to public administration, chaos reigned at the White House . . . not since the administration of Warren Harding has the fundamental competence of the President's top aides been called so frequently into question.[3]

From journalists:

The Carter Presidency [is] an assemblage of well-intentioned people who have given the White House an aura of one-of-these-days-we've-got-to-get-organized.[4]

Outside the White House looking in, there is a general perception that the Carter operation is in disarray. It is a perception that grows out of a trail of unreturned phone calls and broken appointments, of still unfilled high administration jobs, of the sound of harassed Presidential aides rushing from one meeting to the next.[5]

From 'Tip' O'Neill, Speaker of the House, after reportedly telling Frank Moore, President Carter's Congressional Liaison Assistant, to 'stay the hell out of my office':

I'm not mad at Frank. Out of all that damned crowd down there, he's the only one who's ever been very friendly to me . . . I don't know, maybe they don't understand my style. Maybe they don't want to.[6]

How can we explain this contradiction between the apparent competence of particular individuals and the overwhelmingly negative evaluations of the staff as a whole? Perhaps a poor staff structure buried individual competence in organizational chaos. Possibly a poor fit between individuals and their jobs forced basically competent people to rely more on their weaknesses than their strengths. Conceivably, a cultural clash between the Georgia aides and the Washington establishment doomed the staff to fail, not so much because of their performance as because they were 'different'. Maybe a vindictive press distorted a solid staff performance because of an excessively negative and cynical outlook on public officials. Or perhaps inexperience in the arcane ways of Washington prevented basically competent people from showing their true potential.

To explore these possibilities, this chapter first presents an overview of the White House staff during the years Carter was in office. The discussion then explores each of these factors as a possible explanation for the contradiction between the reputations of individual competence and overall ineptness. While each may contribute to the explanation, some factors will emerge as more helpful in providing an understanding of the contradiction.

Evolution of the Carter White House staff

The 'White House staff' is a loose term, variously used to refer to a number of different entities. The largest is the Executive Office of the President (EOP), created on the 1939 recommendation of a Committee on Administrative Management headed by Louis Brownlow. By the time of Carter's inauguration EOP had grown to nineteen units and over 1,700 employees.[7] The nineteen units included the Office of the Vice-President, the Office of Management and Budget, the National Security Council, the Domestic Council, the Council of Economic Advisors, and fourteen other advisory groups. This discussion will concentrate primarily on one of the nineteen units that was the subject of so much criticism during Carter's presidency—the White House Office—which had 485 employees at the start of Carter's term.[8]

All White House staffs undergo changes in both structure and personnel, and on the surface the Carter White House seemed to be constantly evolving. The four years of Carter's term, for example, saw staff reorganizations in each of the first three years. But there was less to these reorganizations than met the eye. The resulting structural changes were modest in their effect on the White House Office, especially for the first two reorganizations, and personnel changes affected appointments at the deputy level and below far more than the principal aides. As Table 1 demonstrates, six of the eight most important assistants initially appointed by Carter remained throughout the term, and the top personnel changes that occurred more often involved additions than replacements.

The young Georgians who had been associated with Carter during his gubernatorial years dominated the most influential positions in the White House staff. Hamilton Jordan, thirty-two years old at the start of Carter's Presidency, was always 'first among equals' in the Carter White House. He had engineered Carter's remarkable drive for the Democratic nomination and the presidency, and he was initially appointed as an Assistant to the President with wide-ranging and ill-defined responsibilities. Jody Powell, thirty-three, was the new Press Secretary; he had come to know Carter well while driving the candidate around the state during Carter's 1971 gubernatorial campaign. Stuart Eizenstat, thirty-four, became the President's Assistant for Domestic Affairs and Policy, analyzing policies and preparing legislative proposals. Zbigniew Brzezinski, one of two non-Georgians on the top staff, directed the National Security Council and advised the President on National Security Policy. Jack Watson, thirty-eight had directed the President's transition team and became an Assistant for Intergovernmental Relations as well as Secretary to the Cabinet. Frank Moore, forty-one, had worked as legislative liaison with the state legislature when Carter was Governor of Georgia, so he became Assistant for Congressional Liaison. Robert Lipshutz, at fifty-five the oldest of the top staffers, became legal counsel to the President. Margaret (Midge) Costanza, the other non-Georgian, had been

Table 1. President Carter's Senior Staff

Original Positions	1977	Principal Aides	
		After 1978 Reorganization	After 1979 Reorganization
Assistant to the President	Hamilton Jordan		to Chief-of-Staff
Press Secretary	Jody Powell		
Assistant for Domestic Affairs & Policy	Stuart E. Eizenstat		
Assistant for National Security	Zbigniew Brzezinski		
Assistant for Intergovernmental Affairs & Cabinet Secretary	Jack H. Watson, Jr.		
Assistant for Congressional Liaison	Frank G. Moore		
Assistant for Public Liaison	Margaret Costanza	Anne Wexler	
Counsel to the President	Robert Lipshutz		Lloyd Cutler
Additional Positions			
Assistant for Communications		Gerald Rafshoon	
Assistant for Political Affairs and Personnel		Tim Kraft	
Chief-of-Staff			Hamilton Jordan Jack Watson
Staff Director			Alonzo McDonald
Senior Presidential Advisor			Hedley Donovan
Special Assistant For Political Affairs			Sarah Weddington

Vice-Mayor of Rochester, New York; she became Assistant for Public Liaison. Ten other aides formed a second tier assisting Carter on appointments, reorganization, personnel, media, special projects, consumer affairs, health issues, administration, organization and relations with minority groups.

One of the Carter Administration's first actions involved restructuring the Executive Office of the President, an effort designed to cut the number of units from nineteen to twelve, reduce the number of employees from 1,712 to 1,459, establish a more effective policy management system and consolidate administrative functions of the various EOP sections into one Central Administrative Unit.[9] The effect of this 1977 reorganization on the White House Office, however, was negligible. The change technically allowed the President to fulfill his campaign pledge to reduce the White House staff by 30 per cent since it cut the number of employees from 485 to 351. But of the 134 positions eliminated, 70 were simply transferred to the new EOP Central Administrative Unit and, with the exception of Midge Costanza, none of the top presidential aides lost a significant number of staff.

While the 1977 reorganization was directed toward the entire Executive Office of the President, a 1978 reorganization focused on the White House Office. Stung by charges of inefficiency and incompetence among the staff, Carter gathered his top advisers at Camp David in April of 1978 to assess their work. As a result, Carter added several new staff members in June of 1978. Gerald Rafshoon, an Atlanta advertising executive who had handled Carter's media relations during the presidential campaign, became a Presidential Assistant for Communications to spruce up the President's image. Tim Kraft, formerly the President's Appointments Secretary, received a promotion to the senior staff as Assistant for Political Affairs and Personnel. And, presumably in response to criticism that the Administration needed more 'insiders' with political experience, Carter brought in as Assistant to the President, Anne Wexler, who had more than twenty years' experience in Democratic Party politics in Connecticut and Washington.

The overall effect of the 1978 reorganization was modest. While Hamilton Jordan took over chairing staff meetings from Robert Lipshutz, the basic structure remained much the same. Most of the personnel changes involved second-level appointments and the Georgia aides continued to hold the most significant senior positions. The only top staff aide to be demoted was Midge Costanza, the 'loud and abrasive' New Yorker; the reorganization limited her duties to women's affairs, moved her office to the basement and cut her staff from sixteen to two. She resigned two months later and Wexler assumed her title as Assistant for Public Liaison.

Not surprisingly, criticism of the Carter staff continued. So the following spring the President once again retreated to Camp David to reassess his staff and the entire Administration, an exercise which led to a major Cabinet shake-up and his famous 'malaise' speech where Carter argued that America had a crisis of confidence. The 1979 reorganization that followed involved more significant changes than the two earlier shifts.

At least eighty-five staff members changed positions although, as was the case in the 1978 reorganization, most of the changes occurred at the deputy level and below. Carter replaced only one member of his senior staff: Lloyd Cutler, an experienced corporate lawyer and quintessential Washington 'insider', took over as Presidential Counsel from Robert Lipshutz. Carter also brought in Hedley Donovan, former Editor-in-Chief of *Time* Inc., presumably to add a little wisdom to White House deliberations. The President also hired Alonzo McDonald, a management consultant, as Staff Director to bring order to the unco-ordinated activities of the senior staff. Tim Kraft, the Presidential Assistant for political affairs and personnel, moved to Carter's re-election committee, with Sarah Weddington taking over his political duties. And, as he had planned to do all along, Gerald Rafshoon returned to his advertising agency to prepare for the 1980 Carter re-election campaign.

The 1979 reorganization also created a significant structural change. Carter named Hamilton Jordan as Chief-of-Staff, and the President gave up two and a half years of trying to act as his own chief. As Jordan described his new job, he would 'try to mold the senior staff into a cohesive unit and resolve disputes and conflicts here at the White House.'[10] While other senior staff did not have to go through Jordan to see Carter, Jordan did try to shield the President from some of the details that had consumed so much of his time. Jordan served as chief-of-staff for a year, after which he moved to the Carter re-election committee and was replaced by Jack Watson.

The 1979 reorganization created some important changes in the staff structure, especially in establishing a clearer chain of command. It did not, however, substantially alter the influence of the senior Georgia aides who had been so close to Carter. Of the six Georgians on the senior staff, only Lipshutz did not serve throughout the term. The following section explores why these senior aides—who generally appeared competent as individuals—suffered such negative overall evaluations of their performance.

Exploring the contradiction between individual competence and overall ineptitude

(i) *Staff structure*

One possible explanation for the contradiction between individual competence and overall ineptitude involves a staff structure that might have submerged the competence of individuals in organizational disarray. Past presidents have, through exceptions and modifications, created their own unique staff structure. But most are variations of two basic organizational designs.[11]

The first is a decentralized model with a 'circle of generalists'.[12] The President gathers around him bright people of broad knowledge without specific areas of responsibility, and then assigns particular tasks, often assigning the same task to more than one aide. The arrangement encourages competition, ensures multiple points of view, and maintains the President at the heart of the decision-making apparatus. It also requires a President and aides who can work effectively in an atmosphere of ambiguity and disorder. Franklin D. Roosevelt's staff provides the purest example of the circle of generalists. The President reserved the chief-of-staff's job for himself, thus ensuring 'mobile manpower and multiple antennae'.[13] John Kennedy used a variation of this structure,[14] although with more of a collegial than a competitive atmosphere. By most accounts, the circle of generalists worked well for these two presidents.

The second basic structure is a centralized pyramid or hierarchy, with a chief-of-staff in charge, and with specialist aides given well-defined responsibilities. The chief-of-staff co-ordinates staff activities and controls access to the president. This arrangement encourages order, provides timely information, and places a responsibility clearly in the hands of a particular aide. With this structure a president must be wary of being cut off from useful information that did not survive the tortuous organization path to his office. In this structure, responsibilities that do not fall neatly into one of the predefined specialties may be ignored. The purest example of the pyramidal structure occurred during Dwight Eisenhower's Administration, and by most accounts that arrangement worked well for him.

President Carter adopted a variation of Roosevelt's circle of generalists which came to be called 'spokes-of-the-wheel'. Each of the senior aides had direct access to the President and no one at the start was chief-of-staff. These aides had more specialized areas of responsibility than Roosevelt's advisers, however (Eizenstat was 'domestic adviser', Moore was 'Congressional Liaison', etc.), often with hierarchically organized staff members of their own, so that the Carter staff structure looked like a 'circle of pyramids'. Consequently, one critic could charge that Carter's 'spokes-of-the-wheel' was in reality a highly bureaucratic organization where staff members were expected to perform their functions within their organizational box but were unwelcome outside of it.[15] But at least at the highest level, each aide initially had direct access to the President and no chief-of-staff was responsible for overall co-ordination.

The Watergate scandal, with its abuse of power by top Nixon aides, cast a stigma on the pyramidal organization. President Ford as well as Carter shied away from a strict hierarchy at the start, perhaps to avoid association with the excesses of the Nixon staff. Carter, however, insists that he relied on a spokes-of-the-wheel structure mainly because 'that's my way of operating. That's the way I structured my warehouse, that's the way I structured my governor's office, and that's the way I structured the White House . . .'.[16]

That structure appears partially to blame for the contradiction between the individual competence of aides and the poor reputation of the staff as a whole. The experience of the Carter Administration, the advice of top aides from previous administrations, and the analysis of some presidential scholars indicate that a circular structure is inadequate for running the modern presidency. What worked for Franklin Roosevelt and a White House staff of a few dozen aides may be less effective for a White House Office of over 400 employees and an Executive Office of the President with over 1,900 personnel.

Chaos reigned at the White House for the first year of the Carter Presidency, with even Jody Powell conceding in the spring of 1978 that 'we need to get our house in order'.[17] The lack of co-ordination and clear assignments produced one misstep after another. In one notable example, the staff apparently had not done sufficient homework on the accusations of questionable banking practices against Bert Lance, Carter's close friend and his first Director of the Office of Management and Budget. A report from the Comptroller of the Currency did not support charges of criminal conduct but did report questionable use of bank overdrafts by Lance and his family. Carter announced on national television, 'Bert, I'm proud of you', only three weeks before Lance was forced to resign. Presidential scholar Richard Neustadt wrote:

Behind the affectionate comment lay a remarkable failure of staff work. Reportedly neither Carter nor his closest aides had read the Comptroller's text, relying instead on a summary from Lipshutz.[18]

After the 1978 reorganization that was supposed to eliminate the mistakes of the previous year, the press began calling Hamilton Jordan a '*de facto* chief-of-staff', but he did not fulfill the chief's traditional role of controlling access to the Oval Office. After the 1979 reorganization Jordan officially assumed the chief-of-staff's title with the power to hire and fire aides ('somebody is going to be in charge here for a change', groused a senior adviser),[19] and Al McDonald became Staff Director. The senior advisers all reported to Jordan, although they retained direct access to the President's office. The change to a more hierarchical structure was an implicit admission of the failure of the earlier arrangement. As Jody Powell commented, 'We found that we needed a greater degree of centralization than we thought at the outset.'[20]

Richard Cheney, President Ford's Chief-of-Staff from November 1975 to January 1977, argues that a structure with no one in charge except the President is unworkable. The President would have to spend all his time managing the staff, while in fact he has other duties of a higher priority. Cheney argues against the idea that a pyramidal structure is inherently subject to abuse. 'Watergate created the idea that there was some moral value in how you organized the White House. There isn't. Organization is neutral. It's people who set the values.'[21] Cheney's position is echoed by one presidential scholar who argues that the emergence of a central figure is necessary for efficient staff functioning.[22]

Perhaps a president can still maintain a circular structure for access of senior aides to the president. The initial use of a structure lacking a co-ordinator with clear authority over the large staff, however, did not serve the Carter Administration well. The Carter White House staff would probably have enjoyed a better reputation had the initial structure included the position of chief-of-staff, filled by someone with substantial managerial experience.

(ii) *Poor fit of individuals*

Another possible explanation for the contradiction between individual competence and overall ineptitude is a poor fit between particular staff members and their jobs. Individuals may have been capable of handling some staff jobs, but not the ones to which they were assigned.

President Carter flatly rejects this factor as an explanation for the negative reputation of his staff. 'The ones that I thought were a poor fit at any time I got rid of. I don't have any particular reticence about replacing someone or changing someone when I don't think they're doing a good job.'[23] Indeed, some of his appointments seem to be excellent fits for particular positions. Press Secretary Jody Powell is quick, witty and willing to stay up half the night drinking with reporters—none of which hurt his relations with the press. Stuart Eizenstat is scholarly, reflective and experienced in issue-analysis—an ideal fit for his position as domestic adviser.

Two staff members, however, seem to have been particularly ill-suited to their positions, and the reputation of the Carter staff suffered as a result. Hamilton Jordan is, by all accounts, an outstanding political tactician, who directed one of the most remarkable victories in American presidential politics. He is also, by his own admission, poorly suited to be chief-of-staff: 'I don't have the range of ability to do it [the chief-of-staff's job]. I'm not an administrator. I understand politics, but I'm weak on the issues . . .'[24] Yet after the 1978 reorganization he ended up chairing staff meetings and was presumably expected to co-ordinate staff efforts; after the 1979 reorganization he was given the title of chief-of-staff.

The result was predictable: poor staff co-ordination, communication breakdowns, and a general appearance of disarray. Even his friend Jody Powell would say of Jordan: 'The fact that the White House as an operation was not as well-run as it should have been was partly his fault.'[25] Jordan was not blind to his weaknesses and Al McDonald was brought in as an administrator under Jordan after the 1979 reorganization, two and a half years after someone of his skills should have been employed. To place a political thinker in a position requiring an administrator is a clear case of poor fit between individual and position. As Richard Cheney said of his former job: 'A lot of it is quite pedestrian and not very creative. It's the wrong place for an artist who wants to go off by himself and think deep thoughts or write great memos.'[26]

Another case of questionable fit between individual and job involved Frank Moore, Carter's Congressional Liaison. A genial fellow, Moore had no particular difficulty dealing with members of the Georgia state legislature when he served in a similar position on Carter's gubernatorial staff. But he had virtually no experience with Congress and he gave the impression of a man out of his league. Only five days after Carter's inauguration, the *Washington Post* reported that 'Frank Moore . . . has already made a bad impression on many of the most important Democratic legislators in both the House and Senate.'[27]

Once again the result was predictable for the Carter White House: relations with a Congress controlled by the President's own party started off poorly and then declined. Complaints about lack of consultation with key congressmen abounded. Carter appointed two Republicans from Massachusetts to high office without first touching base with the Massachusetts Speaker of the House, 'Tip' O'Neill, thereby thoroughly antagonizing a key politician.[28] In another instance, the Administration announced a joint United States–Soviet communiqué on the Middle East without first informing key Jewish congressmen, consequently misreading the reaction of the Jewish community.[29] Inconsistency also damaged the Administration's relations with Congress. As one aide related: 'We'd ask the members to walk the plank on a bill and then change signals on them; we did it on the (proposed) $50 (tax) rebate, the water projects, and the farm bill. They'd tell us, "If you are going to cut us off at the limb, let us know, don't let us commit ourselves and then make us look foolish." '30

One congressman levelled a particularly stinging indictment that summarizes many of the complaints about the Administration's congressional relations:

They haven't got their act together on lobbying the important issues. The vote counts have not been reliable. There's been inadequate use of carrot-stick tradeoffs. And with almost no exceptions every issue that has come down from the White House or agency has been viewed as THE big issue. There is no sense of priorities. Also, they haven't developed an early warning system. They don't know when a problem exists or develops until it's already out of control. That can be potentially fatal. And they're not using their sources of information. There are congressmen—natural allies—they ought to be tapping constantly. They could have saved themselves so much aggravation that way—it's sad.[31]

It is unfair to place all of the blame for Carter's sour congressional relations on Frank Moore's shoulders. Some long-term forces exacerbated presidential difficulties in dealing with Congress. First, a more independent and resurgent Congress appeared, after Vietnam and Watergate, to be less willing to defer to Presidential desires. Second, the erosion of party discipline creates additional difficulties for the President's programme, even when his party controlled both houses of Congress. President Reagan's congressional successes during the first year of his term indicate that these difficulties are not insurmountable, especially when, unlike Carter, the President has won a substantial electoral victory that allows him to claim a mandate for his policies. But these long-term changes do create additional difficulties.

Moreover, Frank Moore served as a convenient lightening rod for criticism of an Administration that repeatedly demonstrated its lack of understanding of Congress. Many of the moves that so antagonized congressmen, such as the effort to cancel pet federal water projects that congressmen view as so important to enhancing their standing with their constituents, should be traced to Carter rather than Moore. In addition, Carter's unwillingness to play coalition politics and trade federal project grants for votes hurt Moore's leverage and influence.[32]

But Moore must bear at least a portion of the blame for poor congressional relations. The widespread complaints about inept lobbying and poor communications are largely the liaison office's responsibility. And the apparent lack of understanding of the Congressional process by Moore plagued the Administration. In the words of Bryce Harlow, Congressional Liaison for Presidents Eisenhower and Nixon,

[Frank Moore is] a likeable, intelligent, and competent fellow. But what I don't know is whether he is tuned into the decision-making process. That is terribly critical to the job. Access alone should not be equated with influence. He has to be in a position to influence the content and timing of programs.[33]

Carter defends Moore in his memoirs as overworked and unfairly criticized because of congressional frustrations at contacting Carter himself. 'He put together an outstanding staff and worked hard to overcome this original stigma of ineptitude.'[34] He never succeeded, and consequently made his own contribution to Carter's poor congressional relations. Frank Moore was not a good fit for the job of Congressional Liaison.

Poor fit between particular individuals and their jobs helps to explain the contradiction between individual competence and general ineptitude. As is so often the case, attention focused on the problem appointments, colouring the reputation of the entire staff. Despite remarkably good fits among some of the top Carter staff such as Powell and Eizenstat, poor fits in the crucial positions of Chief-of-Staff and Congressional Liaison cost the White House dearly.

(iii) *Cultural clash*

Another possible explanation for the contradiction between individual competence and general ineptness is a cultural clash between the 'Georgia Mafia' and the Washington establishment. Perhaps the reputation of Carter's staff suffered simply because some of its members were 'different' and insufficiently deferential to Washington mores.

Key members of Carter's staff, and particularly Hamilton Jordan, did not initially make an effort to conform. In a town where a brown rather than blue or grey suit can start tongues wagging, Jordan showed up in the lobby of the elegant L'Enfant Plaza Hotel wearing boots, corduroy trousers, a plaid flannel shirt, and navy windbreaker.[35] Similar attire worn in the White House shocked Washington society.

Moreover, two widely-reported incidents, whose facts remain

in dispute, added to Jordan's image as impolitic and uncouth. In December of 1977 at a party thrown by Barbara Walters, Jordan reportedly pulled at the bodice of the Egyptian ambassador's curvaceous wife and made a crack about always wanting to see the pyramids of the Nile. The following month a woman accused Jordan of spitting his Amaretto and cream drink down her dress at Sarsfield's bar, leading House Minority Whip Robert Michel to quip that '. . . in one year the Carter Administration has gone from "Great Expectations" to "Great Expectorations".'[36] Jordan denied spitting his drink and claimed that he was harassed by an inebriated woman, but the damage had been done. When Jordan granted an interview to *Playgirl* magazine, and posed with Jody Powell as Butch Cassidy and the Sundance Kid for the cover of *Rolling Stone* magazine, his reputation as a mature and distinguished presidential adviser was not enhanced.

There was a cultural clash with the Washington establishment, but it was more of a generational than a regional clash. As Meg Greenfield pointed out, many prior Georgians in Washington such as Senator Richard Russell and Secretary of State Dean Rusk reflected refinement and gentility, just the opposite of the hooliganism of which Jordan stood accused.[37] Moreover, Jimmy Carter's rectitude stood in sharp contrast to the reputations of some of his aides. The clash was more between the values of some members of a younger generation (both Powell and Jordan were in their early thirties) and those of older-established Washington figures.

Some of Jordan's and Powell's actions indicate an aversion to taking anything too seriously. Many Washingtonians appear to take almost everything, especially themselves, very seriously, and the Powell/Jordan duo would not play along. The reputation of the Carter staff suffered in part because those two aides demonstrated insufficient sensitivity to established mores. Both aides admitted as much during the last year of Carter's Administration. 'I didn't come here with a proper appreciation of the public responsibility of a person who serves in the White House', Jordan said. 'We came up here kind of cocky.'[38] Jody Powell commented about the *Rolling Stone* cover:

It wasn't intended that way, but I think a lot of people saw it as a great big front page thumbing your nose. I think it sort of confirmed everybody's worst suspicions. It probably angered people a little bit, maybe without their even knowing it. To a lot of people, it symbolized a lack of proper respect for the White House, our jobs, the institutions of this city.[39]

The cultural clash contributed to the poor reputation of the staff, but it is probably less important than other factors already discussed. Had the Carter operation been functioning smoothly and effectively in Washington, the powers that be would probably have been less critical of these antics. But, as Powell suggests, the actions reinforced fears that key members of the Carter team were unwilling to defer to the mores of the capital, and therefore less likely to be effective participants in the play of power.

(iv) *A vindictive press*

Another possible explanation for the conflict between individual competence and general ineptitude might be a vindictive press that views public officials as guilty of some wrongdoing until proved innocent. Perhaps the overall reputation of the staff was damaged by a press corps obsessed with unfounded allegations and trivial incidents. President Carter singles out this factor as the main explanation for his staff's poor reputation:

I think [the poor reputation is] primarily an image that you get within the Washington press. There's an inbreeding among the press . . . I think it is primarily the effort among the press to follow one another and I don't have much respect for many elements of the press.[40]

Without exception, every president becomes exasperated with the press, in some cases blaming the messengers for the message. The White House staff under Carter *was* unorganized in its initial years and the congressional relations *were* disastrous; the press reported these problems and obviously upset those involved. The issue here is whether the reporting was basically fair and balanced or vindictive and irresponsible.

Some Carter White House staff members fared very well in the press. Despite the constant sparring that has come to characterize White House press briefings, Jody Powell received very favourable press reviews. A problem did arise, however, once Jordan and Moore developed negative images, because then the press sometimes emphasized incidents, no matter how trivial or poorly-documented, that reinforced those images.

When the owners of Studio 54, a New York City discotheque,

accused Hamilton Jordan of using cocaine, the action seemed to be consistent with his fast-living image. The accusers, Steve Rubell and Ian Schrager, had been indicted on charges of tax evasion, obstruction of justice and conspiracy. Despite a clear motive for these accusers in enhancing their leverage in plea bargaining, despite the lack of any evidence to support the charges except statements from questionable witnesses, and despite Jordan's flat denials, some elements of the press apparently assumed he must be guilty. *Newsweek* magazine printed a picture of Jordan holding a bottle of Coca Cola with a caption 'Jordan at the White House with a legal Coke'.[41] While the accompanying story does not support the caption's insinuation of guilt, the picture and caption itself are at best questionable journalism.

Jordan incurred over $150,000 in legal debts before he was cleared of the Studio 54 charges. The treatment of Jordan even bothered some members of the press: 'When all of it—the press, the new laws, and an atmosphere of unrelenting cynicism —are taken together, it can amount to the equivalent of what in football is called piling on . . . We can maul our public servants, sometimes on the most trivial of all grounds.'[42] President Carter becomes quite heated when discussing the case:

Absolute lies . . . were told about Hamilton Jordan on the cocaine issue. There was never an investigative reporter who tried to find out who lied or who told this tale . . . Nobody ever tried to find out. The presumption was that Hamilton was a cocaine sniffer.[43]

A vindictive or unbalanced press contributed to the poor reputation of Carter's White House staff, but it is less important than the staff structure or personnel fit. To assume that the press was primarily responsible for the poor reputation is simplistic and inaccurate, for the image of staff ineptitude was well established long before the reporting excesses. The gossip-laden columns about Jordan's behaviour occurred after the start of 1978; the poor reputation of the staff was well-developed by the end of 1977.

(v) *Inexperience in Washington*

The underlying problem for so many of Carter's White House staff members—reflected in structural difficulties, poor fits between individuals and positions, and cultural clashes—appears to be a lack of sound judgement. As Richard Neustadt has been quoted as saying, 'Procedure is no substitute for judgement.'[44] Repeatedly the President and his staff exhibited poor judgement about what structure would effectively organize the White House Office, what approach would effectively persuade congressmen, and what attitude would avoid antagonizing key politicians in Washington. Certainly no one would suggest that the staff could have solved all the problems that beset them, for many factors were beyond their control. But all too often the Carter White House made poor use of those factors under its control, thereby creating additional problems.

Since sound judgement is such an elusive quality and so difficult to detect until after the fact, it is not much help to suggest that presidents need advisers with good judgement. But a more objective characteristic that is related to—though not synonymous with—good judgement, is experience in Washington. The lack of experience in Washington that was such an asset for an 'outsider' on the campaign trail became a debilitating impediment to governing effectively.

One presidential scholar wrote in a book that reportedly influenced Carter: 'Those who have excelled at the White House, even the young ones, almost always have had some previous experience and a feel for Washington and the power equations of government.'[45] Yet, except for Stuart Eizenstat, none of Carter's original senior advisers had any Washington experience. As a top aide to President Ford said of Carter's team: 'They're very smart, but very naive'.[46] Powell survived without Washington experience; the rest suffered.

Carter could easily have brought in more experienced hands, but decided against it:

I know that my predecessors had been criticized for installing their 'cronies' in the White House . . . But when I considered the alternatives, I decided without any doubt that my predecessors had chosen wisely. The selection of loyal and well-known associates is the result of a need for maximum mutual confidence and a minimum of jealousy and backbiting within a President's inner circle.

During the campaign we had been embarrassed by a few bad personnel selections. Though never fatal, the consequences were serious enough to arouse caution about bringing new people into our most intimate circle . . . My White House team had been tested in the political crucible and found not wanting in experience, competence, and compatibility with me and with one another.[47]

Carter hoped that reliance on Vice-President Mondale's staff and a diverse Cabinet would overcome the Washington in-experience of his aides.[48] The record indicates that he was wrong. Inexperience in Washington appears to be a significant part of the explanation for the contradiction between the basic competence of individual aides and the overall reputation of ineptitude.

Conclusion

The Carter White House staff included competent individuals who collectively produced an appearance of incompetence. A major part of the explanation lies in lack of Washington experi-ence among the top aides; it is difficult to imagine individuals as bright as Powell and Jordan, for example, so thoroughly antagonizing the capital's powers-that-be after the benefit of four years in Washington. Another major portion of the explana-tion involves an inadequate staff structure and a poor fit of certain individuals for their jobs. The improvement in White House operations toward the end of Carter's term provides evidence for this proposition. In July of 1980 Hamilton Jordan moved to Carter's re-election committee[49] and Jack Watson became Chief-of-Staff with Al McDonald as Staff Director. At long last the Carter operation had developed a more hierarchical structure, run by two individuals with strong administrative skills. A cultural clash between Georgia aides and the Washington establishment, and a vindictive press, also contributed to the negative reputation of the staff, but these two factors appear secondary to those already discussed.

The White House staff's successes and failures can ultimately be traced to Carter himself. It was he who saw the promise in a Powell or an Eizenstat, and placed those people in positions that relied on their strengths. It was also he who, through an aversion to 'outsiders', refused until it was too late to provide proven managers for the White House staff or to bring experi-enced Washington hands into his inner circle of advisers. The result was a collection of capable people who never did com-pletely overcome a reputation for ineptitude.

Notes

1. Robert Locander, 'Carter and the Press: The First Two Years', *Presidential Studies Quarterly*, 10, winter 1980, pp. 107-8.
2. Garrett Epps, 'The Myth of Hamilton Jordan', *Washington Post*, 17 December 1978, p. WPM 3.
3. Michael Medved, *The Shadow Presidents*, New York, Times Books, 1979, pp. 351-2.
4. Martin Schram, 'As Plaster Falls, A Staff is Remodeled', *Washington Post*, 3 September 1979, p. A1.
5. Edward Walsh, 'Central Role for Jordan', *Washington Post*, 22 February 1977, p. A1-6.
6. Mary Russell, 'O'Neill: Simmering but Conciliatory', *Washington Post*, 11 August 1978, p. A1.
7. Dom Bonafede, 'White House Reorganization—Separating Smoke from Substance', *National Journal*, 20 August 1977, p. 1307.
8. This distinction will occasionally appear confusing since top staff members of some EOP units such as the National Security Council are on the White House staff payroll, while the top staff members of other units such as the Office of Management and Budget are not. This chapter excludes any staff members listed under an EOP unit other than the White House Office as indicated by the White House Telephone Directory published by *National Journal*, 30 September 1978.
9. Bonafede, 'White House Reorganization', p. 1307.
10. Dom Bonafede, 'Jordan's New Role Signals an End to "Cabinet Government" ', *National Journal*, 18 August 1979, p. 1358.
11. Stephen Hess, *Organizing the Presidency*, Washington, Brookings, 1976; William D. Pederson and Stephen N. Williams, 'The President and the White House Staff', in Edward N. Kearny (ed.), *Dimensions of the Modern Presidency*, St. Louis: Forum Press, 1981. For a conceptualization of staff structures as formalistic, competitive, and collegial, see Richard Tanner Johnson, *Managing the White House: An Intimate Study of the Presidency*, New York, Harper and Row, 1974.
12. Hess, p. 174.
13. Richard Neustadt, 'Approaches to Staffing the Presidency', in Thomas E. Cronin and Sanford D. Greenberg, *The Presidential Advisory System*, NY, Harper & Row, 1969, p. 15.
14. Steven J. Wayne, *The Legislative Presidency*, New York, Harper & Row, 1978, Chapter 2.
15. James Fallows, 'The Passionless Presidency', Part II, *Atlantic Monthly*, 243, June 1979, pp. 78-9.
16. Jimmy Carter, Interview held in Plains, Georgia, 25 April 1983.
17. Medved, p. 352.
18. Richard E. Neustadt, *Presidential Power: The Politics of Leadership From FDR to Carter*, New York, John Wiley & Sons, 1980,

p. 227. Neustadt includes an insightful summary of the affair on pages 225-8.

19. Martin Schram, 'The Day that Hamilton Jordan Took Charge', *Washington Post*, 18 July 1979, pp. A1-16.
20. Quoted in John H. Kessel, 'The Structures of the Carter White House', Ohio State University, unpublished paper.
21. David Broder, 'Beware the Spokes of the Wheel', *Washington Post*, 25 July 1979, p. A21.
22. Medved, p. 352.
23. Carter interview, 25 April 1983.
24. David Broder, 'A Man Who Declines Power Is Not Just Rare', *Washington Post*, 17 July 1977, p. B7.
25. Epps, 17 December 1978, p. WPM 4.
26. Broder, 25 July 1979, p. A21.
27. Joseph Kraft, 'A Shakedown Cruise for Carter's Staff', *Washington Post*, 25 January 1977, p. A15.
28. R. Gordon Hoxie, 'Staffing the Ford and Carter Presidencies', in Bradley D. Nash (ed.), *Organizing and Staffing the Presidency*, Washington, DC, Center for the Study of the Presidency, 1980, p. 68.
29. Dom Bonafede, 'Carter and Congress—It Seems that "If Something Can Go Wrong, It Will" ', *National Journal*, 12 November 1977, p. 1760.
30. Ibid.
31. Judy Bachrach, 'I Love Those People on the Hill', *Washington Post*, 3 November 1977, p. B12.
32. Eric L. Davis, 'Legislative Liaison in the Carter Administration', *Political Science Quarterly*, 94, summer 1979, pp. 287-301.
33. Bonafede, 'Carter and Congress', pp. 1760-1.
34. Jimmy Carter, *Keeping Faith: Memoirs of a President*, NY, Bantam Books, 1982, p. 45.
35. Sally Quinn, 'Hamilton Jordan and the Washington Power Rush', *Washington Post*, 16 January 1977, p. H1-6.
36. Epps, 17 December 1978, p. WPM 4.
37. Meg Greenfield, 'Georgians On My Mind', *Newsweek*, 91, 16 January 1978, p. 88.
38. Meg Greenfield, 'Hamilton Jordan: Looking Back', *Washington Post*, 2 December 1980, p. A19.
39. Dick Kirschten, 'A Little Humor, a Little Humility Help Powell Weather Stormy Seas', *National Journal*, 26 July 1980, pp. 1229-30.
40. Carter interview, 25 April 1983.
41. 'Now, Ham and Coke?', *Newsweek*, 94, 10 September 1979, pp. 20-1.
42. Richard Cohen, 'Unfair Battering Taken By Hamilton Jordan', *Washington Post*, 7 December 1980, p. 67.
43. Carter interview, 25 April 1983.

44. Dom Bonafede, 'Reorganization Perspective', *National Journal*, September 10 1977, p. 1418.
45. Hess, p. 165.
46. David Broder, 'New Process for Domestic Issues', *Washington Post*, 12 February 1978, p. A14.
47. Carter, *Keeping Faith*, p. 41.
48. Carter, *Keeping Faith*, p. 47.
49. For the story of Jordan's last year in the Carter Administration, see Hamilton Jordan, *Crisis: The Last Year of the Carter Presidency*, New York, G. P. Putnam's Sons, 1982.

9 Carter and the Congress

Tinsley E. Yarbrough

Most students of his presidency have given Jimmy Carter failing marks as a legislative leader. In an evaluation of Carter's legislative prowess with the 95th Congress, for example, Charles Jones concluded that Carter repeatedly demonstrated limited knowledge of the legislative branch; found the coalition-building, compromise-oriented politics necessary for congressional success 'neither natural nor right'; and failed to surround himself with experts in legislative liaison.[1] Others have echoed Jones' impressions.[2]

Of course, a president's legislative skills may be of limited significance in explaining his record of success or failure with the Congress. While generally concurring with pessimistic assessments of President Carter's legislative prowess, George C. Edwards III has observed that Carter's legislative success rate compares favourably with that of Lyndon Johnson, 'the master legislative technician'. In the House of Representatives, Edwards notes, Carter's support rate was only slightly less than Johnson's among Republicans and southern Democrats, though somewhat lower among northern Democrats. In the Senate, Carter did better than Johnson among all Democrats and equalled his Democratic predecessor's support rate among Republicans. In the first year of the 89th Congress, when Johnson's legislative influence was greatest, he received a higher support rate than Carter only among Northern House Democrats.[3]

When Carter's aggregate support rate is compared with that of his Democratic predecessors, the difference appears more substantial. In 1977 Congress voted for 75.4 per cent of his proposed legislation, compared with first-year support rates of 88.0 per cent for Johnson, 81.0 per cent for Kennedy, 58.2 per cent for Ford, 74.0 per cent for Nixon, and 89.0 per cent for Eisenhower. Subsequently, however, Carter's support rate did improve somewhat, reaching 78.3 per cent in 1978, 76.8 per cent in 1979, and 75.1 per cent in 1980.[4] Especially when one considers the highly controversial issues Carter's legislative

programme confronted, moreover, these are respectable support rates.

Furthermore, Carter did develop a modestly successful
legislative record. He obviously failed to realize many of his
legislative goals, and those programmes which Congress enacted
often bore little semblance to Carter's original proposals. His
veto record, moreover, reflected continuing congressional
difficulties. Carter vetoed twenty-nine bills, compared with
thirteen for President Johnson and nine for John Kennedy.
He also became the first president since Truman to have a veto
overridden by a Congress controlled by his own political party.
In his first year, however, he gained authority to create, termin-
ate, or merge executive agencies—authority enjoyed by most
modern presidents but especially important to Carter given his
campaign promise to reorganize the federal bureaucracy. During
his term he also prodded Congress into creating a Department
of Energy and enacting a variety of proposals designed to limit
oil and natural gas consumption, reduce United States dependence on foreign oil, and encourage development of alternative
energy sources. Other legislative successes and partial successes
of the Carter Administration included reform of the civil service
system, elimination of federal regulations stifling competition
in the airlines industry, Senate ratification of the Panama Canal
treaties, creation of federal authority to clear up toxic chemical
dumps and spills, and a 'windfall' profits tax on oil company
revenue increases stemming from de-regulation of fuel prices.[5]

This chapter focuses on those factors which may have worked
to inhibit President Carter's success as a legislative leader.
Arguably, Carter had some degree of control over certain of
these factors, including the structure of legislative liaison
operations in the Carter White House, the consequences of his
status as a Washington 'outsider', and his legislative style. An
underlying theme of the chapter, however, is that many of the
obstacles to Carter's legislative success were beyond his or his
Administration's control.

Legislative liaison under Carter

Every president since Eisenhower has maintained a congressional
liaison office. Given Lyndon Johnson's reputation for skillful
manipulation of Congress, his liaison organization seemed a

likely model for the Carter White House. Under Johnson, the liaison staff had been divided into House and Senate specialists and then further divided to allow specialization corresponding to regional and partisan blocs in the Congress. Different liaison officers, for example, were given responsibility for each of three House groups: the traditional southern Democrats, northern Democrats elected with the strong support of party organizations, and those northern democrats primarily dependent on personal political organizations for electoral support. Under the Johnson arrangement, in fact, each congressional Democrat could feel that he had a specific contact person in the White House. Each executive department also maintained a liaison staff; but the White House team, and frequently the President personally, directed all congressional activities. The White House staff met every Monday morning for specific instructions, and these directives generally included assignments for department liaison staffs as well as White House personnel. The department staffers, moreover, were often obliged to work outside their department spheres of issue concern, attempting to influence congressmen with whom they were closely associated.[6]

The Carter Administration decided, however, not to adopt the Johnson arrangement. President Carter and his aides apparently believed that the congressional blocs underlying the distribution of liaison duties in the Johnson White House were no longer powerful sources of voting cues and that the 1974 and 1976 elections had brought more issue-oriented congressmen to Washington. Consequently, the Carter staff initially attempted to structure the White House liaison office along issue lines, with specialists for energy, foreign policy, tax reform, and other significant issue areas. This arrangement lasted only until the late spring of 1977, however; as one Carter liaison officer later explained:

I don't think that the issue-based organization of the liaison office was a very good idea. Too many members simply fall through the cracks. You might be assigned an issue, and that issue might never come up during the entire two years of a congressional session. Also, with the issue-based system, you don't get around to talking to many members until it's too late. You won't talk to the lowest ranking member of the Energy Subcommittee until you need his vote, and that's not when we should be talking with him. Our job is to serve the members' needs, to hold their hands, to stroke their egos. We have to do all kinds of little things with them that have nothing to do with issues. It's sort of like we're in the Green Stamps business. But we have to give out a lot of stamps before the members will trade them in.[7]

Motivated by such concerns and by general complaints from congressional leaders and in the press of ineptness in its liaison operations, the Administration replaced the issue-oriented approach with an arrangement in which each liaison officer simply worked closely with those congressmen he knew best and thus had the greatest potential to influence. There was Senate and House specialization among White House liaison staffers; beyond that, however, there was no specialization at all.

As his assistant for congressional relations, President Carter selected Frank Moore, a Georgian who had served as Carter's chief legislative lobbyist during the President's term as Georgia's Governor and had been Carter's emissary to Capitol Hill during the 1976 campaign.[8] Typically, White House liaison staffs are small; Kennedy's and Johnson's rarely numbered more than six, Nixon's and Ford's no more than ten. The Carter staff was no exception. Initially, Moore had five professional assistants; in the summer of 1977 two others were added to his staff. Although Moore lacked extensive Washington experience, three of the five assistants originally hired had served as congressional staffers, lobbyists, or in both capacities. With a supporting staff of six or seven, the White House liaison organization handled congressional correspondence and constituency problems as well as lobbying in behalf of administrative proposals. Augmenting the White House staffs were liaison organizations within every cabinet department and most non-cabinet agencies as well. At least 675 agency staffers were directly involved in congressional liaison work.[9]

The liaison staffers were not the only figures who attempted to build congressional support for the President's programmes. As presiding officer of the Senate, Vice-President Walter Mondale maintained an office in the Capitol. A Senate veteran with closer congressional ties than other members of the administration, if not a reputation as a Senate power, Mondale was often assigned liaison duties. Early in Carter's tenure, for example, Mondale played a significant role in securing Senate confirmation of Paul C. Warnke as the President's chief arms negotiator. Mondale's chief liaison assistant—the Vice-President's Senate administrative assistant and a Senate aide since 1965—maintained an office off the Senate lobby.[10] Though with limited success, Hamilton Jordan and other top members of the Carter White House also saw liaison service as did, eventually, a number of prominent Washington Democrats holding no formal position in the Administration. Finally, of course, the President himself played a major liaison role throughout his tenure.

As noted earlier, congressional leaders frequently complained about the quality of the liaison operation during the first six months of 1977. By the end of Carter's first year, however, the liaison system seemed to be functioning more smoothly. By mid-1977, moreover, the White House liaison staff had developed computerized files on every member of Congress, itemizing party affiliation, committee assignments, seniority, election margins, interest group ratings, and voting patterns. The staff had also begun using computer facilities to track the progress of pending legislation and process congressional mail.[11]

On certain issues, in fact, Carter White House lobbying efforts had a masterful quality. Most notable were those directed toward Senate ratification of the two controversial Panama Canal treaties.[12] In an effort to generate popular support for the treaties, the President invited hundreds of opinion-leaders to the White House; answered questions regarding the treaties at various town meetings; and dispatched Secretary of State Cyrus Vance, Defense Secretary Harold Brown, and other top officials around the country for lectures and other forums defending the treaties. Interested senators were flown to Panama for conferences with General Omar Torrijos; influential constituents of undecided senators were invited to the White House for conferences; the Administration contacted each senator; President Carter personally made eighty-seven phone calls to senators in the two weeks before the vote on the first treaty; and influential outsiders such as Washington lawyer and Johnson administration cabinet officer Clark Clifford also lobbied on behalf of the measures. According to Carter's memoirs, the President even read every page of former university professor-administrator S. I. Hayakawa's semantics text in an effort to win the California Republican's vote.[13]

Ultimately, each treaty was ratified by one more Senator than the two-thirds vote mandated by the Constitution. In 1978 aggressive lobbying also helped to account for a turnabout of thirty-one House votes needed to halt development of the B–1 bomber.[14] And there were other successes as well.

In the main, however, the congressional lobbying system in the Carter White House seemed only marginally effective. For one thing, Frank Moore never fully overcame the initial impression of many congressmen that he was a poor choice for the job of chief liaison officer. After eight years of Republican famine, Democratic congressmen bombarded the White House liaison staff with patronage and related requests. On the day following Carter's inauguration alone the White House received 1,100 letters from Congress.[15] Executive agencies were equally innundated. In 1977, for example, the State Department received more than 1,600 letters each month, Defense 112,136 written inquiries and 229,089 telephone requests for the year, and Agriculture an average of 325 inquiries daily.[16]

Initially, the liaison staffs were not equipped to handle such a volume of requests; and many inquiries went unanswered. In recent years, moreover, presidential patronage had dwindled dramatically. Many congressmen had unrealistic expectations regarding the amount of patronage available to the White House, and they were irritated when their patronage requests produced limited results. Indeed, the dispensing of patronage proved such a frustrating experience for liaison officials that one suggested that patronage 'be given to the losers'.[17]

In June 1977 House Speaker Thomas 'Tip' O'Neill met with fifty Democratic congressmen, Frank Moore, Hamilton Jordan, and the head of the White House personnel office. 'We won the election', O'Neill complained, 'but you'd never know it.'[18] Other House Democrats voiced similar sentiments. 'I busted my butt for Carter', said one Alabama congressman, 'and there's nobody I know who got an appointment. I call up [the agencies] and I'm talking to the same people I talked to under Nixon and Ford.'[19] After this session, the liaison system functioned more smoothly. Congressional leaders placed principal blame on Frank Moore for the early difficulties, however, and the impression lingered that Moore was largely inept as liaison chief.

Ironically, the member of the Carter White House most likely to forge an effective congressional relationship was Bertram Lance, the administration's earliest casualty. Lance had been Georgia's highway director during Carter's term as governor and became the President's Director of the Office of Management and Budget. In many respects the charming and affable Lance was an excellent choice for the position, and he seemed particularly well-suited for congressional liaison duties. 'Of all the Georgians I brought to the White House', Carter would later write, 'he was the best at cementing ties with key members of Congress, with Cabinet members, and with business and financial leaders.'[20]

Since April of 1975, however, certain of Lance's practices as President of the National Bank of Calhoun, Georgia, and the National Bank of Georgia in Atlanta had been under investigation by the office of the Comptroller of the Currency. The Comptroller's report found no criminal wrongdoing but did raise serious questions about the propriety of certain of Lance's banking practices, including his approval of huge overdrafts for himself, his wife and friends. By September 1977 Lance was under investigation by Congress and six federal agencies. On 15 September he made an effective appearance before the Senate Government Affairs Committee. Especially in view of Carter's post-Watergate campaign promise of an administration free of any hint of scandal, however, Lance's ultimate fate seemed certain. On 21 September Carter announced that Lance had submitted his resignation.[21]

Students of the Carter presidency have suggested other weaknesses in the Carter liaison operation.[22] Liaison officers are most likely to exert influence with members of Congress if they are perceived as being closely associated with the President and able to make commitments on his behalf. Lyndon Johnson attended meetings of his liaison staff about every other week and saw liaison personnel daily, taking a keen interest in every facet of the congressional relations process. As one Johnson liaison staffer has recalled:

He was right on top of it . . . totally involved. And some days he would say to us, 'I want you to go up there today and find out what the members need. What do they need in the district? Do they need the little wife invited down to the White House, or can we help with a constituent?' Then we would go up to the Hill and say, 'The President asked me to come see you and ask if you need anything.' That was impressive. People felt warmly toward LBJ.[23]

Frank Moore enjoyed regular personal contact with President Carter, but other members of the liaison staff apparently dealt with Carter largely through Moore. Except for Moore and his immediate staff, moreover, the liaison operation was located in the White House's East Wing, physically remote from the President, rather than in the West Wing with Moore where the liaison staffs of previous administrations had been housed. In a city in which physical proximity to authority is itself an attribute of power, placement of the liaison staff largely in the East Wing further contributed to congressional doubts that Carter's liaison staff, apart from Moore, could speak for the President.

Carter's staff also had fewer opportunities than the liaison personnel of previous administrations to offer benefits to congressmen in exchange for support of presidential programmes. John F. Kennedy's patronage 'plum book' had been at least two inches thick, Carter's a fifth that size. Of 135,000 positions in the Department of Health, Education, and Welfare, for example, the White House controlled 115; of 80,000 federal regional positions in Chicago, Carter could fill five. In time, Carter made reasonably effective use of rides on Air Force One, pens from bill-signing ceremonies, social-political gatherings, and other tokens of exchange. But Carter's natural distaste for pork-barrel politics—a facet of his legislative style given more extensive treatment later in this chapter—added measurably to the difficulties confronting his liaison staff.

The Carter arrangement for developing legislative proposals, then lobbying for their congressional enactment, also posed liaison problems. Liaison staffs within the executive agencies were involved in the formulation of substantive policy as well as with lobbying efforts. In the White House, however, the Office of Management and Budget, the Domestic Policy Staff, and related agencies were principally concerned with the formulation of the President's legislative programme; the liaison staff was normally only involved with pushing his programmes through the legislative mill, not with their substance.[24] Greater familiarity with substantive issues might have improved the liaison staff's effectiveness.

The working relationship between the White House staff and

the liaison staffs within the executive agencies reflected another weakness in the Carter liaison arrangement. In the Kennedy, Johnson, Nixon and Ford administrations, the White House heavily influenced the selection of department liaison personnel, closely supervised their work, and co-ordinated their activities with those of the White House staff. Agency staffers were frequently assigned to lobby congressmen with close agency ties, even when the legislation in question lay beyond a particular agency's sphere of concern. The White House made it clear, moreover, that the President's programme, not individual agency interests, was to be the principal concern of all liaison personnel.

Largely because of Carter's campaign commitment to 'cabinet government' as a counterpoint to the elitist White House government which had characterized the Nixon Administration and ultimately helped to account for its downfall, President Carter and his top aides played virtually no role in the selection of department liaison personnel. Moreover, while White House and agency lobbyists met weekly, their relationship seemed to be considerably less developed and hierarchical than that characteristic of earlier administrations. On a number of occasions, too, the White House staffers voiced concern that the department staffers were unduly inclined to defend the agency's turf rather than the administration's interests.

Finally, the Carter liaison staff had greater difficulty than previous Democratic administrations in mobilizing interest groups traditionally aligned with the party for congressional lobbying efforts. Changes in the process for selecting delegates to the Democratic national convention had enabled Carter to win his party's nomination without building a coalition within major Democratic interest groups. A number of the President's policy positions, moreover, alienated substantial segments of these groups, especially labour, urban and Jewish voters. Carter's liaison staff was thus largely deprived of a major source of lobbying talent as well as information regarding the issue preferences of Congressmen with strong interest group ties.

Carter as outsider

It is ironic, of course, that the same institutional changes which allowed Jimmy Carter to win his party's nomination without forging the interest-group coalition normally required of winning Democratic candidates would later obstruct his Administration's congressional liaison efforts. That irony, however, is simply part of the broader irony that Carter's status as a Washington 'outsider' both helped him to become a winning candidate and limited his potential for success as a legislative leader.

In the immediate post-Watergate era, a presidential campaign based on the candidate's distance from the federal government seemed a shrewd strategy. For an obscure ex-southern governor such a theme may have been the only formula for victory. During his campaign for the Democratic nomination, Jimmy Carter spoke to a variety of issues and emotions. He ran principally, however, on a promise to 'clean up the Washington mess'—a mess clearly not of his doing. At a Berlin, New Hampshire, rally early in the 1976 presidential primary season, he exclaimed: 'It's time for someone like myself to make a drastic change in Washington.' His campaign advertisements promoted the same theme, and it soon became apparent that Congress—and those congressmen also seeking the presidency —would be his principal Washington targets. One mailing warned: 'We will not see the kind of change we need in Washington by moving from Congress to the White House.' Another was more direct: 'The candidates from Congress running for President are telling the people . . . about the evils of Washington bureaucracy, when they have been a part of the bureaucracy all along.' Nor were Carter's attacks always general. When Minnesota senator Hubert H. Humphrey reacted to Carter's rhetoric, for example, Carter responded: 'I think Senator Humphrey perhaps is concerned because some of the things that he was influential in passing 15 or 20 or 25 years ago are challenged as being not too perfect. . . . And I think he's also concerned by the fact that some of us don't believe that Washington is the repository of all national wisdom.'[25]

Had Democratic Party rules been of the pre-1972 variety, the congressional leaders Carter attacked would have played key roles in the nomination process, and Carter would have pushed his outsider, anti-Washington theme at considerable risk. Given rule changes that allowed a candidate to win the nomination largely with presidential primary and caucus victories binding convention delegates, however, Carter's strategy posed few short-term dangers. Indiana's Birch Bayh and other Senate Democrats wondered aloud whether peanut farming qualified one for the presidency. But Carter's 'experienced outsider' theme clearly helped him to secure his party's nomination; and while a generally inept general election campaign almost cost him the contest, many voters found Carter a refreshing, if vaguely defined, alternative to the Washington establishment.

Had Carter won a stunning election victory, Democratic congressional leaders might have 'forgiven' the anti-Washington tenor of his campaign. But Carter carried only 50.1 per cent of the total vote, while Democratic House candidates won 56.2 per cent, leading Carter in every region of the nation including the South. Democratic senatorial candidates, moreover, carried 54.4 per cent of the vote; Carter ran ahead of a successful Democratic Senate incumbent only in Tennessee; and Carter lost all five states in which Democratic senatorial incumbents were defeated.[26] As one House aide commented after the election, 'Congress [didn't] owe Jimmy Carter anything'.[27]

The 1976 campaign also affected the attitude of the Carter people toward Congress. Carter called on 'Tip' O'Neill in Washington in early 1975 and spelled out precisely how he would have the nomination won before the convention.[28] But in the early days of his campaign, when Carter was derided as 'Jimmy Who?', congressional leaders largely ignored or ridiculed his candidacy. The tenor of his campaign obviously did nothing to improve the relationship. In achieving the near-miraculous feat of capturing the nomination and in then winning the election, the Carter campaign got little help from congressional Democrats. They were not needed to win the election, and Carter and his top aides apparently believed that they would not be needed in governing the nation, that given sufficient popular support for his programmes, Congress would come around. In 1979 *Atlantic* magazine's Washington editor James Fallows, who had served as the administration's chief speech writer during the first two years of Carter's presidency, wrote a fascinating two-part account of life in the Carter White

House.[29] Much of Fallows' narrative is overdrawn and reflects the frustrations of an aide unable to 'improve' his president's performance. Even so, it is an often insightful analysis. Fallows captures well the feelings of the Carter White House toward the Washington establishment:

> At the start of the Administration, as in the general election campaign, Carter and his captains felt omniscient; they had done what no one else had known how to do. Why should they take pains to listen to those who had designed the New Deal, the Fair Deal, the Great Society? The town was theirs for the taking; it would have required nothing more than allowing the old warriors a chance to help. But [Jody] Powell ánd Jordan and Carter let these people know that they could go to hell. Where had they been, with all their sage advice, when the campaign was out of money and no one knew who Jimmy Carter was? What were they doing when Carter was drawing crowds of ten and twenty in tiny Iowa towns? Spite is an expensive luxury in government, but Carter thought he could afford it, not realizing then how badly his operating account would soon be overdrawn.[30]

Fallows' impression reflects more his concern about Carter's early failure to recruit influential and capable Washington elites into his Administration than the attitude of the Carter White House toward Democratic members of Congress. The sentiments Fallows described, however, seem clearly to have extended to Congress; and such attitudes obviously aggravated Carter White House congressional relations. Early in Carter's tenure they were manifested essentially in petty slights. The White House, for example, billed House and Senate leaders for meals. House Speaker O'Neill, moreover, had difficulty securing inaugural tickets, was seated at the table farthest from the President at a Carter fund-raiser, and soon began referring to Hamilton Jordan as 'Hannibal Jerkin'.[31] Throughout Carter's term, however, the White House attitude toward Congress had more serious, if largely indefinite, effects on the Administration's relations with Congress.

Jimmy Carter's status as an outsider candidate created another uncertain, but potentially meaningful, problem for his Administration and its congressional relations. A Washington outsider free of responsibility for the Washington 'mess', and with no record of national public service against which his campaign platform could be evaluated, Candidate Carter promised much to an electorate eager to believe that he could bring about meaningful change. 'Like a new bridegroom', a reporter wrote, 'promises, made in all sincerity, rolled off his lips, encompassing everything from eternal truth to a balanced budget.'[32] Washington insiders may have winked at his promises to reduce the number of federal agencies from 1,900 to 200 and balance the budget. Carter began his term, however, amid rising public expectations about what his Administration could accomplish. The first-year gap between Carter promise and performance drastically reduced those optimistic expectations and further damaged his influence with Congress.

If Carter's outsider strategy angered members of Congress, tempted him into extravagant campaign promises, and aggravated whatever sense of alienation he and those closest to him harboured for the Washington establishment, the image of austerity he cultivated as part of that strategy posed similar difficulties. Carter's decision to carry his own luggage, take the oath of office in an off-the-rack suit, walk down Pennsylvania Avenue in his inaugural parade, and significantly curtail White House pomp obviously had citizen appeal, as did other symbolic gestures. But well-publicized lapses from this image, such as Carter's decision early in his administration to grant White House staffers sizeable rises, probably hurt his standing in public opinion polls. More significantly for our purposes, the Carter austerity image may have further alienated members of Congress. As Robert Shogan has observed:

The new President's image as a political outsider, which his advisers believed had broad public appeal, grated on the sensibilities of the leaders, whips, and ranking committee chairmen. Nor could these legislative potentates, who jealously guarded their own perquisites, avoid feeling a measure of suspicion and resentment about the new atmosphere of austerity and informality which had become the style of the White House.[33]

Occasionally, the Carter austerity programme had a direct impact on his congressional counterparts. At the first White House breakfast for congressmen, for example, the visitors dined on poached eggs and sausage. On later visits, they complained, the menu was juice, coffee, and a roll. More fundamentally, certain members of Congress may have feared unflattering comparisons of the simplicity characterizing the Carter White House with the Capitol Hill lifestyle.

Carter, of course, was not only a Washington outsider; in many respects, he was also outside the mainstream of his own political party. Sensing growing voter discontent with social welfare measures, big government, and other major elements in the New Deal, Fair Deal, New Frontier, and Great Society programmes of his Democratic predecessors, Candidate Carter stressed a balanced budget, limited government, and related policies traditionally associated with Republican candidacies. His approach may have appealed to voters, but liberal Democrats in the Congress were alarmed that he was rejecting basic Democratic positions and embracing conservative causes. Nor were they enthused when, contrary to his campaign promise to cut defence spending by at least $5 billion, he advocated increases in the defence budget. Conservatives complained, on the other hand, that his domestic policies were unduly liberal and his efforts to promote international human rights focused almost exclusively on right-wing regimes. Like his outsider strategy in general, therefore, his 'Republicrat' policy stance probably helped Carter win the presidency; in Congress, however, it cost him liberal support and won him few conservative friends.[34]

The Carter legislative style

Though a Washington outsider, Jimmy Carter was obviously no stranger to the difficulties of legislative liaison when he assumed the presidency. As Governor of Georgia, 1971–5, he had established a legislative style which would later be reflected in his relations with Congress and would help to account for some of the obstacles he encountered in that relationship.

As Governor, Carter had difficulty adapting to the traditional trappings of effective legislative leadership—the smoke-filled room, pork-barrel politics, superficial friendships. He particularly abhorred the logrolling tactics often so critical to the executive's legislative success, and he generally resisted the suggestion of his executive assistant Hamilton Jordan and other top aides that he aggressively employ pork-barrel politics to bolster his position. Moreover, while he did employ dinners at the Governor's mansion and other tokens of gratitude to loyal legislators, his efforts in that direction seemed only marginally effective.[35]

The sheer volume of Governor Carter's legislative packages created other problems. On the theory that the legislators would inevitably reject much of what he proposed, he chose to inundate them with recommendations in the expectation that enactment of only a few would assure him a successful legislative record.[36] The result was that even sympathetic legislators groaned under the burden of his programme to reform government organization, Georgia's welfare and tax structures, the state's conservative policies, and its approach to consumer protection, among a variety of other proposals. Nor did many of the major elements in his programme enjoy ready popularity with legislators, bureaucrats, or the voters. Government reorganization, for example, clearly has public significance. But it was also a politically volatile issue, enjoyed little or no natural constituency beyond the general appeal it would have for those concerned about the size of government, and produced few tangible benefits likely to attract legislative support. At the end of his first year as Governor, Carter conceded: 'If I have made one mistake, it has been in undertaking too many things simultaneously.'[37] One student of his gubernatorial career, however, has suggested that Carter's statement was designed more to placate legislators than reflect his personal convictions.[38]

Finally, Governor Carter was frequently accused of submitting what he considered the 'best' proposals to the legislature without adequate prior consultation with legislative leaders or due regard for the political risk elements of his programme might pose for supportive legislators or his Administration.[39] His relationship with the Georgia legislature thus proved to be a turbulent one. When asked by a reporter to identify the Governor's faithful supporters in the Georgia House of Representatives, his House floor manager smiled. 'It's not going to be a long article, is it?'[40] When asked during his presidential campaign whether some heifers on a South Dakota farm reminded him of Georgia's legislators, Carter replied, only somewhat enigmatically, 'No. They're more intelligent.'[41]

Carter's congressional style generally tracked his approach to legislative liaison in the Georgia statehouse. As noted earlier, he occasionally employed the prerogatives of his office as effective tokens of exchange; but he still found logrolling awkward and distasteful. In a televised press conference conducted toward the end of his first year in the White House, for example, he observed:

Horsetrading and compromising and so forth have always been very difficult for me to do. I just don't feel at ease with it, and it is a very rare occasion when any member of Congress or anyone else even brings up a subject that could be interpreted by the most severe cynic as a horse-trade. We were interested and amused, somewhat, during the Panama Canal treaty votes that every time a senator came in here, there were a rash of stories saying that certain things must have been promised to that senator to vote for the bill. This is not the case.[42]

In the post-Watergate era, such statements had undoubted voter appeal. Logrolling, however, is a necessary, expected ingredient of legislative politics.

Carter's first rift with congressional leaders over pork-barrel politics arose during the critical early weeks of his administration when the establishment of a workable congressional relationship was especially important. The controversy involved a sacrosanct pork-barrel institution, the water project. Such projects are often of doubtful value and frequently pose environmental problems. For the congressman whose state or district is awarded one, however, its political value is obvious. As Georgia's Governor, Jimmy Carter had opposed numerous Corps of Engineers projects on environmental grounds.[43] During his presidental campaign, he promised to curb dam construction; and even before his inauguration, he earmarked sixty-one projects for cancellation. On 18 February 1977, three days before the congressional deadline for the submission of proposed changes in his predecessor's 1978 budget, the President recommended that funding be eliminated for eighteen water projects. Later, another project was added to the list.[44]

The Administration estimated that dropping the projects would save $268 million in fiscal year 1978 alone, and about $5 billion in all. Among congressmen affected by the proposed cuts, however, were some of the Congress's most powerful members, including House majority leader Jim Wright, Senate Armed Services Committee Chairman John Stennis, and Russell Long of Louisiana, Chairman of the powerful Senate Finance Committee.[45] Long and other congressional leaders complained bitterly to administration officials. Carter was adamant, however, that the projects were a 'gross waste' of taxpayer money and the cuts an important part of his goal to balance the federal budget. Ultimately, Carter obtained approval to eliminate nine of the projects.[46] The cost in congressional goodwill, however, had been enormous.

An aspect of the water-project controversy especially irritating to congressional leaders was the Administration's failure to consult with them before announcing the proposed cuts. Leading a congressional delegation complaining about the cuts, Senator Long, whose state was slated to lose five projects, introduced himself to Carter aides in a voice dripping with sarcasm. 'My name is Russell Long, and I am the Chairman of the Senate Finance Committee.'[47] His meaning was clear. The Administration had decided to kill projects of considerable interest to one of the Senate's most powerful members without even apprising him of the President's intentions.

Nor, in the eyes of congressional leaders, was Carter's failure to consult adequately with Congress on the water-projects issue an isolated event. Early in his term especially, there were numerous similar, if less well-publicized, incidents. Carter, for example, named Republican Elliot Richardson United States representative to the Law of the Sea Conference without informing Speaker O'Neill, even though Richardson was then expected to oppose the Speaker's eldest son in a bid for the Massachusetts governorship. Other Republicans from O'Neill's state were named to the positions of White House Protocol Chief and Ambassador-at-large, again without consultation with the Speaker; and Carter also fired a close friend of the Speaker from the General Services Administration without informing O'Neill. Not all such lapses, moreover, were of limited substantive importance. When Carter reversed his position and announced his opposition to development of the B-1 bomber, congressional leaders backing his original stance learned of his decision only minutes before the press. In his first year also, Carter dropped his proposal for a $50 income tax rebate without informing certain key members of the congressional tax committees. Finally, the Administration apparently developed its first comprehensive energy package without any prior congressional consultation.[48]

When the water-projects controversy arose Frank Moore claimed that he had been unaware that the White House traditionally consulted with key congressmen while formulating legislative proposals.[49] President Carter was obviously familiar, however, with both the tradition of advance consultation and its political significance. In an interview with Neal Peirce during the 1976 campaign, for example, he had observed: 'If the legislative leaders can be involved in the initial stages of a project, if they can take credit for what is done, and not be placed in a combative attitude, then most of the disharmonies can be avoided.'[50] At his first press conference after becoming President, Carter apologized for early failures to consult Congress and said that he was then in almost daily contact with the Capitol.[51] As his administration progressed, the President did consult more frequently during the formulation stage of the legislative process, as well as on other matters. It is doubtful, however, that the congressional leadership considered his efforts adequate. In his memoirs, Carter wrote:

It seemed that Congress had an insatiable desire for consultation, which, despite all our efforts, we were never able to meet. It was not for lack of trying. Important committee chairmen were frequent visitors to the White House; and in addition to regular working breakfasts with the elected Democratic leaders in Congress, I held frequent sessions with entire committees or larger groups . . . I spent many good evenings having supper and then a lively discussion of domestic and foreign affairs with groups of as many as a hundred members of Congress.[52]

As noted earlier, President Carter's failure to appreciate the need to cultivate support for proposals before their submission to the legislative process and to consult with legislators on numerous other matters had been characteristic of his gubernatorial style. As Governor, Carter had also frequently threatened to go over the heads of Georgia legislators, taking his case directly to the people. In his 1976 interview with Neal Peirce, Carter spoke of this element in his legislative style:

I've never had the inclination nor the knowledge about the process to twist arms or force people to vote different from what they thought. But I've always seen the effectiveness of convincing the constituents back home about the question and then giving the legislative members maximum credit for the success achieved.[53]

In one of his first conversations with 'Tip' O'Neill, Carter told of going over the heads of the Georgia solons to the people;[54] in an otherwise harmonious breakfast meeting with O'Neill and other Democratic leaders five days after his inauguration, he reiterated this theme.[55] On each occasion, O'Neill warned him that such a tactic would be a grave mistake with Congress. In fact, Carter's opinion-moulding efforts appear to have been no more aggressive than those of his predecessors. Combined with his outsider campaign strategy, however, such threats did little to improve his position with the Congress.

Another aspect of Carter's gubernatorial legislative style was even more evident in his presidency. Governor Carter inundated the legislature with proposals, giving little indication of the priority he assigned to each. He followed essentially the same pattern with Congress. During the first months of his administration, he recommended more legislation to Congress than any other first-term president since Franklin Roosevelt— in February, government reorganization; in March, an energy department, election law reforms, abolition of the electoral college, public financing of congressional campaigns, and a new approach to foreign aid; in April, an anti-inflation programme, major food stamp provisions, a new consumer protection agency, restrictions on hospital costs, a comprehensive energy programme; in May, ethics-in-government legislation and major increases in social security taxes; in July, a plan to reorganize the White House staff and labour law reforms; in August, a programme for control of illegal aliens and comprehensive welfare reform.[56]

Though the sheer volume of Carter's legislative packages itself posed enormous problems, the schedule might have been manageable had the Administration made clear the relative significance of each proposal. The White House largely failed, however, to send Congress such signals.

James Fallows has characterized Carter's as a 'passionless' presidency largely because he discovered little genuine commitment to substantive issue positions among the President's lieutenants or in Carter himself.[57] Carter's favourite speech format, Fallows claims, was the list—an address listing what his Administration had accomplished, what it intended to do, in no particular order of importance. 'Carter's passionate campaign commitments turned out to be commitments to generalities, not to specific programmes or policies. After taking office he commissioned panels of experts to tell him what to do, usually giving them instructions no more detailed than his repeated exhortation to "Be bold!" '[58] In Fallows' judgement, the election-oriented Georgians closest to the President were even more devoid of specific policy commitments. After two years as Carter's top speech writer he could not recall a single 'serious or impassioned' issue discussion with a senior member of the White House staff.[59] Like Fallows' other impressions of the Carter White House, these seem overdrawn. Whatever the reason, however, Carter's programme lacked the focus and ordering of priorities that may have enhanced his chances for legislative success.

A new Congress

This chapter has focused on those aspects of effective legislative leadership over which President Carter had varying degrees of control. Given changes in the Congress over the past decade, however, it is likely that any president's congressional influence will be limited, and especially so if he enjoys no strong electoral mandate and focuses on energy, environmental, and other highly controversial, seemingly intractable public issues. Ronald Reagan, for example, has been successful in his dealings with Congress largely only in achieving tax cuts and other goals of modest scope and reasonably broad voter appeal. His promises to effect fundamental changes in federal-state relations and balance the budget, among other basic planks in Candidate Reagan's platform, are now almost entirely elements of Reagan rhetoric.

As Georgia's Governor, Jimmy Carter had faced an assertive General Assembly. The legislature had elected Carter's pre-decessor, arch-segregationist Lester Maddox, when Maddox's Republican opponent failed to win the electoral majority mandated by state law; and the Assembly dominated Georgia government throughout Maddox's term. As Lieutenant-governor during Carter's tenure, moreover, Maddox sided with Assembly forces seeking to obstruct Carter's legislative programmes and perpetuate legislative supremacy.[60]

President Carter confronted a similarly independent, assertive national legislature. During the latter days of the Nixon Administration, the Congress imposed restrictions on the President's war powers and assertions of impoundment authority, among other presidential prerogatives.[61] In the aftermath of Watergate and Vietnam, moreover, Congress seemed unwilling to yield to the presidency any power advantages it had derived from those twin national tragedies. As one Democratic senator observed in 1977, 'We got such fun out of popping Nixon and Ford, we don't want to give it up and be good boys any more.'[62] An impressive victory at the polls might have moderated congressional assertiveness. But a president who ran behind most congressional victors could hardly claim a popular mandate.

Following his election, congressional leaders frequently stressed to Carter their institution's growing independence from the executive. In a meeting at Carter's Georgia home in December 1976, 'Tip' O'Neill emphasized that Carter would face an assertive, independent legislative branch. At a breakfast meeting with the Democratic leadership early in February of his first year, Carter complained that his Cabinet officers were spending too much time testifying before congressional committees. O'Neill retorted that the Congress was an equal branch of the government and would call on members of the executive for testimony and other assistance whenever necessary.[63] In other settings, O'Neill, Senate majority leader Robert Byrd, Hubert Humphrey and other congressional veterans reiterated this theme. Their import was obvious: to be effective, Carter must treat the Congress with considerable deference; even then, success was not assured.

Not only was the Congress more assertive than in the days of the recent Democratic presidents with whom Carter is most commonly compared, Carter also confronted a Congress in which power was more widely dispersed than at any other period in the recent past. This diffusion of power was particularly evident in the House of Representatives. In 1971, 1973 and 1974 three reform committees, chaired by Republican Julia Butler Hansen (D–Washington), made recommendations which led to a number of fundamental changes in House institutions. One reform established a procedure, for example, whereby the Democratic caucus could elect standing committee chairmen by a secret ballot vote and without regard to seniority. Another substantially increased the number of House subcommittees as well as their independence from parent committees.[64] Beyond these and similar products of the Hansen committees' work, significant growth in the size of congressional staffs had made members of both chambers less dependent on both executive agencies and their own leadership. In such a setting, Speaker O'Neill, Robert Byrd and other Democratic leaders attempting to muster support for presidential programmes confronted special obstacles relatively unknown to the congressional leadership during the Kennedy and Johnson administrations.

Recent changes in electoral politics have also worked to disperse legislative power and limit the degree to which party leaders supportive of a president's programmes can deliver votes. Just as reform of the delegate selection process in the Democratic Party enabled Jimmy Carter to win nomination without forging the party and interest group coalition normally required of victorious hopefuls, congressional candidates now often conduct highly personalized campaigns with few ties to traditional party machines. As a result, James Sundquist of the Brookings Institution has observed, they are 'self-selected, self-organized, self-propelled, self-reliant, with no habit of being deferential to the establishment and the powerful, and they will not be so in Congress, either in committee or on the floor.'[65]

In such a setting even the most skilful party leader would be expected to encounter difficulty in delivering votes for controversial presidential programmes, especially given the problems the Carter White House itself had created. It seems clear, however, that the Democratic leaders on whom Carter depended lacked the legislative skills of certain of their predecessors. Speaker O'Neill is reasonably capable; and he gave the appearance, at least, of working hard in behalf of Carter's legislative proposals even though many were too conservative for his tastes and Carter had not been his first choice for the presidency.[66] But O'Neill was no Sam Rayburn. In the Senate the situation was even more critical. Robert Byrd's early relations with Carter were strained at best and improved only slightly during the President's term. In his memoirs, Carter would write of Byrd, himself a 1976 presidential hopeful: 'Sensitive about his position, he made certain I paid for my mistake whenever I inadvertently slighted him.'[67] More critically, Byrd was a relatively ineffectual majority leader, particularly when compared with Howard Baker, the capable Tennessee Republican who became leader after the 1980 elections gave the GOP a Senate majority. Following the 1982 elections in which the Republicans narrowly retained control of the Senate, columnist David S. Broder claimed that many Democratic senators, concerned by the prospects of a return to the Byrd era, were actually relieved at the election outcomes.[68]

The Carter burdens

In a perceptive analysis of deep-seated contemporary trends making effective presidential leadership more difficult, James Sundquist has written:

A party's nominee for president now is someone who has been able to devote enough time to shaking hands in the early primary and caucus states and to forming an effective get-out-the-vote organization there, who has raised enough money to put himself on television throughout the primary season, and who has proved to have popular appeal. He may be an outsider to the national political process. He may have no experience in the federal government he seeks to head. He may be a neophyte in dealing with complex issues of foreign relations and the domestic economy. He may be in no sense the natural leader of large and crucial elements of his own party. If elected, he may be a stranger to the people in Congress with whom he has to work, and he may have little sense of how to get along with them. He may have little idea of the kind of talent he needs to help him run the executive branch, and no network of experienced advisers to help him find them. All this was true of Jimmy Carter.[69]

Sundquist's statement reflects many of the weaknesses in President Carter's approach to legislative leadership examined in this chapter as well as their proximate causes. Carter obviously could have improved his relations with the Congress in a number of respects and to a greater degree than he attempted. In fairness, however, it is doubtful whether such efforts would have made for much difference in his legislative success rate. As indicated earlier, he faced a more independent, assertive Congress than had Kennedy and Johnson even though, like them, he had the advantage of Democratic-controlled Congresses. Perhaps more fundamentally, Kennedy and Johnson benefited from a relatively stable economy and low level of inflation; nor were they forced to cope with dwindling energy resources, growing environmental problems, and other critical issues which occupied much of Carter's attention. To date, the Reagan Administration·has shown itself to be more skillful than the Carter White House in matters of legislative liaison. Thanks somewhat at least to Carter policies, however, Reagan has enjoyed an international oil glut and the stagnant fuel prices and declining inflation rate that glut has helped to provide. As a 'fiscal conservative', he has also been able largely to ignore the issue of a spiralling national debt, indeed to pursue policies aggravating the deficit, without serious political fallout, much as anti-communist Richard Nixon was able to establish closer ties with mainland China after years of ascribing communist motives to Democrats inclined in that direction. Had the contexts within which Kennedy and Johnson functioned been more similar to Carter's, their reputations in legislative leadership, and congressional support scores, might also have been closer to his. So, too, might Ronald Reagan's.[70]

Notes

1. Charles O. Jones, 'Congress and the Presidency', in Thomas E. Mann and Norman J. Ornstein (eds), *The New Congress*, Washington, American Enterprise Institute, 1981, pp. 238-9.
2. See, for example, Reo M. Christenson, 'Presidential Leadership of Congress', in Thomas E. Cronin (ed.), *Rethinking the Presidency*, Boston, Little, Brown & Co., 1982, pp. 255-70.
3. George C. Edwards, III, *Presidential Influence in Congress*, San Francisco, W. H. Freeman, 1980, pp. 190-3.
4. A summary of congressional support rates for presidents since Eisenhower is contained in *Congressional Quarterly Almanac*, Vol. XXXVII, p. 17-C.
5. Ibid., Vols. XXXIII—XXXVI, contains excellent summaries of Carter's legislative successes and failures.
6. On the Johnson legislative liaison system, see especially Eric Davis, 'Legislative Liaison in the Carter Administration', *Political Science Quarterly*, 94, summer 1979, 287-301. Davis' study of legislative liaison in the Carter White House draws frequent and useful comparisons to the Johnson system.
7. Ibid., p. 289.
8. For brief profiles of Moore, see Haynes Johnson, *In the Absence of Power*, New York, Viking Press, 1980, p. 25; Robert Shogan, *Promises to Keep: Carter's First Hundred Days*, New York, Crowell, 1977, pp. 208-10.
9. Davis, pp. 290-2; Barry M. Hager, 'Tighter Coordination: Carter Seeks More Effective Use of Departmental Lobbyists' Skills', *Congressional Quarterly Weekly Report*, 4 March 1978, p. 579.
10. Mercer Cross, 'Carter and Congress: Fragile Friendship', *Congressional Quarterly Weekly Report*, 26 February 1977, p. 362.

11. Edwards, p. 179.
12. For a brief summary of White House lobbying for ratification of the treaties, see Edwards, pp. 176-7; for President Carter's version of the treaty battle, see *Keeping Faith: Memoirs of a President*, New York, Bantam Books, 1982, pp. 152-85.
13. Carter, p. 175.
14. Hager, p. 581.
15. Stephen J. Wayne, *The Legislative Presidency*, New York, Harper & Row, 1978, p. 211.
16. Hager, p. 584.
17. Wayne, p. 211.
18. Ibid.
19. Ibid.
20. Carter, p. 128.
21. For discussions of the Lance affair, see Johnson, pp. 199-214; Carter, pp. 125-37.
22. Unless otherwise indicated, this discussion is drawn primarily from Davis, pp. 291-301.
23. Hager, p. 586.
24. Wayne, p. 206. Among other agencies, the counsel's office was involved in all legislation pertaining to the Department of Justice, including intelligence questions; the President's assistant for intergovernmental affairs dealt with legislation involving disaster relief and various state and urban policy problems; and an Economic Policy Group was evolved to review economic issues and make recommendations to the President. Ibid., pp. 206-7.
25. Betty Glad, *Jimmy Carter, In Search of the Great White House*, New York, Norton, 1980, pp. 250-1.
26. *Congressional Quarterly Weekly Report*, 19 March 1977, pp. 488-9.
27. Daniel J. Balz, 'Carter's Honeymoon on the Hill—How Long Can It Last?', *National Journal*, 13 November 1976, p. 1618.
28. Johnson, pp. 20-1.
29. 'The Passionless Presidency', *Atlantic*, May 1979, pp. 33-48, June 1979, pp. 75-81.
30. Ibid., p. 46.
31. Eric Davis, 'The President and Congress', in Arnold J. Meltsner (ed.), *Politics and the Oval Office*, San Francisco, Institute for Contemporary Studies, 1981, p. 117.
32. Dom Bonafede, 'A Report Card on Carter—Lowered Expectations After a Year', *National Journal*, 14 January 1978, p. 44.
33. Shogan, p. 124.
34. On this point, see generally Johnson, pp. 162-3.
35. For an examination of Governor Carter's legislative leadership style, see Gary M. Fink, *Prelude to the Presidency: The Political Character*

and Legislative Leadership Style of Governor Jimmy Carter, Westport, Conn., Greenwood Press, 1980.
36. Balz, p. 1620.
37. Quoted in Fink, p. 165.
38. Ibid.
39. Balz, p. 1620.
40. Quoted in Fink, p. 169.
41. Shogan, p. 207.
42. Quoted in Edwards, p. 175.
43. Johnson, p. 159.
44. Shogan, pp. 212-13.
45. Ibid.
46. *Congressional Quarterly Almanac*, XXXIII, p. 65-A.
47. Shogan, p. 213.
48. These and other examples are discussed in Richard E. Cohen, 'The Carter-Congress Rift—Who's Really to Blame?', *National Journal*, 22 April 1978, pp. 630-2; Cross, pp. 361-3; Johnson, pp. 159-64; Edwards, pp. 174-5; Shogan, pp. 125-6.
49. Glad, p. 420.
50. Neal R. Peirce, 'The Democratic Nominee—If I Were President . . .', *National Journal*, 17 July 1976, p. 994.
51. Shogan, p. 125.
52. Carter, p. 71.
53. Peirce, p. 994.
54. Glad, p. 421.
55. Johnson, p. 155.
56. For an excellent overview of Carter's legislative programmes and the relationship between his rising and falling congressional fortunes and his standing in public opinion polls, see Austin Ranney, 'The Carter Administration', in Austin Ranney (ed.), *The American Election of 1980*, Washington, DC., American Enterprise Institute, 1981, pp. 1-36.
57. Fallows, pp. 40-2.
58. Ibid., p. 40.
59. Ibid., p. 42.
60. Fink, *passim*.
61. For a survey of recent congressional limitations on presidential power, see Thomas E. Cronin, *The State of the Presidency*, second edn., Boston, Little, Brown, 1980, Chapter 6. Also see generally James L. Sundquist, *The Decline and Resurgence of Congress*, Washington, Brookings Institution, 1981. In *Immigration and Naturalization Service* v. *Chadha*, 51 L. W. 4907 (1983), the Supreme Court declared the legislative veto approach to limiting presidential discretion unconstitutional.

6 2. Edwards, p. 196.
63. Johnson, pp. 156-8.
64. For a more detailed summary of the Hansen reforms, see Lawrence C. Dodd and Bruce I. Oppenheimer, 'The House in Transition: Change and Consolidation', in Lawrence C. Dodd and Bruce I. Oppenheimer (eds), *Congress Reconsidered*, second edn., Washington, Congressional Quarterly Press, 1981, pp. 36-88.
65. James L. Sundquist, 'Congress, the President, and the Crisis of Competence in Government', in ibid., p. 363.
66. In his memoirs, Carter writes that O'Neill 'flinched visibly' when the President spoke of balancing the federal budget. Carter, p. 73.
67. Ibid.
68. *News and Observer*, Raleigh, NC., 6 January 1983, p. 5A.
69. Sundquist, 'Congress, the President . . .', p. 359.
70. President Reagan's congressional support score was 82.4 per cent in 1981 but dropped to 72.4 per cent in 1982.

10 Carter and the bureaucracy

Donald A. Marchand

A major dilemma of democratic government is whether it can be responsive and effective at the same time. Responsiveness points in the direction of narrowing the gap between the preferences of the community and the decisions of elected officials and administrators. Effectiveness on the other hand highlights the need for decisions to lead to intended outcomes —however praiseworthy the policy and programme, they must work.[1] Even a cursory review of presidential intentions in recent years highlights the fact that liberal Democratic presidents have tended to focus on the responsiveness of government even if not all the programmes they launched worked effectively; while more conservative, Republican presidents have focused on lowering the expectations of the community concerning the responsiveness of government at the same time as they have emphasized the need for effective government in those areas where governmental involvement was deemed appropriate.

Interestingly enough, Jimmy Carter as a presidential candidate and as president wanted to achieve both goals at the same time: that is, to make government *both* more responsive and effective. In direct contrast to traditional Democratic liberalism which resolved the dilemma in favour of responsiveness and to Republican conservatism which resolved the dilemma in favour of effectiveness, Carter's Southern populist beliefs led him to emphasize the need for government that was responsive to the poor, uneducated and minorities on the one hand and, on the other hand, to strive for effectiveness in government as well (that is, a government that was fiscally prudent and managerially efficient). To anyone born and raised in the South, such views were not contradictory, but rather represented the essence of Southern Democratic populism: a set of beliefs based on the notion that fiscally prudent, but well-run governmental programmes were also, in the long run, the most responsive to those citizens in need of government's assistance.

It is no wonder that during his presidential campaign, Jimmy Carter could elicit support from Democrats and Republicans alike since he sounded a little like both, but really was like neither. In the context of the mid-1970s, Carter's appeal to the theme of responsive government fell within the traditional Democratic appeals for social programmes and policies that met the needs of the poor, minorities and the uneducated; while, at the same time, his appeal to the theme of effectiveness and efficiency in government came on the heels of the chaos of Watergate and an unprecedented proliferation of social programmes through the Johnson and Nixon administrations. In effect, by appealing to these dual themes, Carter the candidate hit a responsive chord. Moreover, nothing in Jimmy Carter's previous political experience suggested that any aspect of the pursuit of these dual themes was contradictory. As Governor of Georgia, Carter had initiated massive reorganization and consolidation of government agencies, had introduced reforms such as Zero-Based Budgeting (ZBB), as well as other measures which sought to improve the delivery of government programmes to the citizens of the state, especially the poor and minorities. All that was needed was strong executive leadership and an effective team of appointees and staff in the executive office and agencies—ingredients which Carter as candidate felt he could duplicate in Washington, DC. Therefore, as Jimmy Carter's transition team approached the White House in the fall of 1976, making the Federal government more responsive and effective were to be the critical criteria by which the Carter presidency was to be judged.

The Carter Programme: making government work

Having campaigned for more than two years as an outsider to Washington and as a critic of the way the Federal government was run, Jimmy Carter as President launched four initiatives on which his theme of making government was based.

(a) Cabinet government

The first initiative that Carter launched aimed at creating a new balance in policy-making and management between the White House staff and the department heads and staffs. Invoking in part the excesses and problems of centralizing policy control in the White House which had arisen during the Nixon Administration, Carter declared that he believed in Cabinet administration and that there would never be an instance while he was President where the members of the White House staff dominated or acted in a superior position to members of the Cabinet.[2] These sentiments were reinforced in July 1977 when Jack Watson, Jr., the Cabinet Secretary, defined four key principles of Cabinet government:

— Cabinet officers should be free to appoint subordinates of their own choice;
— Cabinet officers should be able to set their own priorities for their appointments;
— Cabinet officers should be able to administer their bureaucracies free of White House interference; and
— Cabinet officers should be delegated significant policy-making authority.[3]

However, having defined the principles, both Carter and Watson found them difficult to implement. While the role of individual Cabinet members was enhanced, the role of the Cabinet as a deliberative body for policy-making quickly deteriorated. Cabinet meetings became more informational than deliberative and the White House staff quickly assumed a preeminent role in policy-making. After the first year, Cabinet meetings declined in frequency as individual Cabinet members and their staffs increasingly dealt directly with White House staff and the President on key issues. Moreover, on the weekend of 15 April 1978, Carter held a series of meetings at Camp David with his White House Staff and other trusted advisers which precipitated a major realignment of policy-making responsibilities from the Cabinet to the White House staff and which ultimately led to a major shake-up of the Carter Cabinet. During the months following the Camp David meeting, Hamilton Jordan emerged as the White House chief-of-staff whose task was to co-ordinate the policy development responsibilities in the White House and to redefine the relationship between the Cabinet officers and the White House in four areas: (1) to undertake a personnel review of sub-Cabinet political appointees; (2) to reassert control over the patronage system of departmental appointments; (3) to clean up the Administration's image as indecisive and contradictory and

(4) to take over more responsibility in policy-planning in the White House.[4] In addition, by July 1979, Carter decided to accept the resignations of four Cabinet officers who had proved in one form or another troublesome to the Administration:

Joseph A. Califano, Jr., (HEW) intensely disliked by White House staff as high-minded and disloyal to the President; W. Michael Blumenthal (Treasury), also out of favor at the White House for his policy disagreements with the President's staff; James R. Schlesinger (Energy), regarded as a liability at a time of long gas lines and an approaching re-election campaign; and Brock Adams (Transportation), safe until he refused a White House directive to get rid of his deputy.[5]

By the end of 1979, Carter's collegial approach to management of the Federal government had yielded to a tighter and more conventional system of policy co-ordination and development between the White House domestic policy staff and the individual department heads and their staffs. 'Cabinet government' as a concept had proved both unfeasible and a political liability.

(b) Government reorganization

The second initiative which Carter set in motion during his first year in office concerned frequently-expressed plans to reorganize and consolidate the many agencies and departments of the government in a similar manner to what he had done as Governor of Georgia. To accomplish this ambitious task, Carter took three key steps: (1) he created the role of Special Assistant to the President for Reorganization; the task here was to direct and co-ordinate the reorganization effort from the White House; (2) he reorganized the Office of Management and Budget (OMB) to create a structure to carry out the necessary reorganization studies; and (3) he drafted legislation requesting congressional authority to submit reorganization plans which could be automatically approved if Congress took no action to specifically disapprove a plan within sixty days.[6]

On 31 March 1977 Carter won approval from Congress to proceed with reorganization of the Federal government under the revised procedures. During 1977 and 1978 the OMB created over twenty-eight different task forces to study the Federal government. The task forces were divided along two lines: some task forces were directed at studying specific substantive areas such as social services, law enforcement, health, etc; while other task forces studied cross-cutting management concerns of government agencies such as cost-accounting, data processing, communications, etc.

Originally, the task forces were to be made up of federal employees detailed to the task forces from agencies and private sector executives and university representatives brought in through the Executive Loan Program (ELP). The intention of the ELP was to recruit private sector executives whose firms would pay their salaries, travel and board in Washington, DC, for the duration of a study project. Although a few of the projects were successful in recruiting a substantial number of private sector executives and academics to serve in the task forces, most were not. Therefore, most of the Presidential Reorganization Projects (PRP) that were launched were made up of representatives from the agencies to be reorganized.

Despite these recruitment difficulties, the Presidential Reorganization Projects were successful at defining reform proposals in key substantive areas such as energy, social services, law enforcement, education, natural resources and health insurance. In addition, the management task forces drew up plans for redefining government policies over computers, communications, accounting systems and procurement policies. Not since the Hoover Commission reviews in the 1950s had the Federal government received such a comprehensive management review.

However, studying reorganization and getting Congress to go along with specific reorganization proposals were two different activities. In the latter case, the Carter Administration over the next three years attained major victories in the areas of Civil Service Reform, and in creating new Departments of Energy and Education. In other areas, Carter proposals did not receive support from Congress. The Administration's social service and health programme reforms were only partially successful, while Carter's proposal to create a Department of Natural Resources met with significant agency and congressional opposition.[7]

(c) Zero-Based Budgeting

The third initiative which Jimmy Carter desired to launch in his first year involved a revision of the budget review process in the executive branch called Zero-Based Budgeting (ZBB). Originally developed by an executive in Texas Instruments Inc., the essence of ZBB was to make agencies review and justify each year from the bottom up how they were going to use their existing and requested funds to achieve their programme goals. In contrast to the incremental form of budgeting where the agency only had to justify the additional monies it was requesting over last year's base, ZBB required an evaluation of both the effectiveness and efficiency of the agency's programmes and operations.

OMB was authorized to revise the executive branch's budgetary process to introduce the ZBB concept to the agencies. Coming on the heels of efforts by the Johnson and Nixon administrations to introduce similar programme evaluation and budgetary approaches, the ZBB was not well received in the individual agencies. Although all agencies complied, they tended to perceive the ZBB process as an additional paperwork exercise which the limited OMB staff was ill-prepared to assume. While several state governments had introduced the ZBB concept with some success, the Carter Administration efforts to impose ZBB on the Federal executive and budgeting process did not prove very useful or efficient. The incremental budgeting process proved very resistant to change.[8]

(d) Regulatory reform

The fourth initiative which Jimmy Carter launched came as an outgrowth of concerns previously raised during the Ford Administration and focused on the 'de-regulation' of major industries that had at some point over the last hundred years come under Federal government regulation. During 1977 and 1978, the Carter Administration launched efforts to reduce paperwork regulatory burdens as well as promote competition in the airlines, trucking, railroad, banking and other financial institutions and the communications industries.[9] Although the Administration was not completely successful in accomplishing de-regulation in all these industries before the first term expired, it is clear that the Administration did set the course on which Congress, the courts and the interest groups representing the industries have continued to play key roles. In an effort to reduce regulating burdens on industries and increase competition for the benefit of consumers, the Carter

Administration set into motion a series of initiatives whose consequences have already had profound effects on the American economy in the 1980s.

The limits of presidential management initiatives

There has probably been no other president in modern times who has had such a keen interest in management of the Federal government as Jimmy Carter. However, like other presidents, Jimmy Carter had to go through a period of on-the-job training to understand the types of constraints a president must face in launching new initiatives. Although some of the constraints the President faced were of his own making, many of the problems he confronted were largely beyond his control or ability to significantly influence. For the sake of analytical convenience, I have defined below three types of constraints the President faced:

(a) *Structural constraints*

When Jimmy Carter was elected, his governmental management training had been based on his term of office as Governor of Georgia where executive authority was strong and management could be accomplished with the top-down approach. The existing federal bureaucracy, in contrast, was not managed from the top-down but from the bottom-up. Federal agencies were loose confederations of largely independent bureaux with close ties to interest groups and congressional subcommittees. These 'iron triangles', as Jimmy Carter recognized, were highly resistant to top-down management directives. It is not surprising, therefore, that Carter's attempts to develop a Cabinet form of government floundered when his Cabinet officers became more allied with the concerns and interests of their agencies than with the policy priorities of the White House.

A second structural constraint that the Carter Administration confronted was the fact that the Executive Office of the President did not really manage or execute policy directly, but rather guided and, in some limited cases, co-ordinated implementation of policy. Moreover, the largest agency in terms of personnel in the EOP was the Office of Management and Budget, which traditionally had been more concerned with the federal budget process and not with direct management control of agency activities.[10]

Finally, a third structural constraint which provided Jimmy Carter with his most difficult problems was the fact that Congress and its committees and subcommittees and support agencies like the U.S. General Accounting Office exercised management oversight over the activities of OMB and the agencies.[11] Thus, at every point in the Presidential Reorganization Projects, the President and his staff needed to build consensus for new proposals with members of the House and Senate serving on government operations committees or on substantive area committees. Without their support, the President had very little room to manœuvre independently in seeing his reorganization plans and management initiatives move forward.

In many ways, Jimmy Carter as President was confronted with exactly the opposite management situation he had dealt with as Governor of Georgia. The model of overhead administration that had served him so well in Georgia was largely inoperative in the Federal government where management control (if there was any) was bounded by the influence structure of 'iron triangles'.[12]

(b) Political constraints

The political constraints on Jimmy Carter's management reform initiatives were even more severe than the structural limits. During his campaign for the presidency, Jimmy Carter continuously emphasized the issue of re-organization and management reform of the Federal government. As a campaign theme, the issue of good government was a very useful one: that is, 'everyone' was for good government. The almost universal appeal of the issue provided, therefore, a useful avenue for Carter's image as a competent outsider who would go to Washington to make government work.

On the other hand, once the candidate Carter was elected, the issue of good government had three fatal drawbacks which made government reorganization and management reform difficult to pursue: first, the issues had no 'natural' constituency (everyone was for good government, but there were no significant political supporters organized around this issue); second, vigorous pursuit of the issue guaranteed that the costs of change were going to be borne by the federal agencies and employees (a constituency you could not afford to alienate if you wanted your key *policy*, as opposed to management initiatives, to succeed); and third, the average voter or citizen really didn't understand how he/she benefited directly as a result of government reorganization and the introduction of management initiatives like ZBB. For example, it was difficult to explain the 'success' of management initiatives when the benefits were long-term in nature (such as creating a Department of Education and Department of Energy) or not clearly identifiable (such as introducing a Cabinet form of government or ZBB).

In comparison with visible policy issues such as tax policy, energy supplies, hazardous waste disposal and environmental regulation, the politics of reorganization and management reform were relatively low visibility concerns which were sustained largely by the personal concern of the President for improved government performance.

In addition, two other political constraints limited the President's effectiveness. First, most of the political appointees responsible for the reorganization efforts were unfamiliar with the complexities and intricacies of the Federal government. Coupled with the limited knowledge of agencies which many new department heads and staff had, the White House and Executive Office staff had to look to the career civil servants themselves for help in reorganizing their agencies and/or programmes. Second, despite President Carter's early efforts to achieve civil service reform by expanding the numbers of positions in agencies subject to political appointment or oversight, the President's initiatives were bounded by the limited interest that the typical political appointee displays in long-term management reform. Since the average 'career' of a political appointee was eighteen months, it is not difficult to see that these individuals were often more concerned with selective *policy* issues and thus delegated the matter of management reform to the career civil servants.

(*c*) *Personal constraints*

In addition to the political and structural constraints which limited the pursuit of improved management in the Federal government, Jimmy Carter, as President, was also restricted by some personal constraints.

The first problem which the new President had to deal with was that there was a lot to learn about many policy as well as management issues. As both a businessman and governor, Jimmy Carter had developed a management style which depended on a paper-flow system which emphasized attention to detail. Although Carter had a keen mind which absorbed information quickly, the President was often tied down to long hours of reviewing detailed analysis and option memoranda (called PDMs, or Presidential Decision Memoranda). During the first two years of his Administration, Carter was personally involved in reviewing PDMs from the multiple reorganization projects which he had launched, in addition to the 'normal' responsibilities of the President in foreign and domestic policy matters. It is not surprising, therefore, that over time the matters of management reform and reorganization consumed less and less of Jimmy Carter's precious time as President. While many commentators have suggested that Carter spent too much time on the 'details' of administration, it is difficult to understand how the President could have avoided such matters when he launched more than twenty-eight Presidential Reorganization studies during the first two years of his term!

A second personal constraint on Jimmy Carter's ability to deal with management reform issues came from the initial presumptions he made that as President he really was the chief executive with at least the same amount of management authority that he had enjoyed as Governor. For example, as Governor of Georgia, Jimmy Carter had reduced and consolidated the number of state agencies from 300 to 22. On 17 November 1976 President-elect Carter suggested that he could reduce the number of federal agencies from 1,900 to 200. In fact, Carter learned over the first two years of his Administration that the President as manager is even more severely constrained than the Governor of a state. In large measure this is due to the fact that the 'overhead' model of administration does not apply in the Federal government where agencies are often loose confederations of semi-autonomous bureaux and where the President's appointees represent a relatively small number in the Federal executive workforce. Therefore, as 'chief executive', Jimmy Carter was severely bounded in the exercise of management authority in the Federal government—a fact which he had not fully anticipated and appreciated when he assumed office.

The final personal constraint on the President's pursuit of reorganization and management reform politics revolved around the tendency of the President to underestimate the White House and OMB staff required to assure management initiatives are implemented in the agencies. Since, during the early days of his Administration, the EOP staff grew considerably, during his second year Carter reduced the EOP staff and the positions available to OMB for reorganization at precisely the point at which the Presidential Reorganization Projects were completing their work and moving toward the implementation of management changes and policies. Thus, there were often inadequate numbers of EOP staff to follow up on the many detailed recommendations of the PRP task force reports. The limited staff that did remain concentrated on only selected initiatives and largely left the detailed follow-up to the discretion of line agencies. During 1978, one high level OMB official responsible for reorganization typified the problem as 'management by snowflakes'. OMB or the White House would approve policies and management reforms, by the time the agencies got around to responding, the management reform had evaporated like new snow with little or no trace.

Achievements and lessons learned

Jimmy Carter did not achieve everything he set out to do in reorganization and improving the efficiency of government. Neither was he entirely successful in doing things his way. His cabinet form of collegial administration did not work very well. Zero-Based Budgeting was not accepted by the federal agencies and was, in the end, perceived as either another management 'fad', or as a grand paperwork exercise. In reorganizing the government Carter had some notable successes, such as establishing the Departments of Energy and Education as well as pushing through civil service reform, and some dismal failures such as his inability to consolidate agencies as he had done in the Georgia state government. In other instances, Presidential Reorganization Studies launched by Carter resulted in significant, if not very visible, reforms in government administration in areas like the management of information resources and technology in the Federal agencies. Finally, his regulatory reform initiatives led to significant deregulation of major industries which are still being carried out today.

Jimmy Carter did not so much fail in accomplishing the objectives of reorganization and management reform in the Federal government as much as he did not fully appreciate the structural, political and personal constraints to success. The Federal government could not be managed like state government since the President was only one of several key actors in the management reform process. Moreover, while Carter recognized that the revenues available to the government were declining, he underestimated the difficulties of restructuring government in a period of fiscal retrenchment. Finally, it became increasingly clear as his Administration progressed, that the foreign and domestic pressures on the President left little time or energy for pursuing the details of management reform and administration. Despite his intentions and mind for management detail, Carter was, after the first eighteen months of his Administration, increasingly involved in foreign crises and domestic problems.

In reviewing the legacy of the Carter efforts to improve the management of the Federal government, several lessons can be drawn for future Presidents to consider. First, it is clear that the selection of one's targets of management reform is critical. If there was one problem which hampered Jimmy Carter throughout his management reform efforts, it was the perception that he took too many projects on too fast. Moreover, it is clear that Carter himself deliberately chose this course, as revealed in this entry in his personal diary on 28 January 1977: 'Everybody has warned me not to take on too many projects so early in the administration, but it's almost impossible for me to delay something that I see needs to be done.'[13] Therefore, by both inclination and design, Jimmy Carter was susceptible to undertaking many more management reform efforts than he could possibly complete. Instead of targeting on key areas or agencies, Carter simply proceeded with a comprehensive approach even when neither he nor his staff fully appreciated the complexities of the issues they were dealing with nor realized the constraints influencing their progress across so many fronts.

Second, for a President to be successful in bringing management reform to the Federal government, it is clear that he must get the support of the business community and leadership behind him. Without such a constituency interested in efficient management, the efforts of the President are likely to be politically weak and uneven. The history of management reform in the government has always included the clear support and involvement of business leaders. The latter represent one of the only 'natural' constituencies for internal reform in government. In this regard, Jimmy Carter's management reform efforts, especially in the Presidential Reorganization Projects, never had the real involvement or support of big business. Indeed, as suggested earlier, as the Presidential Reorganization Projects were organized, the Carter staff had significant problems in recruiting business representatives for service on the reorganization studies. During the first year of his Administration many businessmen were as ambivalent about Jimmy Carter as the Washington bureaucrats he aimed to reform.

Third, it is important early in management reform efforts that the President develop a clear strategy for getting the co-operation of congressional leaders whose interests are affected. If Jimmy Carter failed in accomplishing his objectives in this area, the causes of failure had to do more with his lack of clear congressional strategy than any other factor. The President is simply too weak in management authority and support within the EOP to pursue major management reforms without congressional involvement and support. In large measure, the difficulties Jimmy Carter had with the Congress were not just due to inadequate staffing of his Congressional Liaison Office, but, more importantly, were a product of underestimating the intimate links between the congressional committees and sub-committees and the agencies and programmes they supported and oversaw. Only later in his term did Carter and his staff begin understanding and successfully using the close ties that Congress had with the agencies to achieve successes.

Fourth, the key to the long-term success of management reforms resides in the ability of the President and his staff to convince the agencies that the reforms are worth pursuing. No president can afford to take a We/They approach to the agencies and expect to have his reorganization and management reform proposals accepted. Significantly, during the first two years of his Administration, Jimmy Carter had great difficulty in shaking off the confrontational We/They image he had fostered towards the civil servants and agencies during his campaign. The threats of massive agency shake-ups, Zero-Based Budgeting and civil service reform did nothing to allay the concerns of Washington civil servants that the President had limited appreciation of their programmatic concerns and interests.

Fifth, it is important that the President should not involve himself in the details of management reform efforts. While he should use his office to marshall support and visibility for such efforts, he should refrain from engaging in detailed review of all the changes to be made. As an engineer by background and as a manager by choice, Jimmy Carter approached every problem as a puzzle to be solved if only all the appropriate information could be digested. As a president, Carter confused the role of leader with the role of manager. As management reformer, Carter immersed himself in the details of Presidential Reorganization Project studies and recommendations which left little or no time for exercising leadership in building support and consensus for his proposals. In the latter part of his term Carter had to reduce his involvement in the details of management to act as a forceful political leader and strategist in getting congressional approval for his reform proposals.

Finally, it is critical that the President recruit managers with business and government experience to lead the management reform efforts. It is not enough to appoint staff with business backgrounds and assume they will learn the ways of Washington. Rather, it is critical that the leadership of the reform efforts be well versed in Washington administrative politics as well as have current experience as managers in business. Without such a combination of skills among staff persons, the President will be isolated from the critical judgements which must be made in making reform proposals both politically feasible and administratively acceptable. To a great degree, most of the full-time staff who were involved in the management reform efforts were outsiders to Washington and, in some cases, lacked business management consulting expertise as well. Thus, it is not surprising that many of the management reform efforts were either not approved or not successfully implemented.

Conclusion

Jimmy Carter's attempts to introduce significant and lasting management reforms in the government must be perceived in the context of what the modern administrative state has become. Top-down management of the government is largely an illusion. While the modern presidency is a powerful post from which to exercise leadership and to influence the tide of domestic and foreign events, it is nevertheless a very poor position from which to manage the details of administration. Neither the White House staff nor the Executive Office of the President, including the Office of Management and Budget, can influence the day-to-day management and operations of agencies and bureaux. Moreover, it is clear that within the current decentralized system of government, Congress, the agencies and interest groups have a greater impact on the management of the programmes of government than the president himself. For this reason, it is important for a newly-elected president to target his management initiatives carefully to assure some measure of success, rather than to ambitiously undertake sweeping reforms that create undue fears and expectations of results which a president is in a poor position to assure. Today, the modern administrative state provides only limited opportunity for presidential management initiatives. The execution of policy and administration of programmes remain largely outside the purview of the president unless he selects his targets for reform carefully and appropriately. Trying to do too much can be as problematic for the modern president as not doing enough.

Notes

1. See Francis E. Rourke, *Bureaucracy, Politics and Public Policy*, Boston, Little, Brown & Company, p. 3.
2. Stephen J. Wayne, *The Legislative Presidency*, New York, Harper & Row, 1978, p. 202.
3. R. Gordon Hoxie, 'Staffing the Ford and Carter Presidencies', Chapter 3 in Bradley D. Nash, ed., *Organizing and Staffing the Presidency*, New York, Center for the Study of the Presidency, 1980, pp. 72-3.
4. Dom Bonafede, 'Carter's Recent Staff Shake-up May Be More of a Shake-down', *National Journal*, 17 June 1978, pp. 952-7.
5. 'What to Expect from Carter's New Cabinet', *National Journal*,

28 July 1979, p. 1241. 'Jordan's New Role, Signals An End to "Cabinet Government" ', *National Journal*, 18 August 1979, pp. 1356-60. Griffen Bell, the Attorney-General, also left the Administration.

6. Joel Haveman, 'Reorganization—How Clean Can Carter's Broom Sweep?', *National Journal*, 1 January 1977, pp. 4-8.
7. Joel Haveman, ' "Turf" Battles Threaten Reorganization Plan', *National Journal*, 20 May 1978, pp. 788-92.
8. Joel Haveman, 'The Budget—A Tax Cut, Little Else', *National Journal*, 28 January 1978, pp. 124-32.
9. Richard E. Cohen, 'Carter Has Landed Running in Regulatory Reform Issues', *National Journal*, 16 April 1977, pp. 592-3.
10. See Larry Berman, *The Office of Management and Budget and the Presidency, 1921-1979*, Princeton, New Jersey, Princeton University Press, 1979, pp. 105-30.
11. See Randall B. Ripley and Grace A. Franklin, *Congress, The Bureaucracy and Public Policy*, Homewood, Illinois, The Dorsey Press, 1976, pp. 1-70.
12. See also Emmette S. Redford, *Democracy in the Administrative State*, New York, Oxford University Press, 1969, pp. 38-82.
13. Jimmy Carter, *Keeping Faith*, New York, Bantam Books, 1982, p. 65.

11 Conclusion: the legacy

Dilys M. Hill and Phil Williams

Many scholars now reject that pessimism which contends that in an era of complex issues, declining party support, bureaucratic intransigence and congressional fragmentation, presidents can no longer govern.[1] Nevertheless, as this book has shown, the president faces formidable barriers from both political structures and political processes in his search for effective decisions. Indeed, the contributors almost invariably agree that the problems facing Jimmy Carter were of enormous complexity: the Carter Presidency coincided with a period when, in relative terms at least, American power *vis-à-vis* its allies and adversaries was declining, and when internal problems were becoming increasingly intractable. And these were trends for which the President was not responsible and over which he had little or no control. Yet there is also agreement that the President's own style of government did little to help him overcome the problems facing the United States and at times may have actually added to them. In response to the question whether Carter jumped or was pushed, therefore, most of the contributors suggest that he fell. There is also broad agreement that his downfall cannot be adequately explained either by reference to the difficulties of presidential government in the latter half of the 1970s or by focusing on shortcomings in Carter's approach to politics and policies. It was the combination of both these things which gave the Carter presidency its distinctiveness and, indeed, much of its chararacter.

One of the major difficulties for the Carter Administration was political fragmentation, especially in the Congress. The changes that had taken place in the legislature prior to 1976 meant that Carter had to contend with a Congress characterized by increased individualism, lack of party cohesion, and the diffusion of power among an unprecedented number of sub-committees. In such circumstances it was hardly surprising that the lobby had become more pervasive and more powerful. The result was what Carter's Secretary for Health, Education

and Welfare, Joseph A. Califano described as 'molecular government'. In Califano's view, Washington had become a city of
political molecules with the fragmentation of power encouraging alliances between interest groups and their counterparts
in Congress and in the departments.[2] The discussions in the
preceding chapters suggest that it was this, together with
the changes in procedure in Congress after 1974, and not
just the inexperience of the President or the introversion
and ineptitude of his Georgia aides, which reduced Carter's
influence on Capitol Hill and thereby undermined his effectiveness. Nor was the President helped by the fact that many
Democrats in Congress had never served with a Democrat
in the White House: Carter's uneasy relationship with his
party and his weak claim to lead it both exacerbated his difficulties with Congress and weakened his Presidency.

Although such problems were very real, and were specifically
bounded in the post-Watergate unease, they must also be seen
in perspective. Indeed, there have only been three periods in
the twentieth century when the relationship between presidential leadership and congressional compliance was strong
enough to achieve major changes in domestic policy—Wood-
row Wilson's Administration, FDR's first term and Lyndon
Johnson's first two years.[3] Similar bursts of innovation have
now become very much harder. The pluralism of Congress and
the decline of party has meant that over the last two decades
presidents—regardless of style, personality or preference—
have increasingly been compelled to build the equivalent of
a presidential party for governing.[4]

Jimmy Carter tried to achieve this through organizational
subdivisions in the White House dealing with women's issues,
group liaison, Hispanic affairs, ethnic matters and civil rights.
Although these efforts were buttressed by the President's
well-known efforts to 'appeal to the people' directly through
his grass-roots tours and televised 'fireside chats', they were
undermined at source. The internal reorganizations of 1977
and 1979 meant that, almost from the outset, the efforts to
build a presidential party were afflicted by uncertainties.
Carter's reluctance to establish a firm chief-of-staff post until
mid-1979 added to the problem of establishing priorities and
co-ordinating issues. This is not to deny that there were attempts
to bring a degree of order to the activities of the White House.

During the first two years of the Administration Carter used Vice-President Mondale and his staff to draw up half-yearly lists of policy issues emerging from the executive branch: after review by senior advisers, these lists provided the policy agenda for the next six months. Nevertheless, this system did not provide the sense of direction that was required.

Carter's failure to recognize the need for a chief-of-staff until it was too late was part of a broader managerial problem. As James Sundquist has pointed out, one of the most effective ways to ensure that an Administration functions efficiently is to appoint to 'the key managerial positions in the executive branch persons whose capacity to administer large organizations' is 'tried and tested'.[5] Although some of Carter's appointments met this requirement, these were the exception rather than the rule. Furthermore, the President himself seems to have given scant consideration to the problems of implementation. This shortcoming was particularly serious when set against Carter's aspirations and the political obstacles to their fulfilment. Without the total commitment of the power and prestige of the Presidency, there was little prospect that Carter's good intentions could be translated into policy outcomes.

Although the failure to follow through decisions and ensure that they were not undermined by bureaucratic and congressional intransigence was one of the main weaknesses of the Carter Presidency, it was not entirely surprising in the light of Carter's background and experience. Indeed, we see in Jimmy Carter the extension to the Presidency of the American belief that amateurism is no barrier to office; any citizen can do any public job. Carter's Presidency embodied this belief: he was inexperienced in the ways of Washington and had had little opportunity to become acquainted with those who had served as Washington administrators. The difficulty of operating without the Washington 'insiders' became apparent during the Bert Lance affair and it is noteworthy that the Administration turned for help in defending Lance to Clark Clifford, a prominent Washington lawyer whose experience in government dated back to the Truman Administration. For the most part, though, Carter proceeded as if Washington was simply Atlanta writ large.[6] And although the Administration learned fast, Carter's first two years in office 'have been characterised as the most expensive—and most risky—on-the-job training course ever taken'.[7] In defence policy, for example, the President so damaged his credibility during 1977 and 1978 that nothing he did thereafter could redeem his position with his more conservative critics. Although the hostage crisis which bedevilled Carter's last year was an important factor in undermining his bid for re-election, the damage had been done much earlier.

Part of the problem was the President's failure to project an image of strength and decisiveness. Whatever his private convictions—and more often than not they were strong and clear-cut—publicly Carter appeared ambivalent or ineffectual. In domestic policy, for example, it was alleged that after presenting Congress with the avowed imperative of welfare reform, the President then 'walked away' from the issue for four or five months. Nor did Carter's reputation for stubbornness lead to a follow-through over water projects where the President in fact backed down from his initial position. Nowhere was Carter's ambivalence more pronounced, however, than in the area of national security. Until the Soviet invasion of Afghanistan Carter failed to develop a consistent policy towards the Soviet Union. This was partly a reflection of the fact that his Presidency coincided with a period of considerable uncertainty in Soviet–American relations: *détente* had been called into question but it was not clear what the alternatives were. Yet Carter compounded the problem by his unwillingness or inability to decide between the conflicting prescriptions of Secretary of State, Vance, and National Security Adviser, Brzezinski. Not only did the President oscillate between toughness and conciliation from one speech to the next, but some of his statements themselves appeared to be an uneasy and confusing amalgamation of disparate advice and contradictory themes. In the last eighteen months of the Administration, Brzezinski emerged as the dominant figure, especially after Afghanistan appeared to confirm his judgement of Moscow's intentions. Until then, Carter rarely appeared comfortable with Brzezinski's demands for a more vigorous approach to the Soviet Union. Indeed, it is one of the ironies of the Carter White House that the President himself came to rely on an adviser who was fundamentally lacking in sympathy with many of his most cherished foreign policy objectives.

Brzezinski's influential role in national security issues was to some extent paralleled in domestic affairs by Carter's reliance on Stuart Eizenstat. Indeed, Eizenstat enjoyed a closer relationship with the President than any domestic Cabinet member. His position was enhanced by the fact that, despite Carter's commitment to 'Cabinet government', policy-making continued to be centred in the White House as it had been with all recent Presidents. In addition, Carter encouraged Eizenstat to adopt a more active role in economic affairs. Eizenstat was a member of the Economic Policy Group (the President's principal economic advisory body), though there were reportedly clashes of ideology, and, indeed, of temperament between him and Blumenthal, the Secretary of the Treasury.[8] And although such clashes were not as damaging as those in foreign policy, they add credence to claims that Carter did not exert sufficient control or leadership over his officials. Differences of perspective and interest among high level officials, of course, were not unique to the Carter Administration. Nevertheless, it is difficult to avoid the conclusion that these differences were more debilitating for Carter than for other presidents because of his failure to exert his own authority. A system based on multiple advocacy and conflicting advice has many virtues and was a refreshing departure from the secretive and insulated decision-making of the Nixon Presidency. Nevertheless, such a system can only work if the President himself is decisive, as was Roosevelt. Carter was probably more open-minded and receptive to new information and advice than any other recent President. Instead of this being a positive virtue, however, it contributed to his image as being vacillating and indecisive. There were also occasions when the President would have been better trusting his own instincts than those of his advisers. Perhaps the most notable example of this was the admission to the United States of the Shah of Iran. In making this decision Carter capitulated to pressure not only from Brzezinski but also from Rockefeller and Henry Kissinger (whose support for the SALT II Treaty was deemed essential).

It was partly because of this indecision at the top that the Carter Administration was never seen as standing for clear political goals and suffered from accusations of being a 'passionless Presidency'. Carter's own style—decisions were made one at a time and without any overall strategy or design—created the impression that the White House lacked a sense of cohesion or purpose.[9] Yet the President's programme, for all its

shortcomings, was the only one available. Although certain
individuals in Congress did promote alternative legislation to
that proposed by the President on health and welfare, the
party leadership had no programme of its own to offer.[10]
At the same time, the fact that committees and individuals
jealously guarded their rights and prerogatives over legislation
and appropriations added to Carter's difficulties. One way to
deal with this would have been for Carter to have concentrated
his efforts on a narrower range of issues in the hope that by
reducing his agenda he would achieve those goals which really
mattered. Yet the President was very reluctant to do this.
Influence is a scarce resource in Washington, and by diffusing
his efforts Carter squandered what limited resources he did
possess. The one exception to this was the Panama Canal
Treaties on which Carter launched a massive and ultimately
successful lobbying effort. Even this success brought difficulties in its wake, however, and many of the senators who
had voted for Panama at some political risk to themselves
decided that prudence demanded a much more circumspect
and critical approach to SALT II.

Indeed, the links between Panama and SALT demonstrated
how difficult it had become for the President to exert sustained and effective leadership. Carter may not have been
a naturally assertive president, but on those occasions when
he did attempt to wield presidential power, he found that he
faced almost insuperable difficulties. As Etzioni has pointed
out, American society was going through a period in which
many factors militated against strong presidential leadership.[11]
The changes in Congress which had made it 'semi-anarchic'
were, in fact, symptomatic of the state of the Union.[12] While
it is true that Carter was not particularly skilled at building
coalitions—with the result that many of his proposals went
to Congress politically naked and therefore a prey to interest
groups—it had become much more difficult to do so than it
had been in the 1960s under Johnson. There were growing
divergences between different parts of the country: the interests
of the sunbelt differed from those of the frostbelt; the interests
of oil and gas-producing states were at odds with those of
consumer states. The result of this was an erosion of party
unity and support. Furthermore, the old Democratic coalition
was weakening. Liberals were declining in both number and

enthusiasm, the labour unions were losing their power, and the solid South was dissolving. In the face of these changes, Carter found that it was less and less effective to use the White House as a 'bully pulpit'. His attempt to mobilize public support for his energy programme was a particularly telling illustration of the difficulties that would have confronted any president in the latter half of the 1970s. The implication of this is that Dom Bonafede's charge that all too often Carter 'offered the sanctimonious homilies of a country preacher instead of the forceful declarations of a strong President' is too harsh.[13] Leadership is much more effective when there are willing followers—and willing followers were an asset that Jimmy Carter lacked.

Another criticism of Carter which needs to be put into perspective concerns his relations with the members of his Cabinet. Conflict between Cabinet members and White House staff is not unique to the Carter years. What was new and different, though, was that the President emphasized his support for Cabinet government and his desire to ensure that Cabinet members had a major input into policy development— thereby giving Cabinet members a greater sense of their own importance. The disillusionment, therefore, was all the greater when Cabinet officials found that all their policy recommendations were reviewed by OMB and other units in the White House. In domestic policy this amounted to a treaty-making process inside the White House.[14] In foreign policy it meant that there were frequent disputes between the NSC and the State Department. Indeed, Carter fell between two stools in his conduct of foreign affairs. Although his initial intention was that Vance should be the leading figure in the policy-making process, and that Brzezinski's role should primarily be that of 'policy thinker' he did not give Vance the kind of presidential backing that had been received by previous Secretaries of State such as Dean Acheson and John Foster Dulles. At the same time, Carter's commitment to the principle that Brzezinski should not become another Kissinger, inhibited the emergence of one dominant figure capable of introducing a greater degree of coherence into US foreign policy. This is not to suggest that injecting greater coherence would have been an easy task even with a less fragmented policy-making process. Carter's foreign policy was formulated in a world characterized by complex interdependence, fragmented issues, and the relative decline of American power. It is to the credit of the Administration that instead of seeking refuge in traditional but simplistic notions of military superiority —as its successor has done—it made a concerted, if ultimately futile attempt, to cope with complexity. The difficulty was that complex problems demanded clear procedures, well-established lines of authority, and an overall conception of the objectives to be attained and the most appropriate means to be adopted. Almost all these characteristics were lacking, thereby undermining the endeavour itself and provoking the kind of reaction that is evident in the policies of the Reagan Administration.

The complexities which confronted President Carter in foreign policy had their counterpart in domestic politics. Indeed, domestic issues were much more complex than in the Johnson years. President Johnson had addressed a relatively small number of issues, such as civil rights and medicare, on which it was possible, albeit not easy, to develop a consensus. But by the mid-1970s the government's domestic activities had expanded considerably. Their cost had also risen, jumping from around 8 to about 14 per cent of GNP. In view of the sheer scale and complexity of government policies Carter's decision to be his own chief-of-staff was somewhat inappropriate to say the least. The result, as discussed above, was that the decentralization of power to Cabinet and White House units combined with the centralization of final decision-making in the Oval Office to create a 'multitude of semi-autonomous fiefdoms, quarrelling bitterly among themselves and speaking with different voices to the public'.[15] In these circumstances it was inevitable that the President appeared in an unflattering light. Carter's own background and personality combined with a decision-making structure that encouraged advice from competing interests within his own staff to encourage the President to concentrate excessively upon detail. Although Carter grasped the details of complicated issues far better than most presidents, this was no substitute for the sense of purpose and vision that only the Chief Executive can provide. Nor did it help Carter in his search for solutions which would find common acceptance in an increasingly intractable political environment.

This is not to argue that alternative decision-making arrangements would have solved all Carter's problems. The thrust of much of the earlier analysis is that at least some of these problems were not amenable to solution. Nevertheless, the President's failure to resolve fundamental disagreements among his advisers, his lack of a coherent staff organization, and his inability to establish clear priorities among differing policy areas, exacerbated the difficulties and turned improbable successes into almost certain failures.

Carter's first year in particular saw a vast series of initiatives, reviews and proposals which over-burdened the policy process in both the executive branch and the Congress. By the end of this year, the President's energy package was deadlocked in Congress and Carter's actions were being seen as more memorable for their symbolism and pace than for their accomplishments. In an attempt to offset criticism that his Administration was long on ideas and short on achievements Carter declared that the legislative activism of his first year would be followed by a period of consolidation involving fewer legislative proposals. Certainly, by the end of 1978 the campaign against inflation had become the driving force behind Carter's policy agenda, giving it a sense of direction and purpose that had hitherto been lacking. But the preoccupation with inflation also brought a new set of problems: it led to a reversal of what had traditionally been the major concerns of the Democratic Party with supporting the cities, providing jobs, aiding the poor, the sick and the elderly, and striving to improve the prospects for international peace and security. Indeed, the main thrust of policy, particularly in the domestic field, became negative cost-cutting rather than positive innovation, while defence was by and large exempted from the concern with controlling government expenditures. The criticism which this provoked revealed one of the main weaknesses of the Carter Presidency. Because the President himself lacked a well-conceived grand design he was less able to withstand the attacks that followed these cuts and came from those groups and individuals who had traditionally provided the bulk of the support for Democratic presidents. In his election campaign, Carter had promised to balance the budget by fiscal year 1981 while maintaining domestic programmes and promoting tax cuts. The hope was that economic recovery would provide the necessary resources to facilitate the attainment of these objectives. The failure to deliver on these promises meant that the Administration was in deep political trouble. Nor could it easily overcome the image of incompetence and ineptness which, by 1979, had become deeply entrenched, and was to be reinforced the following year.

To his credit, Carter did attempt to re-invigorate his Presidency during the Summer of 1979. His 'crisis of confidence' speech of July 1979 was heralded as a rejuvenation of his Administration. In the event, it was no such thing—and not simply because its impact was dissipated by the Cabinet sackings which followed. By then the pattern had been set. As one commentator observed:

Presidents cannot easily reverse their course after 30 months in office. By that time their people and policies are already in place. All they can do—and this is what Carter is trying to do—is salvage what they can from their defeats and disappointments.[16]

Nor did the nature of the problem change. Despite the President's exertions, the Administration still appeared to lack a sense of direction. It was not clear whether the President was trying to break new ground or simply attempting to build on what had gone before. And although there were areas such as defence in which Carter did have a clear set of priorities, these were the exception rather than the rule. This is not to deny that the Administration had strengths as well as weaknesses. Furthermore, there were successes: the ratification of the Panama Canal Treaty was a major achievement, while Carter's peace initiatives in the Middle East displayed a high degree of resolve and skill. Furthermore, in assessing the Administration's record it is necessary to consider the mood of the country. The United States, for a variety of reasons, was becoming much more conservative during the latter half of the 1970s. Although the Carter White House is open to criticism for its poor planning and inept public relations, it must also be acknowledged that public and congressional sentiments were hostile to traditional liberalism—and that a Hubert Humphrey or a Henry Jackson would have encountered similar problems to those which beset Carter. Jackson might have won greater public approval for his defence and foreign policies, but on domestic issues would not have been markedly more successful than Carter. There was widespread public disenchantment with government, which appeared as intrusive as it was ineffectual. In the aftermath of Watergate there was also conflict between Congress and successive presidents over the control of the federal system while the disintegration of the political parties destroyed one of the major channels for consensus building.[17] If Watergate typified the political system of the early 1970s, Proposition 13 was the appropriate metaphor for the late 1970s and the early 1980s as the 'age of limits', prophesied by California's Governor, Jerry Brown, became a political reality. Indeed, the Carter Presidency can be understood in terms of these two phenomena—it was a product of the reaction against Watergate and a victim of the age of limits. At the same time, it is hard to escape the conclusion that Carter's managerial inadequacies and conceptual inconsistencies made him much more vulnerable than was necessary. Indeed, the dominant theme of this book is that the age of limits and the limits of the Carter Administration were mutually reinforcing.

Notes

1. Arnold J. Meltsner (ed.), *Politics and the Oval Office: Towards Presidential Governance*, San Francisco, California, Institute for Contemporary Studies, 1981.
2. Joseph A. Califano, Jr., *Governing America*, New York, Simon & Schuster, 1981, p. 451.
3. James L. Sundquist, 'The Crisis of Competence in Our National Government', *Political Science Quarterly*, Vol. 95, 2, Summer 1980, p. 190.
4. Hugh Heclo, 'The Presidential Illusion', in Hugh Heclo and Lester M. Salamon, *The Illusion of Presidential Government*, Boulder, Colorado, Westview Press/National Academy of Public Administration, 1981, p. 9.
5. James L. Sundquist, 'Jimmy Carter As Public Administrator: An Appraisal at Mid-Term', *Public Administration Review*, 39, January/February, 1979, p. 4.
6. Ibid., p. 4.
7. Ibid., p. 5.
8. Dom Bonafede, 'Stuart Eizenstat—Carter's Right-Hand Man', *National Journal*, 6 September 1979, pp. 944-8.
9. John H. Kessel, 'The Structure of the Carter White House', unpublished manuscript, University of Ohio. The authors are grateful to Dr Kessel for allowing them to consult his manuscript.

10. Sundquist, *Political Science Quarterly*, op. cit., p. 199.
11. Amitai Etzioni, 'The Lack of Leadership: We Found It—In Us', *National Journal*, 23 February 1980, p. 334.
12. Ibid., p. 335.
13. Dom Bonafede, 'A Turning Point', *National Journal*, 23 June 1979, p. 1048.
14. Timothy B. Clark, 'The Power Vacuum Outside the Oval Office', *National Journal*, 24 February 1979, p. 296.
15. Ibid.
16. Dom Bonafede, 'Singing the Same Old Tune', *National Journal*, 21 July 1979, p. 1216.
17. Richard E. Cohen, 'The Political System Attempts to Cope with Public Loss of Faith in Government', *National Journal*, 19 January 1980, p. 10.

Index

Aaron, David, 72
Abortion, 116, 117
Adams, Brock, resignation from Cabinet, 29, 195
Afghanistan invasion, 103, 211
  effect on re-election chances, 137
  effect on US foreign policy, 65
  influence on defence policy, 7
Air Force
  cutbacks, 90
  effect of 1979 budget, 93
Airlines, deregulation, 30
Anderson, John, 139
Angola, invasion of Katanga, 64
Anti-Recession Fiscal Assistance Act (1977), 14
Army
  effect of 1979 budget, 93
  withdrawal from Korea, 90-1, 99

B-1 bombers, cancellation, 90, 181
Babcock, Barbara, 107
Balanced budget, 13, 36
Barber, James, 1-2, 56
Bell, Griffin, 107
  resignation from Cabinet, 29
Blumenthal, Michael, 42, 50, 212
  resignation from Cabinet, 29, 195
  Treasury Secretary, 40-1
Bonn economic summit meeting (1978), 49
Brooks, Jack, 24
Brown, Harold, 90, 169
  capabilities, 71-2
  foreign policy implementation, 61
  increased defence spending favoured, 96
  role in defence policy questioned, 92
  stance on SALT II, 98
Brown, Jerry, 218
Brzezinski, Zbigniew, 6, 146, 211
  capabilities, 71
  defence budget, 89
  increased defence spending favoured, 96
  on neutron bomb, 95
  role in foreign policy, 61-3, 67-8

views on foreign policy, 60-1
views on Soviet intentions, 64
Budget deficit
  at beginning of administration, 35
  effectiveness of policies, 43
  see also Balanced budget; Zero-based budgeting
Bugging, see Electronic surveillance
Burns, Arthur, 39, 41-2
Byrd, Robert, 186

Cabinet government, 26, 173, 193-5
  Carter's relations with members, 214
  principles, 194
Califano, Joseph A., Jr., 22, 24, 209
  appointed to Health, Education and Welfare, 19
  friction with White House aides, 20-1
  resignation from Cabinet, 29, 195
  views on health insurance, 23
  Welfare Reform Consulting Group formed, 20
Camp David Agreement, 67, 68, 69
Campbell, Ann, 134
Carter, Hodding, Jr., 61
Carter, Jimmy
  as 'outsider' candidate, 127, 128
  as 'outsider' president, 9, 174-8
  attack on Nixon-Ford foreign policy, 55-7
  constraints on policies, 2
  election campaign, 1, 126-32
  first TV 'fireside chat', 14
  growth as foreign policy-maker, 68-9
  lack of Washington experience, 210
  legislative performance, 9, 165-91; limitations, 187-8; style, 178-84
  managerial reforms, 9-10
  personal constraints on government reform, 200-2
  political career, 1
  political temperament, 127-8
  presidency: at time of declining US power, 208; evaluation, 4; limitations, 218; style, 1-2, 10, 212
  relations with Cabinet, 214
  relationship with Democratic Party, 8, 125-43, 178, 209